Pension Policy in an Integrating Europe

Edited by

Onorato Castellino and Elsa Fornero

University of Turin and Center for Research on Pensions and Welfare Policies

Edward Elgar
Cheltenham, UK • Northampton, MA, USA

Published by
Edward Elgar Publishing Limited
Glensanda House
Montpellier Parade
Cheltenham
Glos GL50 1UA
UK

Edward Elgar Publishing, Inc.
136 West Street
Suite 202
Northampton
Massachusetts 01060
USA

A catalogue record for this book
is available from the British Library

Library of Congress Cataloguing in Publication Data

Pension policy in an integrating Europe / edited by Onorato Castellino and Elsa
Fornero
  p. cm.
  "This book mainly draws from the proceedings of the conference 'Pension policy
harmonization in an integrating Europe', held on 21 and 22 June, 2001 in
Moncalieri (Turin)"—Ackn.
  Includes bibliographical references and index.
  1. Pensions—Government policy—European Union countries—Congresses. 2.
Old age pensions—Government policy—European Union countries—
Congresses. 3. Payroll tax—European Union countries—Congresses. 4. Pension
trusts—Taxation—European Union countries 5. Retirement income—Taxation—
European Union countries—Congresses. I. Castellino, Onorato. II. Fornero, Elsa.

HD7164.P46454 2003
331.25'2'094—dc21

               2003049038

ISBN 1 84376 254 4

Printed and bound in Great Britain by MPG Books Ltd, Bodmin, Cornwall

Contents

Figures

Tables

Contributors

Vincenzo Andrietti Dipartimento di Scienze, Università 'G. D'Annunzio' di Chieti and Departamento de Economía, Universidad Carlos III de Madrid

Frits Bolkestein European Commission, Internal Market Directorate-General

Axel Börsch-Supan Mannheim Research Institute for the Economics of Aging and Economics Department, University of Mannheim; National Bureau of Economic Research, Cambridge, Massachusetts

Onorato Castellino Department of Economics, University of Turin and Center for Research on Pensions and Welfare Policies, Turin

Bruno Contini Department of Economics, University of Turin and LABORatorio R. Revelli, Turin

Francesca Cornaglia Department of Economics, University of Turin and LABORatorio R. Revelli, Turin

Francesco Daveri University of Parma and Innocenzo Gasparini Institute for Economic Research, Milan

Elsa Fornero Department of Economics, University of Turin and Center for Research on Pensions and Welfare Policies, Turin

Richard A. Ippolito George Mason University School of Law, Arlington

Surachai Khitatrakun Department of Economics, University of Wisconsin–Madison

Melanie Lührmann Mannheim Research Institute for the Economics of Aging and Economics Department, University of Mannheim

Cheti Nicoletti Institute for Social and Economic Research, University of Essex

Claudio Malpede R&P Ricerche e Progetti, Turin

Franco Peracchi Faculty of Economics, University of Rome 'Tor Vergata'

xi

Pierre Pestieau   Centre de Recherche en Economie Publique et de la Population, Université de Liège; Center for Operation Research and Econometrics, Université Catholique de Louvain; Centre for Economic Policy Research, London; Département et Laboratoire d'Economie Théorique et Appliquée, Ecole Normale Supérieure

Enrico Rettore   Department of Statistics, University of Padova

John Karl Scholz   Department of Economics and the Institute for Research on Poverty, University of Wisconsin–Madison

Acknowledgments

This book mainly draws from the proceedings of the Conference 'Pension Policy Harmonization in an Integrating Europe', held on 21 and 22 June, 2001 in Moncalieri (Turin) and organized by the Center for Research on Pensions and Welfare Policies (CeRP; http://cerp.unito.it).

The re-organization and structuring of the different papers into this volume has not been an easy task to accomplish for the editors; without the cooperation of each contributor in providing revised versions of the conference drafts and in patiently answering the many questions and remarks raised during the editing phase, the realization of this project would have not been possible; many sincere thanks go to each of them.

Particular thanks are due to the Compagnia di San Paolo, whose funding is a precious support for the activities of the centre, and which enabled CeRP to organize the conference. We are also indebted to the conference discussants and participants for helpful suggestions, and to all CeRP researchers for encouragement and support. The debt of thanks of each contributor are acknowledged in the respective chapters.

Finally, we would like to thank Alberto Crosta for his careful cooperation in formatting the final typescript and, in particular, Silvia Maero for her care and commitment in coordinating the whole project.

Onorato Castellino and Elsa Fornero

Introductory remarks[*]

Frits Bolkestein

Pension reform is more than ever at the top of the political agenda in Europe. There isn't a day when one doesn't read or hear about the challenges raised by an aging society, the threats to our public health and pension systems, all the initiatives envisaged by governments to tackle those challenges. And this conference is therefore particularly timely, but its title, namely 'Pension Policy Harmonization in an Integrating Europe' is, I believe, deliberately somewhat provocative.

Indeed, pension policy harmonization is not on the agenda of the European Union, nor does it fall under its competence. Each Member State retains full responsibility for the design and organization of its pension system and for meeting the many pensions challenges. And each Member State has to make the political choices and take the sometimes tough but necessary measures in that field.

The EU can bring some added value to Member States' pension policies and reforms, in particular through greater coordination within the framework of the Internal Market. The Stockholm European Council in March emphasized the need to review public pension systems in the context of the broad economic policy guidelines and of the long-term sustainability of public finances.

Community action may notably contribute to relieving some of the financing pressures on public systems by allowing private pension funds to take full advantage of the euro and of the internal markets, and to operate more efficiently. The establishment of an effective EU framework for occupational pension funds is one of my key priorities as Commissioner

[*] Message from F. Bolkestein, 20 June 2001 – EUROPEAN COMMISSION, Brussels.
Since this statement has been made, substantial progress has been achieved in the Council, especially under the Spanish Presidency in the first half of 2002. Political agreement was within reach and the Spanish Presidency was intending to submit it to Finance Ministers in June 2002. [The Council agreement on the Commission's proposal was reached on 4 June 2002; after approval by the European Parliament on 12 March 2003, the Council adopted the Pension Funds Directive on 13 May 2003].

1

responsible for the Internal Market. The proposal for a directive on the supervision of institutions for occupational retirement provisions, which was adopted by the Commission in October 2000, follows that objective and has three aims:

- firstly, ensuring a high degree of security of pensions and of protection of the beneficiaries, through a qualitative approach combining a set of basic prudential rules with qualitative rules on pension funds liabilities;
- secondly, making supplementary pensions more affordable by avoiding unduly restrictive prudential rules which would result in lower returns. The Commission insists that the prudent-expert rule which has operated successfully for decades remains the key principle governing asset allocation;
- thirdly, allowing pension funds to provide their services in another Member State, thereby making it possible to have cross-border membership so as to reduce costs and to encourage cross-border mobility within the firm.

The discussion in the Council has clearly demonstrated that some Member States remain concerned about the qualitative approach proposed by the Commission. They argue in favour of some quantitative limits for investment rules as the best means to safeguard the interests of the beneficiaries. For its part, the European Parliament completed its first reading of the Commission proposal in July 2001, so as to allow for swift progress on that proposal for a directive.

That directive will however only deliver its full benefit if it is accompanied by similar progress to eliminate the tax obstacles to the cross-border provision of occupational pensions. The Commission adopted in April 2001 a Communication which proposes to follow a coordinated approach, adapted to the diversity of national tax systems and it calls for the elimination of unduly restrictive or discriminatory tax rules.

This conference intervenes at the moment when we are becoming more confident about our ability to meet the challenges of aging. The onus is now on the Member States, the European Parliament, the supervisors and regulators who start preparing for a modern and open EU pension market which will benefit all future pensioners. The European Commission stands ready to fully contribute to the work undertaken to make progress in that area.

1. Overview

Onorato Castellino and Elsa Fornero

1.1 Pensions have become a source both of pride and concern for advanced economies. There is pride in recognizing that, largely thanks to social security systems, the living standard of the elderly has made incomparable progress over the past hundred years or so. There is concern over the mounting troubles of these same social security systems: financial imbalance, perverse redistribution, misdirected incentives.

Increased relevance of the pension systems' role in transferring purchasing power from the young to the old has added to the intricacies and interrelations between payroll taxes, pension benefits, work-leisure and consumption-saving choices by individuals, hiring and firing policies by firms, budget balances, intergenerational equity, political differences over principles and ideologies.

Different national systems of social security mirror different historical paths and political choices, so that heterogeneity dominates over convergence, and variability of rules over uniformity. Among the main differences are the mix between public and private component, the balance between PAYG and funding, the insurance or redistributive nature of pension formulas, and the sources of financing, which can be based more on general or more on payroll taxation, with important impacts on savings and the labour market.

Some countries, such as Italy and Spain, have generous PAYG public systems, while others (such as Great Britain, the Netherlands and Ireland) rely more heavily on the second pillar (firm-based or industry-based pension funds) and on the third one (insurance policies), both originating more private saving to be invested in financial markets. Furthermore, some countries use (or at least have used) social security for redistributing income (within or between generations, even if the result is not always a correct redistribution from rich to poor); or for industrial policy (as when early retirement has been used for financing industrial restructuring); or else for political aims, perhaps on the eve of an election period, when promises are made without taking their costs into account. In other countries, the system is less redistributive in its purposes, with lower payroll taxes and more actuarially-oriented pension formulae.

Despite these differences, there are common problems all over Europe. The 2001 EU's Göteborg summit squarely put pensions very nearly at the top of European issues, in the face of a very rapid population aging. Like unemployment in the 1990s, pensions in the first decade of the New Century are being upgraded from national to European issues. In an integrating continent, financial sustainability of individual countries' pension systems can no longer be treated as a mere national problem. Pensions policies are increasingly perceived as an integral part of economic policies and indirectly but effectively influence growth and employment, not only of the country that adopts them but of the EU at large.

Demographic changes exert a strong pressure on public pension systems based on PAYG. This method works reasonably well in a young demographic framework where the dependency ratio is low, while it has difficulties in supplying the resources necessary to finance the flow of benefits in mature systems where such a rate is comparatively high. The resulting financial imbalances impose reforms which, although of many different types, cannot but pursue one single strategy: to reduce aggregate benefits, since payroll taxes are already very high. All countries must therefore resort to converging, or similar, measures, such as those which lengthen working life or promote the development of private pensions in order to relieve the budget of the increasing burdens of aging. Correcting financial imbalances according to the stability pact therefore implies greater uniformity and better sustainability of social security.

Pension formulae must then be corrected towards actuarial fairness, achieving a double correlation: between contributions and benefits, so that the higher the former the higher the latter; and between life expectancy at retirement and benefits, so that the lower the former the higher the latter, perhaps with a few and clear exceptions (it must unfortunately be recalled that these criteria are widely disregarded in the early retirement provisions of many European countries).

This implies bringing payroll taxes closer to forced savings. At the same time, a mixed system is gaining increasing favour at the European level: a system which combines, in various proportions, the public PAYG and the private funded component. The latter usually offers a higher expected return but also a higher risk; as with any other type of saving, diversifying pension wealth seems to be a wise rule.

1.2 In June 2001, the Center for Research on Pensions and Welfare Policies (CeRP) – an independent research institution operating in association with the University of Turin – devoted its yearly conference to *Pension Policy Harmonization in an Integrating Europe.*

We were of course aware that the term 'harmonization' could be considered provocative, since, at the European Union level, pensions, as well as taxation, are subject to the subsidiarity principle, as Mr Bolkestein was quick to point out. We however decided to tackle the harmonization issue for one good reason: pension systems, in their fullest sense, including both the PAYG and the funded component, cannot move too far apart without interfering with two vital aspects of the European Union. Free movement of workers would be gravely hindered by difficulties in transferring pension rights across national borders and in benefit calculation, and competition would be hampered by significant differences in payroll tax burden.

Similar observations of course also apply to general taxation, another relevant field where it is considered important that member states should keep their autonomy. It must furthermore be noted that it is difficult to draw the dividing line between payroll taxes, as a sort of forced saving, and general taxation, since this depends upon the degree of actuarial fairness of the overall design of the social security system. We are anyway convinced that, quite apart from what the Commission and the European Parliament can or cannot do, scholars should not stop short of addressing the problem.

Moreover, if we turn to the more restricted item of the funded component, Frits Bolkestein reminds us that '(t)he establishment of an effective EU framework for occupational pension funds is one of my key priorities as Commissioner responsible for the Internal Market'. The supervision of the institutions and the extent to which it should entail specific investment rules are the subject of a directive which was proposed by the European Commission two years ago (October 2000), and whose core principles were approved by the Council of Economics and Finance Ministers in June 2002. The reason why it has taken such a long time to reach this intermediate stage is partly due to some disagreement between the member states on the choice of the balance between quantitative and 'prudent man' rules, but the need for a common framework for occupational pension funds is widely shared. This is why, while deciding to take the word *harmonization* out of the title of this collection of papers, we do think that pension policy must be seen as a matter of common concern within a unifying Europe.

Side by side with this broadening of policy horizons from a national to a European perspective, a shift in emphasis can be detected in the academic approach to pensions from the financial sustainability of present systems to the microeconomic features of pension provisions, notably their effect on the labour market, on the formation of savings, and therefore on economic performance at large.

Within this framework, we chose to tackle the general issue of our conference by focussing on three topics:

- effects of the huge differentials in payroll taxes existing in Europe on labour choices and the labour market;
- taxation of pensions;
- portability of occupational pensions.

In our view, the first is perhaps the most intriguing, certainly the most frustrating of the three topics. We are confronted with greatly different payroll taxes in countries constituting a single market; these taxes range from 9 per cent in Denmark to 33 per cent in Italy and 37 per cent in Spain; and yet labour costs are more or less competitive. What makes this happen? A cutback in the net wages of workers? Compensations in other items of the public budget? The presence of a large irregular sector in the economy? These questions are difficult perhaps because they are too general.

So we have to be more specific, take one step backward and focus upon more limited phenomena, like early retirement being attributed to pension formulas that are unfair to the continuation of work, or the fact that the young seem in the position only of having jobs with less social security. It is by now widely recognized that the parameters of the system go a long way in explaining retirement decisions, since implicit taxation can bring about such huge losses in pension wealth as to make continuation of work wildly irrational. Although this is merely a first approximation, the idea that labour is too heavily taxed also because of implicit taxes in our pension systems seems fairly grounded.

The second set of relevant questions relates to the fiscal treatment of pensions. While taxation of public pensions leads us back to the comparison between pension systems, taxation of the private component touches directly upon the subject of *tax competition* between member states with the possibility of double taxation in certain countries and tax heaven conditions in others. Proper comparisons are complicated by the fact that taxation and tax exemption may take place at different time periods, i.e may affect contributions, the return from the investment or the collection of benefits by the worker now turned pensioner. There is a discussion in this country (Italy), as well as in others, about the effectiveness of fiscal incentives to encourage savings for retirement in the presence of a high level of compulsory participation in the public PAYG system; but it is unfair, at least in Italy, to attribute the lack of demand for private pensions predominantly to an ungenerous fiscal treatment.

The third set of questions concerns labour mobility, which may well be discouraged by loss of pension wealth due to worker migration from one country to another in conditions of incomplete portability of accrued pension rights. Agreements between member states generally guarantee full portability of public pensions, while portability of the private component – especially in the case of occupational pensions – is still largely incomplete, although it is difficult to assess its importance in restricting mobility.

Pension policy in Europe is therefore a complicated and multifaceted problem and both theoretical and applied analysis has a long way to go. With the Göteborg summit, however, harmonization of pension policies has ceased to be an abstract theme. If pensions are considered not just an important part of the welfare system but also an efficient way to reallocate income towards old age, the road to follow must include the elimination of dead-weight losses, the application of coherent taxation principles and the implementation of greater portability of pension rights. These three guidelines are essential to guarantee greater solidity to European growth in the present and future decades.

1.3 Cheti Nicoletti and Franco Peracchi (*Aging in Europe: A cross-country comparison*) use European Community Household Panel (ECHP) data based on a common questionnaire – originally covering 12 countries, with Austria, Finland and Sweden joining later – to analyse the conditions of the elderly as regards health status, labour market activity, income and wealth.

The importance of micro data can hardly be overstated. Features which could formerly be only qualitatively studied can now be measured. Differences between member states as well as within each member state can be clearly shown. Nicoletti and Peracchi separately adapted for each country the models adopted for econometric estimation to allow for specific country effects. These are reflected in the wide difference in coefficients estimated for the same variable.

The importance of this method is evident in the study of health status. It is common knowledge that health deteriorates with age: at 20 one is usually in better shape than at 75. But is this process linear or exponential? The answer is important in assessing the relative impact of pension and health care expenditure and in finding out how, beyond age and age squared, health is influenced by income, education and marital status.

Employment rates and exits into retirement are two features well documented in this paper. Taking both genders together, in all the European countries except Sweden, the number of persons out of the labour force at age 60 is greater than the number of persons employed; the gap widens rapidly, also in Sweden, between ages 60 and 65 (see Fig. 2.2 in Nicoletti and Peracchi). Age profiles of retirement, however, are quite different between countries, and often also between genders. Nicoletti and Peracchi try to identify – separately by country and gender – the main explanatory variables of these related phenomena (employment and retirement). Age, educational attainment, having a spouse and health are identified as explanatory variables. Either the dummy for age 60 or the one for age 65 is usually significant. In most cases social security systems appear to have induced workers to retire earlier than they previously used to.

Finally, income and wealth. Here we all have some qualitative priors: but, again, the devil is in the details, and quantitative measures are definitely more important and useful. Thus we need (and Nicoletti and Peracchi lavishly supply us with) more precise knowledge on the relationship between income (what income? – three measures are offered) and age; on the composition of income (earnings, pensions, other); on the structure of earnings and pensions; on replacement rates; on poverty. Of course, when plotting the sources of income against age, the curve showing earnings decreases and the one showing pensions increases. A (perhaps unexpected but reassuring) result is that in some countries (Finland, Italy, the Netherlands and Sweden) poverty, as measured by the percentage of households living with less than 50 per cent of median equivalent household income, decreases with age, and in some others does not increase. This is of course good news: pensions often reach their goal as a means for supporting the well-being of the elderly. From a different viewpoint, (median baseline) replacement rates range between a minimum of 23 per cent in Finland to over 100 per cent in Luxembourg, Portugal and Spain.

These are only examples of the magnitudes considered and of the results (both descriptive and analytical) found by Nicoletti and Peracchi. There are some limits to these results, and the authors frankly mention them in their conclusion. But the whole picture is an important example of the work which is needed on microeconomic data, and suggested reading for all who wish a better and more informed ground for their research on pension systems, health policy and savings incentives.

1.4 A very important question – is there a positive relationship between labour taxes and unemployment? – is tackled by Francesco Daveri (*Labour taxes and unemployment: A survey of the aggregate evidence*).

Some contributions in the literature have come to the conclusion that unemployment is partly due to taxes on labour (where 'taxes' means both general taxation and social security contributions). Of course, this point is of paramount importance. Centre-right politicians usually promise to increase employment by reducing taxes (not only on labour); reforms purporting to prune social security and related taxes are often based, among others, on the expectation of a favourable effect on employment. Unfortunately, barring an increase in the budget deficit, cutting any kind of taxes means reducing some kind of expenditure, and therefore raises objections and disagreements. Since other contributions in the literature come to different conclusions, the evidence of the effect of decreasing taxes is not clear-cut, and the case for overcoming those objections and disagreements is weakened.

Daveri tackles the problem by first of all offering summary data on the biggest OECD countries. Neither cross-country correlations nor within-country time correlations lead to a clear answer, also because of a timing mismatch between labour taxes and unemployment, but suggest that the topic is worth pursuing. Some theory follows. The results are straightforward in a simple setting; the very important point is made that a payroll tax is the more similar to forced saving (rather than to general taxation), the stronger its relationship with the benefits accruing to the worker who pays it. But these results are blurred within a more general framework, such as one with capital accumulation.

Turning to econometric estimations based on aggregate data, earlier evidence led to negative results, while the more recent seems to conclude in favour of sizable effects of labour taxes on unemployment. But even in the latest papers the parameter of the tax rate fluctuates rather widely; omitted variable biases or endogeneity biases may partly explain these differences.

Micro data offer a different viewpoint for studying the taxes-employment relationship; so does simulation. In this connection, the endogeneity problem and the timing mismatch are again addressed. So is the question whether what really matters are labour taxes *per se* (irrespective of what happens to aggregate taxation) or government size *per se* (irrespective of how it is financed).

Daveri's is a very useful survey (where some of the papers mentioned are co-authored by himself). The conclusion is unfortunately not a clear-cut one: 'we still don't know whether labour taxes have statistically significant and economically important effects on labour costs and employment'. In a previous paper by himself and Tabellini (2000), the results were more straightforward: 'the high positive correlation between tax rates on labour income and unemployment is clearly a phenomenon of continental Europe, not present in the Anglo-Saxon or Nordic countries', the reason being that 'higher labour taxes have been shifted onto higher real wages. This has led firms to substitute labour with capital and it has slowed down growth and investment' (pp. 52 and 87). Daveri ends up with the statement that the scope for comparison across macro-econometric, micro-econometric and simulation studies 'does exist and may be fruitful for future research'.

1.5 Bruno Contini, Francesca Cornaglia, Claudio Malpede and Enrico Rettore (*Measuring the impact of the Italian CFL programme on job opportunities for young people*) inquire into the effects of 'Contratto di formazione e lavoro', introduced in Italy since 1985. CFL basically offers both a rebate on

Social Security taxes and (after an 18- or 24-month working spell) more flexibility in firing. Eligible workers are those between 15 and 29 years of age.

Contini *et al.* first formalize the benefit scheme. They consider the interdependence between current and future periods, since (after 1991) new workers can be hired under the CFL scheme only if at least 50 per cent of the ones already hired, who have concluded their spell over the previous two years, have been kept on a permanent basis. They further consider the firing costs which apply to a non-CFL worker. This first step leads to the definition of the ratio between the cost of a CFL and the cost of a non-CFL worker.

The second step is a model at the individual level, where the binary dependent variable y_{it} is 1 or 0 according to whether individual i is at work or not in period t. The explanatory variables include (among others) the dummy being/not being eligible for CFL multiplied by the ratio between the cost of an eligible and a non-eligible worker.

The third step translates the model in aggregate terms (subjects are grouped according to year and cohort); the dependent variable y_{ct} is now the number of subjects belonging to cohort c at work at time t. The time for estimation has come. Twenty cohorts (those born between 1958 and 1977) are observed for the time interval 1986–96 (or part of it). The upper age limit, depending on the cohorts considered, varies from 34 to 19; for about one half of the cohorts, it covers some ages above 29, so as to include non-CFL workers. Two specifications are tested: one in first (time) differences; the other in across cohorts differences of the time differences.

The main result, reached by the authors after their sophisticated econometric test, is that during the eligibility period the chance to work of those belonging to the relevant age bracket is not made higher by a lower eligible/non-eligible cost ratio. Taken literally, this result means that the CFL program has missed its target.

Putting together Daveri's blurred and Contini *et al*'s negative conclusions, one should be persuaded, if not to mistrust policies aimed at increasing employment by decreasing taxes on labour, at least to suspend one's judgment on them. We believe that before taking a firm view about the ineffectiveness of these policies, more evidence is needed.

1.6 Pierre Pestieau (*Are we retiring too early?*) tackles an awkward question, of great political weight. Many statements by experts, international institutions and political parties claim that European countries should raise their average retirement age. Leaving payroll taxes and pension levels unchanged, this would of course improve the financial stability of PAYG systems. A satisfactory answer to Pestieau's question is therefore very relevant.

Pestieau splits it into a number of separate, although connected, sub-questions. The first one is, are we really retiring too early? Two sets of figures suggest a positive answer. All over Europe, effective retirement age for both men and women has decreased by about five years (ten years for women in Ireland and Spain) between 1960 and 1995. In the same time span, life expectancy at birth has increased by about six years for men and seven years for women; and also life expectancy at 55 or 60 years of age, an even more relevant figure for social security, has risen considerably. Retirees' life has therefore extended both due to an earlier beginning and a later end.

In principle, this might be the result of a rational choice: one could argue that higher productivity (such as that actually achieved between 1960 and 1995) has been exploited for working less and enjoying more leisure. But a third trend must be taken into account: decreased fertility. Combining it with the previously mentioned ones, it follows that the pensioners/workers ratio, which has been steadily increasing for decades, is bound to keep rising until the middle of the century. In a PAYG framework, this means that payroll taxes should continuously go up or replacement ratios down. The well-known financial stress which has already hit most social security systems leads us to conclude that we should consider an increase in the age of retirement.

But why has this age decreased? Is this due to the strong effect of the rules of social protection? Pestieau develops a model of maximizing choices, where life is made up of two periods. In the first one, everybody is working and the supply of labour is given. In the second one, everybody chooses how much to work by comparing at the margin, given his wage rate, the (decreasing) utility of consumption with the (increasing) disutility of work.

If we introduce social security, this condition still applies provided the pension formula is actuarially fair. But suppose now that the formula is only partly fair, i.e. only part of the payroll tax paid during the second period of life enters into the pension formula. Suppose further that benefits are paid only after retirement, without actuarial correction for the expected life period. Both burdens reduce the incremental consumption obtained from a unit of additional work, while not reducing its marginal disutility. The equilibrium condition is therefore satisfied at a lower level of activity, i.e. by retiring earlier. A number of studies present 'strong evidence that these implicit taxes induce most workers to retire at the earliest possible stage'.

It is then shown that the equilibrium condition following from a *laissez faire* maximization happens to coincide with the one which would be chosen by a social planner. Obstacles (i.e. not actuarially fair social security) against attaining the former are at the same time obstacles against the latter. The ensuing policy lesson is clear: social security systems should be actuarially fair, at least at the margin relevant for older workers. In fact, the opposite is generally true: many systems are more than fair up to an age limit, and then discriminate against working more.

Why, then, has it become so difficult to increase the statutory retirement age and to reduce subsidies for early retirement? Pestieau looks for the answer in the mechanics of political choices. The level of benefits chosen in a democracy (including the minimum age at which they can be received) is the one preferred by the median-age voter. Such a voter has already acquired, owing to his past contributions, a considerable amount of 'social security wealth'. He is therefore usually reluctant not only to abandon, but also to cut both contributions and benefits (or to rebalance the rules) of the present system. This is why it is difficult to find a majority in favour of a combined move (less for the younger and more for the older pensioners).

Pestieau's result therefore amounts to a particular case of a general rule: it is easy to create (or expand) a PAYG system, but it is difficult to abandon (or reassess) it. The general point has already been made long ago by Browning (1975). A number of surveys, quoted by Pestieau, show that public opinion is generally unsympathetic to raising retirement age – as well as to other cuts in the present system.

The final point is that 'workers can be differentiated not just according to productivity but also to their health at work'. Following Pestieau's analysis, this very fact partly explains and justifies some downward distortions in the retirement age. Although he furthermore looks with approval to the redistributional aims of social security, he leaves us with the message that, in view of the desire to strenghthen the financial viability of PAYG systems, a move to raise retirement age should be strongly encouraged.

As the recent experience of several countries has shown, severe upheavals of existing PAYG systems are possible only under particular conditions. The median voter is more apt to accept a sacrifice (or what he considers a sacrifice) when the monetary and financial conditions of his country appear to be in a state of strain, or the very survival of the social security system is at stake. Let us hope that some dose of intergenerational solidarity will help in voting the necessary reforms even in the absence of such unfavourable conditions.

1.7 Surachai Khitatrakun and John Karl Scholz deal with *Saving incentives in the US*. A preliminary question is whether today's saving rates are too low. But what is the benchmark? The optimization of investment choices in an infinite horizon model? The level of investment adequate for fully exploiting the benefits of technological progress? The rate of savings of the past decades? Only the last one seems to offer a practical rule of thumb, but of course it lacks any logical foundation unless one can prove that in the past some optimization rule was followed, and that the parameters which enter this optimization rule have not changed over time.

Should past experience be the benchmark, we could be led to think that the US saves too little if we consider that personal savings rates have come down from about 10 per cent in the 1970s to about zero today, and Flow of Funds personal savings follow a similar downward path (although at a higher percentage level). But a look at national savings rates is less disturbing. They were slightly above 20 per cent in the 1960s, around 20 per cent in the 1970s and have then oscillated between 15 and 20 per cent. Apparently, improvements in the budget deficit have offset most of the decline in private saving.

The authors are therefore (and quite reasonably) quick in skipping the question of how adequate US national savings are. A different, although related, question is whether Americans are adequately preparing for retirement. The answer, after defining what is meant by adequate, must jointly consider Social Security, employer provided pensions and private saving. Adequacy might be appropriately identified by a life-cycle model or simply by expecting, as a consequence of rational intertemporal choice, a limited fall of consumption after retirement. Results – as surveyed by Khitatrakun and Scholz – are mixed, if only because of the difficulty of assessing the standard against which actual behaviour is evaluated.

Let us anyway assume that American savings (both in aggregate terms and for old age) are too low. This seems the opinion underlying public policy, since a number of saving-for-old-age instruments have been introduced in the last decades, assisted by tax incentives of some sort. In the case of 401(k) plans, both contributions and returns on them are tax-exempt. Contributions for ordinary IRAs and earnings grow tax-deferred until withdrawal (for other types of IRAs, tax exemptions follow different rules). In a word, there is a patchwork of retirement incentives, more often due to historical accident than to a coherent framework, where it is not easy for each individual to find the form best suited to him. Morever, tax incentives often happen to be positively correlated to income, so as to produce inequitable results.

Be that as it may, do tax incentives increase retirement security and national savings? In other words, how can we separate their 'creation' from their 'diversion' effects? A rational individual must take two (intertwined) decisions: how much to save and how to allocate his accumulated savings between different assets. It is apparent that different tax treatments (and more generally post-tax rates of return) impact on the asset allocation. On the other hand, it has long been debated whether a high rate does increase personal savings, and if so whether the increment is consistently higher than the cost of the related tax exemptions; if it is not, higher personal savings have been offset by a worsening of the budget balance.

As far as saving for retirement is concerned, previous research has not led to generally accepted results. Khitatrakun and Scholz suggest new tests, based on data from the Health and Retirement Study. Respondents are treated separately by income quintiles, so as to isolate the effect of different levels of income. A first test is based on the subjective view about retirement expressed by those interviewed. Apparently, 401(k) eligibility reduces the probability of being worried about income in one's old age; these results are however not robust to the treatment of respondents who say they will never retire. The second test looks into the correlation between net worth and 401(k) eligibility: the result is that this correlation is very weak, except in the highest income quintile, where it is significant but negative (instead of positive as should be expected).

Although with a number of caveats, the authors conclude that there is little compelling evidence that 401(k) wealth significantly increases overall wealth accumulation. In their opinion, 'the patchwork of private savings incentives' is not worth emulating. This is an extremely important point; it is therefore necessary to extend similar research to other countries, especially to those (such as Italy) which are trying to boost retirement savings through tax concessions.

A more subtle question (not tackled by the authors) is: should tax incentives be conditional on the accumulated savings being cashed at least partly as an annuity and not entirely as a lump sum? The problem could arise if people were shortsighted and unable to foresee correctly their old-age needs. In this case, tax treatment 'distorting' private choices in favour of an annuity could be a paternalistic intervention aimed at correcting sub-optimal individual decisions.

1.8 Axel Börsch-Supan and Melanie Lührmann (*Retirement benefit and pension taxation principles*) examine the rules applying in the Federal Republic of Germany. The topic is of great importance not only as such, but also in its connection with the choice between PAYG and funding, with the international mobility of labour and capital and with the possibility for pension funds to operate outside national borders.

Börsch Supan and Lührmann start by tackling the old query, whether taxes should be levied on consumption or income. Much has (and can) be said for both solutions, but the authors list themselves in favour of the former, and think that a comprehensive income tax has a discriminatory impact on the formation of savings. Furthermore, they think that discrimination, if any, should act in favour of savings and not against it. Here are the reasons: savings rates are very low in many countries; funded pensions should be encouraged because many people are shortsighted and do not fully grasp the force of compound interest; and also in order to offset the tendency to self-selection in the market for old-age annuities.

Turning from first principles to taxation variants, the authors compare four different methods. If one considers three time periods (when contributions are paid, when income accrues on the accumulated balance, and when benefits are paid), the four methods are, as is well known:

F, F and T (only benefits are taxed)
T, F and F (only contributions are taxed)
F, T and T (contributions are tax-free, but both income and benefits are taxed)
T, T and F (contributions and income are taxed, benefits are free).

Assuming flat-rate taxation and no inflation, a simple example shows that, in terms of the final result, the first two methods are equivalent, and so are the last two, but with a lower result for the pensioner, owing to the taxation of income (absent in the first two). With progressive taxation, retirees presumably pay a lower rate, and therefore: FFT is better than TFF; FTT is better than TTF. With inflation, the taxation of income is also applied on a fictitious component, and the gap between the first two and the last two methods widens. The authors end up with the conclusion that the most rational principle is FFT.

After dealing with some practical problems, Börsch-Supan and Lührmann turn their attention to the impact of tax incentives on savings. The first question is whether state support of specific forms of retirement savings impacts on individual behaviour. The answer is yes: for instance, IRAs and 401(k) plans in the USA have attracted huge amounts of money. But the second and more relevant question is: have these instruments increased aggregate saving or have they only had a diversion effect? As has already been seen, Khitatrakun and Scholz favour the second conclusion. Börsch Supan and Lührmann take a more doubtful position, saying that the question is a matter of dispute, and that only the Chilean experience leads one to think that the overall savings rate has increased.

The authors then turn to examining taxation practice in Germany. Six different schemes, some applying to PAYG and some to funding, are considered. No common rule can be found as far as contributions, capital income or benefits are concerned. Tax-free allowances and deductions complicate the picture even further, without introducing any element of rationality. Since some forms are compulsory while others are voluntary, it is not generally possible to eschew this patchwork by simply choosing the most favourable scheme. Furthermore, occupational pensions and investment funds are unfavourably treated, which is difficult to justify in view of the general opinion that more funding should be called for.

Börsch Supan and Lührmann conclude in favour of a uniform system of deferred taxation on all retirement income. This would automatically benefit from the redistributional effect of progressive taxation. They are aware of the problems involved in transition, but express the hope that the German Government will find the courage to face them.

1.9. In the USA, between the early 1980s and today, defined benefits plans have continuously lost ground as compared with defined contributions plans. Richard A. Ippolito (*Tenuous property rights: The unraveling of defined benefit contracts in the US*) examines the reasons behind this trend.

The essence of a defined benefits plan rests on the promise of a pension proportional to the final wage. At any point during the working career, a 'termination' benefit has been earned, on the basis of the current wage. If the worker stays with the firm, past seniority (together with the future one) will earn a bigger ('ongoing') benefit, on the basis of the final wage. The difference between the two is called 'contingent' benefit.

Firms usually try to accumulate, year by year, not only assets corresponding to termination benefits, but also (at least part of) contingent benefits, so as to spread their burden more evenly over time. But beware. Workers are not sure, even if they are ready to stay with the firm until retirement, of receiving the contingent benefit. First of all, the firm may go bankrupt or face serious financial conditions. But there are other traps. One is 'termination for reversion', whereby firms unilaterally terminate the plan, and the excess assets (i.e. those set aside for contingent benefits) go into corporate profits. ('Reversion' means creating a new plan, but this may be of the defined contributions type). Apparently this should not be permitted, but oddly enough the Internal Revenue Service allowed it in the early 1980s. This gave rise to a high number of terminations. Congress reacted in 1988 by imposing, on excess assets so acquired by the firm, a (non deductible) tax of 10 per cent, later raised to 15 and ultimately (1990) to 50 per cent.

The second occurrence is defunding, whereby firms decrease yearly contributions until the fund comes closer to termination benefits. This clearly happened between the end of the 1980s and the mid-1990s, and appears to be one of the main consequence of the increased reversion tax. Another device is the 'cash balance plan'. An individual account is opened in the name of each participant; the firm guarantees a given return on this account, and the plan is therefore still considered of the defined benefit type. No reversion tax applies, even if the future mechanism is basically of the defined contributions type.

These developments lead to what Ippolito calls a 'lemons model'. Workers choose between defined benefits and defined contributions plans, given the present expected value of wages plus pension. Under defined contributions, assuming that the rate of return is certain so is the present value. Under defined benefits, the expected value depends on the probability that the firm does not default and does not renege (the latter being a 'contract default'). The higher the probability of a contract default, the higher the wage which is necessary to offer an expected value equal to the defined contributions sort. But the higher this wage, the larger the cost of maintaining a defined benefits plan.

Suppose further that workers do not perceive the difference between one firm and another, and ascribe to them all an average degree of trustworthiness. This leads to an overstatement of the contract default risk of firms that are actually more trustworthy than the average. These firms perceive the unjustified mark-up of the wage level and are the first ones to discontinue their defined benefits plan. But this lowers the average level of trustworthiness of the remaining ones; sooner or later workers perceive this trend and raise the premium asked for staying in a defined benefits firm. A self-reinforcing process ensues.

Ippolito's results may therefore be summed up as follows. In the old times, prudent and long-sighted firms accumulated assets that covered not only termination benefits but also (at least part of) the contingent ones. No gimmicks were played on these assets. When it became clear that excess assets (i.e. those corresponding to contingent benefits) could be turned into profits, many firms, perhaps in conjunction with take-overs or leveraged buyouts, exploited this opportunity. When taxation became too heavy, new ways were found to reach a similar goal. But these devices eroded the implicit contract embedded in defined benefits plans, which therefore lost part of their appeal for both parties. Since defined benefits plans offer a safer bonding, they are on the increase.

1.10 Proposals for strengthening the portability of pension rights within the European Union are usually based on the argument that this would enhance workers' intercountry mobility. Vincenzo Andrietti (*Occupational pensions and job mobility in the European Union*) remarks that, if lack of portability is an impediment, it should be so also inside each country. This is the topic addressed in his chapter.

Defined contributions plans usually imply that, perhaps after a vesting period of a few years, the accumulated value of contributions (with interest) may be transferred without any loss to another plan. On the contrary, as has already been seen, defined benefits plans typically link benefits to the final wage, so that a transition to another job implies, even after vesting, freezing the accrued rights to the level corresponding to the current wage (at most with price indexation for the future). In other words, the subsequent real wage increases will not impact, as far as past seniority is concerned, on the amount of benefits. The pension loss from changing job is even higher, of course, if vesting has not yet been reached.

When defined benefits apply, we therefore expect (negative) correlation between pension coverage and mobility, which is, on the face of it, a loss of efficiency. But Andrietti warns us that non-portable pensions might raise productivity 'by preserving productive jobs matches, stimulating investment in workers, or creating incentives not to shirk'; that efficiency wage premiums rather than backloaded pensions accrual patterns could be the primary cause for lower turnover rates; and that individuals might simply be less likely to leave 'good' jobs.

The chapter purports to find out whether the lack of portability characterizing most defined benefits plans actually represents an impediment to within country mobility. Some evidence is available for the USA, but not for Europe. Andrietti therefore looks at the four European countries (Denmark, Ireland, the Netherlands and the United Kingdom) where occupational pension plans are particularly important in terms both of population covered and of contribution to retirees' income.

Individual mobility choices are modelled as being driven by a comparison between benefits (expected lifetime earnings in the new job) and costs (expected lifetime earnings in the old one plus costs of mobility). But there arise many problems: lifetime earnings are not observable (only current ones are); the counterfactual wage for each individual, i.e. the one he would have earned had he not taken the actual choice (move or not move), is again not observable; nor are the mobility costs. Andrietti resorts to ingenuous econometric devices in order to tackle these problems, and ends up with a probit equation which allows us to obtain estimates of the structural parameters related to the main determinants of the individual mobility choice.

Data are taken from the European Community Household Panel, and more precisely from the 1995 and 1996 waves. With good, although not perfect, approximation all pension plans are supposed to be of the defined contributions type in Denmark and of the defined benefits type in the other three countries. Two different specifications are estimated. Model 1 enters mobility costs only through a dummy variable indicating pension coverage; model 2 maintains the dummy but also includes, between the explanatory variables, an estimate of the pension portability losses.

The results are carefully examined. As far as the pension variables are concerned, the existence of an occupational pension plan has a negative and significant coefficient only in the UK. Adding the portability loss does not change the result for the UK; for Ireland the coefficient is negative, but surprisingly offset by a positive coefficient on the dummy. All in all, and with some caveats on possible shortfalls in the data and in the assumptions, Andrietti concludes that his results cast doubts on the effectiveness of reforms aimed at improving labour market efficiency through portability measures.

1.11 The many-sided survey offered by this collection of papers shows how many complex and interrelated problems arise in the interconnection of labour markets, payroll and general taxes, social security systems and supplementary pensions. Even when these problems have been – as they usually have – the object of widespread and intensive research, the results are often provisional and debated, and the need for further inquiry everywhere present.

Different countries show similar but not identical problems. The experience of one of them is generally useful to the others; so are the results of individual researchers and scholars. CeRP intends to be a meeting point where such diverse sources are analysed and compared, and itself a centre for new research.

REFERENCES

Browning, E. (1975), 'Why the Social Insurance Budget is Too Large in a Democracy', *Economic Inquiry*, **XII** (September), 373–88.

Daveri, F. and G. Tabellini (2000), 'Unemployment, Growth and Taxation in Industrial Countries', *Economic Policy*, **30** (April), 47–104.

PART 1

Payroll taxes, the labour market and retirement choices

2. Aging in Europe: A cross-country comparison[*]

Cheti Nicoletti and Franco Peracchi

2.1 INTRODUCTION

In this chapter we describe what the first five waves of the European Commmunity Household Panel (ECHP) can tell us about health status, labour force behaviour, income and wealth of the elderly across the European Union (EU). Information of this kind is very important for public policy given the rapidly growing fraction of elderly in the European population.

The ECHP is an annual longitudinal survey carried out throughout the EU under the coordination of the Statistical Office of the European Communities (Eurostat). The survey began in 1994 as a three-wave panel and was later extended to eight waves. Its main purpose was to collect comparable information on demographic characteristics, income (especially earnings and public transfers), labour market behaviour (including job search activities), health, education and professional training, housing, migration and geographical mobility, at both the household and the personal level. In order to ensure a high level of comparability, the survey design was highly standardized across countries. The ECHP ended in year 2002 and will be replaced by the new survey EU–Statistics on Income and Living Conditions (EU–SILC), whose design and structure is not entirely clear yet. It is therefore important to understand what we can learn from the ECHP and what its limitations are as a source of information on the characteristics and behaviour of the elderly in Europe.

This chapter extends and updates a previous paper by the same authors (Nicoletti and Peracchi, 2001) along two dimensions. First, we use the 2002 User Data Base (UDB) of the ECHP, which includes the fifth (1998) wave of the survey.[1] Second, our analysis now covers all 15 countries of the European

---

[*] Financial support by the MIUR (Cofin2001 No. 2001138514_002) is gratefully acknowledged.

Union, including Sweden that only started participating to the ECHP from the fourth wave.

The remainder of the chapter is organized as follows. Section 2.2 describes the data and some of their problems. The next four sections describe what we can learn from the ECHP about some basic trends associated with aging and the role played by observed individual characteristics, such as sex, education and marital status. We focus attention on health status (Section 2.3), labour market activity (Section 2.4), income (Section 2.5) and wealth (Section 2.6). Finally, Section 2.7 offers some conclusions.

2.2   THE DATA

This chapter uses the anonymized microdata from the first five waves of the ECHP. After a brief description of the survey, we discuss a number of preliminary issues related to the data quality that ought to be taken into account when analysing the sample evidence. They include the types of response patterns, construction of the survey weights and representation of the target population, item non-response and income imputation, and the anonymization criteria adopted by Eurostat.[2]

2.2.1   Brief Description of the ECHP

The target population of the ECHP consists of all individuals living in private households within the EU. In its first (1994) wave, the ECHP covered about 60 000 households and 130 000 individuals in 12 countries, namely Belgium, Denmark, France, Germany, Greece, Ireland, Italy, Luxembourg, Netherlands, Portugal, Spain and UK.

In Belgium and the Netherlands, the ECHP was linked from the beginning to already existing national panels. In Germany, Luxembourg and the UK, instead, the first three waves of the ECHP ran parallel to already existing national panels, respectively the German Social Economic Panel (GSOEP), the Luxembourg Social Economic Panel (PSELL) and the British Household Panel Survey (BHPS). Starting from the fourth (1997) wave, it was decided to merge the ECHP into the GSOEP, the PSELL and the BHPS. Thus, for Germany and the UK, the current version of the UDB contains two data sets for the first three waves, one obtained from the original German and British ECHP, and the other derived from the GSOEP and the BHPS. From the fourth wave, the UDB only contains comparable data sets derived from the GSOEP and the BHPS. For Luxembourg, the current version of the UDB only contains the original data for the first three waves of the ECHP.

Austria, Finland and Sweden began to participate to the ECHP later, respectively from the second (1995), third (1996) and fourth (1997) waves. For Finland, however, the current version of the UDB only contains data for the third and fourth waves. The ECHP data for Sweden are derived from the Swedish Living Conditions Survey.

Table 2.1 presents, for each country, the achieved sample size in the first, third and fifth wave of the ECHP.[3] We also present additional detail for the age groups that represent the focus of this chapter, namely people aged 50–69 and 70 or older (70+). The largest sample size is for Italy and Spain, the smallest for Luxembourg and Denmark. The wide variation across countries reflects both differences in the planned sample size in the first wave and differential non-response and attrition across waves. As the table makes clear, the loss of sample units in the early waves of the ECHP has been substantial in some countries, such as Ireland and the UK.

Table 2.1 Achieved sample size by age group in the first (1994), third (1995) and fifth (1998) wave of the ECHP

	1994			1996			1998		
	50–69	70+	Total	50–69	70+	Total	50–69	70+	Total
Austria				2 024	840	7 271	1 853	808	6 560
Belgium	1 666	815	6 710	1 501	785	6 145	1 383	685	5 339
Denmark	1 523	775	5 903	1 273	612	4 994	1 117	472	4 187
Finland				2 297	598	8 173			
France	3 773	1 612	14 333	3 330	1 494	13 050	3 000	1 423	11 209
Germany	3 009	895	9 490	2 779	923	8 746			
Germany-SOEP	3 416	988	12 233	3 311	990	12 295	3 161	1 003	11 562
Greece	3 853	1 592	12 492	3 529	1 587	11 602	3 036	1 500	9 985
Ireland	2 486	975	9 904	1 945	773	7 487	1 680	707	6 324
Italy	4 877	1 724	17 729	4 915	1 834	17 736	4 435	1 814	15 934
Luxembourg	532	160	2 046	511	172	1 915			
Netherlands	2 295	953	9 407	2 336	942	9 277	2 318	926	8 826
Portugal	3 620	1 610	11 621	3 468	1 664	11 706	3 270	1 743	11 412
Spain	5 018	2 265	17 893	4 101	2 120	15 640	3 503	1 985	13 779
Sweden							2 786	1 200	9 461
UK	2 960	1 445	10 517	1 918	962	6 940			
UK-BHPS	2 149	1 107	9 028	2 162	1 118	8 949	2 247	1 133	8 868

The ECHP divides sample participants into sample and non-sample persons. Sample persons are all individuals belonging to the sample drawn for each EU country in the first year of participation plus children born after the first wave to a sample woman. Non-sample persons are all other individuals. Sample and non-sample persons may or may not be eligible for interview. Sample persons are eligible if they belong to the target population (that is, they live in a private household within the EU) and are aged 16+. In addition, eligibility of non-sample persons also requires them to live in a household containing at least one sample person.

Sample persons who are ineligible (homeless, institutionalized or live outside the EU) are 'traced' and interviewed again if they return to the target population. Not being able to follow people who become institutionalized is clearly a drawback if attention focuses on aging. Ineligible non-sample persons are not traced. Sample and non-sample persons whose refusal to respond is considered 'final' or did not return a complete questionnaire in two consecutive waves are dropped from the sample. Households not interviewed in two consecutive waves are also dropped.

The ECHP is carried out by National Data Collection Units (NDU), with Eurostat providing centralized support and coordination. The NDUs are responsible for sample selection, adaptation of the questionnaire, fieldwork, basic data processing and editing, and initial weighting of the data. Although Eurostat sets general guidelines in order to ensure comparability of survey results, the NDUs largely rely on their normal rules and routines.

All national samples are selected through probability sampling. Sampling frames and sampling procedures are not standardized across countries, however, and each NDU relies on its own methods. In most countries, the sampling frame is either the population register or a master-sample created from the latest population census. Depending on the sampling frame, we may have non-coverage of small portions of the target population, such as households recently arrived in a country (Ireland, Italy) or non-residents unable to speak the national language (Greece, Netherlands). The most common sampling procedure is two-stage sampling, with geographical areas (usually the municipalities) as primary sampling units, and households or street addresses as secondary sampling units.

An essential feature of the ECHP is the adoption of a common questionnaire centrally designed by Eurostat. The questionnaire consists of a household register, mainly for record keeping and control of the sample, a household questionnaire submitted to a 'reference person' (usually the household head or the spouse/partner of the head), and a personal questionnaire submitted to all eligible household members.

The interviewing method recommended by Eurostat is face-to-face personal interviewing, but other interviewing methods have also been used (e.g. telephone or proxy interview). In Greece, Netherlands, Portugal and the UK, interviews are carried out, at least partly, using computer-assisted personal interviewing (CAPI). All other countries rely instead on the conventional 'paper and pencil' method.

After going through standard checking routines, the microdata files collected by the NDUs are sent to Eurostat and stored in the so-called Production Data Base (PDB). Because the PDB contains information considered confidential on the basis of EU Statistical Law and has a rather complex structure, its access is confined to Eurostat and the NDUs. People interested in the ECHP may negotiate with Eurostat the purchase of the UDB, which is an anonymized and user-friendly version of the data.

2.2.2 Response Patterns

A person eligible for interview is said to be unit non-respondent in a given wave if her/his personal questionnaire is not available. Since the 2002 UBD contains five waves of the survey, a response pattern is described by the 5-tuple $D = (D_1, D_2, D_3, D_4, D_5)$, where D_j is a 0–1 indicator of unit response in wave j ($D_j = 1$ for sample respondents). The $2^5 - 1 = 31$ possible response patterns may be classified into four types:

1. regular participation: $D = (1,1,1,1,1)$,
2. monotone attrition: $D = (1,0,0,0,0)$, $(1,1,0,0,0)$, $(1,1,1,0,0)$ or $(1,1,1,1,0)$,
3. monotone entry: $D = (0,1,1,1,1)$, $(0,0,1,1,1)$, $(0,0,0,1,1)$ or $(0,0,0,0,1)$,
4. irregular response patterns: all the remaining ones.

Regular participation is the most frequent response pattern at all ages.[4] The fraction of people characterized by monotone attrition ranges between 15 and 25 per cent for most countries, but is higher than 30 per cent for Ireland and the first three waves of the ECHP in the UK. In general, the frequency of attrition shows no clear relationship with age except for Denmark and the Netherlands, where it sharply increases after age 70, and for Ireland and the UK, where it is higher for people younger than 25. The fraction of people characterized by other response patterns is low, with the exception of new entry of people younger than 30 in the Netherlands.

2.2.3 Weighting

Issues of sampling design and non-response affect the quality of the inference that can be drawn from survey data. If the sampling design is such that individuals in the target population have different probabilities of sample participation, then selection probabilities should take into account explicitly. The ECHP provides a specific set of weights for this purpose.

The ECHP also deals with three distinct types of non-response, namely household non-response (the household interview is not completed), unit non-response (the personal interview is not completed), and item non-response at either the household or the personal level (the household or the personal interview are completed but there is missing information on some questions). The ECHP provides weights to take into account household and unit non-responses, and deals with item non-response by applying an imputation procedure described in the next section. We remark that non-response may not only cause efficiency losses relative to the complete-data case, but may also bias inference. As shown by Horowitz and Manski (1998), the seriousness of the problem is directly proportional to the amount of non-response.

The ECHP provides three types of weights: (1) 'design weights' to take into account sampling design, (2) 'base weights' for household non-response, and (3) 'cross-sectional weights of interviewed persons' for unit non-response. The basic idea is to assign to each unit a weight inversely proportional to the probabilities for an individual to belong to the sample, to be resident in a responding household, and to return the personal questionnaire. The weights, however, are not the simple product of these inverse probabilities factors. Their computation is complicated by a post-weighting or 'calibration' procedure intended to reflect the population structure by sex and age, and the marginal distributions of a number of variables (household size, tenure, number of economically active persons and region).⁵ As shown in Nicoletti and Peracchi (2001), these weights succeed in correcting, at least in part, the distribution by age and sex. There are some important exceptions however for Greece, Portugal and Spain, where the use of the weights does not lead to improvements.

2.2.4 Item Non-response and Income Imputation

The ECHP deals differently with unit (or complete) non-response and item non-response. The first is dealt with by weighting, the second by imputation. Given the relevance of the information about income, in this section we briefly describe the procedure used to compute total household income when some household members are unit non-respondents, and the imputation procedure used for item non-response to income variables at the individual level.

Computation of total net household income starts by summing the personal incomes of responding household members. The ECHP corrects for unit non-response in responding households by multiplying this sum by an 'inflation factor' greater or equal to 1. To construct the inflation factor, individuals are divided into classes (depending on auxiliary variables, such as sex and age) and a weighted average of income is computed for each class. This class average is then assigned to all individuals belonging to the class, whether respondents or not, and the inflation factor of a household is computed as the ratio between the sum of the assigned personal incomes of all its members and the sum of the assigned personal incomes of its responding units.

The ECHP distinguishes among six income categories: wages and salaries, income from self-employment or farming, pensions (old-age-related benefits and survivors' benefits), unemployment/redundancy benefits, any other social benefits or grants (family-related allowances, sickness/invalidity benefits, education-related allowances, any other personal benefits, assigned social assistance, assigned housing allowance), and non-work private income (capital income, property/rental private transfers received). The same inflation factor used for total household income is also used for single components of household income.

The income imputation procedures in case of item non-response at the individual level have changed through time. The first wave of the ECHP uses random hotdeck imputation within classes and predictive mean matching. Starting from the second wave, a procedure called Imputation and Variance Estimation (IVE) has been used. This procedure may be viewed as a variant of the EM algorithm[6] because it iteratively repeats the imputation of missing values until convergence. In the first step of the IVE algorithm, imputation is carried out for variables with a low fraction of missing cases using the information from variables without missing data. In the second step, imputation is carried out for variables with more severe problems of missingness, conditioning both on variables without missing data and variables imputed in the first step; and so on. The specific model used for the imputation depends on the type of variable to be imputed.[7]

2.2.5 Anonymization Criteria

Construction of the UDB required extensive negotiations with the NDUs and various bodies of the European Commission. The anonymization criteria adopted restrict the information available on age, occupation and industry of employment, income, health status, geographical mobility and region of residence. The criteria are not the same for all countries and are generally more severe for Netherlands and the original German ECHP data.

Specifically, information on the upper end of the age distribution has been restricted by bottom-coding year of birth at 1909. Information on school attainments has been collapsed to the very coarse three-category ISCED level. Occupational codes and sector of activity are restricted to a level of aggregation intermediate between one and two digits.

Income components are aggregated at an intermediate level and converted to annual net amounts. In particular, most of the survey detail about pensions is lost in the UDB, which only distinguishes between three aggregates: old-age-related benefits, survivor pensions and sickness/invalidity benefits. Comparability of income across countries is further affected by the fact that in France all income variables (except total household income) and in Finland and all labour incomes are collected as gross instead of net. Also notice that in Sweden several income variables and all imputation indexes are unavailable, in Germany (ECHP) several income variables are not provided for confidentiality reasons, while wage and salary lump sums are missing in Austria, Finland, Germany (ECHP), Netherlands, Spain, Sweden and in the first and third waves of the BHPS.

Concerning health, the first wave only provides the total number of visits to a doctor, optician or dentist for all countries, whereas the information on the number of nights spent in a hospital as in-patient is always available for all countries except Germany.

No information on migration trajectory is available for Germany, whereas the information on foreign country of birth and last foreign country of residence is not available for Germany, Greece and the Netherlands. Finally, no regional information is available for Germany and the Netherlands, whereas for all other countries, except Finland and Portugal, the breakdown is at the coarse level of NUTS 1.

2.3   HEALTH STATUS

We now look at what the ECHP can tell us about health status, labour market activity, income and wealth of the elderly across Europe. We begin with health status because of the important role played by this variable in determining labour market outcomes for the elderly.[8]

Figure 2.1 shows the age profile of three synthetic measures of personal health status, namely the fraction of people who report themselves in bad (or very bad) health, the fraction of people who report to be severely hampered in daily activities by any physical or mental health problem, illness or disability, and the fraction of people who report having been admitted to a hospital as in-patients during the last 12 months.[9] The figure is obtained by pooling all the available waves and computing weighted frequencies using the cross-sectional personal weights. As discussed in Section 2.2.3, these weights are introduced to correct for sampling design, household non-response, and unit non-response within responding households. For Germany and the UK, we use the data from the GSOEP and the BHPS for all five waves.

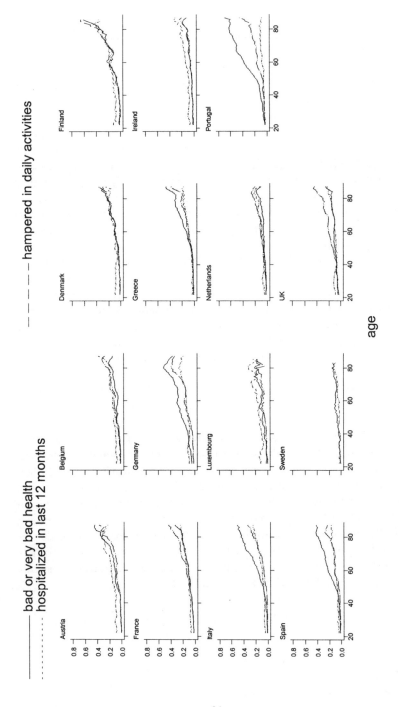

Figure 2.1 Fraction of people in bad health by country and age. Pooled data 1994–98

31

For all three measures considered, cross-country variation is substantial at all ages. Interestingly, self-reported health status tends to be worse in Southern European countries where, in fact, life expectancy is known to be higher than the European average. For all countries, aging is associated with a gradual deterioration of health status (however measured) but there is no evidence that this deterioration accelerates with age, at least over the range of ages considered (essentially 50 to 85 years).

To understand the role played by other factors besides age, we estimate a simple model for the conditional probability $p(X)$ of being in bad health given observable individual characteristics X. Our measure of health status is a binary indicator equal to one if the person is severely hampered in daily activities by any physical or mental health problem, illness or disability, and equal to zero otherwise. The model is a standard logit model of the form $p(X) = \exp(\alpha + \beta' X)/[1 + \exp(\alpha + \beta' X)]$, where α and β are parameters to be estimated and the covariate vector X includes age, age squared, the level of equivalized household income (see Section 2.5), and indicators for the highest level of completed education (2 dummies, one for college and one for secondary education) and not having a spouse. The intercept α corresponds to the log-odds of being severely hampered in daily activities for a person aged 60, married, with only primary education completed and equivalized household income equal to the country median for people aged 50+.

Table 2.2 reports the estimates obtained by fitting the model to the subsample of people aged 50+ separately for men and women and by country. Although the goodness of fit (as measured by the pseudo R^2 in the last column of the table) is rather low, indicating the importance of other factors that are left out of the model, the estimates confirm the worsening of health status with age. More interestingly, we find that the probability of being in good health is strongly positively related to educational attainments, especially for men, and is higher for those who are married than for those who are not. Household income is found to have an important effect, even after controlling for education and marital status. In fact, the probability of being in bad health falls significantly with equivalized household income, especially for men. A comparison of the estimated intercepts shows that the baseline odds of being in bad health are lowest for men in Ireland and Italy, for women in Austria, Ireland and Italy, and are highest for both men and women in Finland, France, Germany and the UK.

Table 2.2 *Estimated logit models for the probability of being severely hampered in daily activities by any physical or mental health problem, illness or disability. (** denotes an observed significance level below 5%, * denotes an observed significance level between 5 and 10%)*

Country	Intercept	Age	Age^2	Tertiary	Second.	No spouse	Hh.Income	n	R^2
					Men				
Austria	-1.842**	0.032**	0.001**	-0.927**	-0.664**	0.085	-0.004	4 994	0.055
Belgium	-1.978**	0.037**	0.000	-0.753**	-0.159	0.111	-0.010**	4 970	0.043
Denmark	-2.304**	0.043**	-0.001*	-0.399**	-0.077	0.240**	-0.070**	4 433	0.062
Finland	-1.549**	0.069**	0.000	-1.472**	0.065	0.206	-0.005	2 823	0.100
France	-1.671**	0.042**	0.000	-0.755**	-0.179**	0.356**	-0.037**	10 659	0.062
Germany	-1.491**	0.041**	0.000	-0.710**	-0.286**	-0.001	-0.024**	7 907	0.038
Greece	-2.149**	0.043**	0.000	-0.751**	-0.124	0.221**	-0.049**	11 366	0.049
Ireland	-2.596**	0.025**	0.001**	-1.339**	-0.474**	-0.201*	-0.046**	6 763	0.054
Italy	-2.495**	0.050**	0.000	-0.613**	-0.755**	0.419**	-0.029**	15 070	0.068
Luxembourg	-2.459**	0.010	0.002*	-0.726	-0.927**	0.574**	-0.036**	985	0.073
Netherlands	-1.984**	0.033**	-0.000	-0.282**	-0.242**	-0.027	-0.048**	7 434	0.035
Portugal	-1.762**	0.042**	-0.000	-0.737**	-0.440*	-0.070	-0.067**	11 211	0.045
Spain	-2.144**	0.036**	-0.000	-0.602**	-0.592**	0.216**	-0.049**	13 644	0.032
Sweden	-2.289**	0.010	0.001	-1.080**	-0.107	-0.121	-0.045**	2 460	0.038
UK	-1.204**	0.030**	-0.001**	-0.427**	-0.124	0.143**	-0.018**	7 115	0.024

Table 2.2 (continued)

Country	Intercept	Age	Age²	Tertiary	Second.	No spouse	Hh. Income	n	R²
					Women				
Austria	−2.478**	0.026**	0.002**	−0.815**	−0.290**	0.244**	−0.014**	6 000	0.082
Belgium	−2.176***	0.034**	0.001**	−0.672***	−0.279***	0.327***	0.000	5 890	0.052
Denmark	−2.009***	0.039***	−0.000	−0.338***	−0.397***	0.159*	−0.021**	4 884	0.043
Finland	−1.720***	0.048***	0.001**	−1.215***	−0.308***	0.045	0.003	2 928	0.093
France	−1.657***	0.040**	−0.000	−0.599***	−0.223***	0.200**	−0.025***	12 268	0.047
Germany	−1.720***	0.038***	0.001**	−0.082	−0.141***	−0.141***	−0.015***	8 874	0.043
Greece	−2.246***	0.047***	−0.000	−0.483***	−0.344***	0.159***	−0.023***	13 061	0.042
Ireland	−3.051***	0.054***	0.000	−0.539***	−0.232	0.344***	−0.018***	6 855	0.069
Italy	−2.337***	0.062***	0.000	−0.516***	−0.611***	0.135***	−0.017***	16 389	0.074
Luxembourg	−2.511**	0.001	0.001	1.052***	0.352	0.182	−0.027***	1 042	0.021
Netherlands	−2.012***	0.024***	0.001*	−0.240*	−0.255***	0.200***	−0.009***	8 393	0.027
Portugal	−1.742***	0.040***	0.000	−0.379	−1.646***	−0.012	−0.021***	13 630	0.034
Spain	−2.246***	0.041***	0.000*	−0.510***	−0.833***	0.066	−0.036***	16 265	0.047
Sweden	−2.289***	0.010	0.001	−1.080***	−0.107	−0.121	−0.045***	2 460	0.038
UK	−1.334**	0.005	0.002**	−0.236***	−0.415***	0.138**	−0.018***	8 865	0.039

2.4   LABOUR MARKET ACTIVITY

The ECHP collects detailed information on labour market activity. We focus on current labour force status and adopt the standard International Labour Office (ILO) classification in three categories: employed, unemployed and inactive (out of the labour force). The employed are those whose current activity is paid employment, paid apprenticeship, or training under special schemes related to employment or self-employment.[10] Following the ILO definition, the unemployed are those who are looking for a job, are ready to work and have carried out some search activity in the last month.[11] The inactive are those who are neither employed nor unemployed. We adopt the convention of classifying people aged 65+ as inactive if they report themselves as unemployed.

This section only considers people in the 50–69 age range and analyses employment rates and exit from employment into either unemployment or inactivity. We are mainly interested in documenting cross-country differences in the characteristics of the retirement process and how they relate to observable individual characteristics.

2.4.1   Employment Rates

Figure 2.2 shows the distribution of current activity status by country and age.[12] In all countries, the fraction of people employed (the employment rate) declines with age while the fraction of inactive people increases. The various countries differ, however, in the initial level of the two profiles, and in their subsequent slopes at the various ages. The fraction of people unemployed also tends to decline with age, although in some countries (Austria, Belgium, Denmark, Finland, France, Germany and Spain) it rises again immediately before age 60. This phenomenon largely reflects the role played by unemployment insurance as one of the pathways of exit from the labour force. In fact, the fraction of people unemployed drops to almost zero in all countries around the age of eligibility for early retirement benefits, lending some support to the view that, at least for the elderly, unemployment and inactivity are not behaviourally distinct labour force states (Flinn and Heckman, 1983).

To control for the effect of observable individual characteristics, Table 2.3 shows the estimates of a simple logit model for the probability of employment fitted separately by country and gender. The model includes among the covariates a cubic polynomial in age, and indicators for educational attainments (two dummies, one for college and one for secondary education), not having a spouse and bad health. The intercept of the model

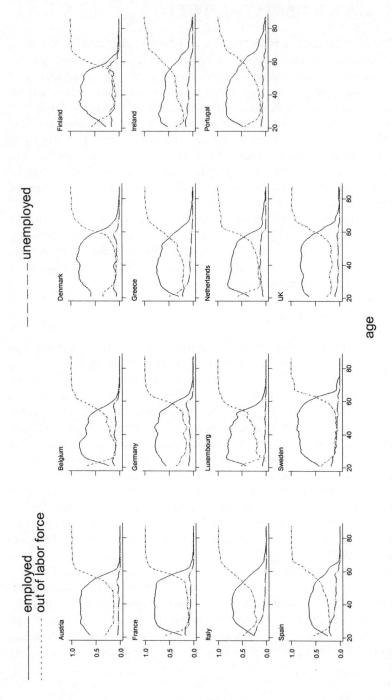

Figure 2.2 Distribution of labour force status by country and age. Pooled data 1994–98

Table 2.3 Estimated logit models for the probability of being employed (** denotes an observed significance level below 5%, * denotes an observed significance level between 5 and 10%).

Country	Intercept	Age	Age^2	Age^3	Tertiary	Second.	No spouse	Bad health	n	R^2
					Men					
Austria	-1.450**	-0.519**	0.003	0.002**	1.215***	0.499**	-0.510**	-1.647**	3 810	0.422
Belgium	-0.855***	-0.372**	0.002	0.001**	0.785***	0.583**	-0.577***	-2.659**	3 498	0.384
Denmark	0.463**	-0.361**	-0.001	0.002**	0.649**	-0.073	-0.885**	-1.684**	3 184	0.338
Finland	-0.271**	-0.260**	-0.002	-0.000	0.422**	0.172	-0.591**	-0.891**	2 149	0.276
France	-1.090**	-0.540**	0.002	0.002**	1.107**	0.165**	-0.374**	-1.460**	7 742	0.496
Germany	-0.295**	-0.358**	-0.004**	0.001**	0.681**	0.031	-0.047	-0.785**	8 218	0.312
Greece	0.549**	-0.282**	-0.003**	0.001**	-0.097	-0.579**	-0.381**	-1.857**	8 454	0.288
Ireland	0.680**	-0.187**	-0.005**	0.000	0.619**	-0.050	-0.568**	-2.611**	5 014	0.195
Italy	-0.272**	-0.217**	-0.004**	-0.000	1.579***	0.418**	-0.327**	-1.003**	11 681	0.242
Luxembourg	-1.672**	-0.463**	0.015**	0.003**	1.248***	0.270	-0.342	-2.189**	809	0.433
Netherlands	-0.603**	-0.417**	0.008**	0.002**	0.571***	0.246**	-0.676**	-1.803**	5 424	0.361
Portugal	1.003**	-0.128**	-0.004**	-0.000**	0.259	-0.318**	-0.237**	-1.418**	7 901	0.192
Spain	0.089**	-0.267**	-0.020**	-0.001**	0.959**	0.309**	-0.530**	-1.411**	9 825	0.332
Sweden	1.150**	-0.311**	-0.015**	0.000	0.504**	0.020	-0.508**	-2.328**	1 511	0.357
UK	0.542**	-0.242**	-0.010**	0.000	-0.035	0.203**	-0.327**	-0.779**	5 077	0.244

Table 2.3 (continued)

Country	Intercept	Age	Age²	Age³	Tertiary	Second.	No spouse	Bad health	n	R^2
					Women					
Austria	-2.406**	-0.333***	-0.009*	-0.000	1.065**	0.440**	0.115	-0.572**	4 093	0.259
Belgium	-2.614***	-0.304***	0.001	0.001**	1.298***	0.774***	0.337**	-1.006***	3 977	0.271
Denmark	-0.787***	-0.289***	-0.009***	0.000	0.971***	0.606***	-0.097	-1.916***	3 317	0.302
Finland	-0.502**	-0.336***	-0.012***	0.000	0.644***	0.194	-0.304***	-1.259***	2 203	0.301
France	-1.602***	-0.393***	-0.008***	0.001**	0.544***	0.115	0.575***	-1.089***	8 542	0.303
Germany	-1.602***	-0.394***	-0.010***	0.001**	0.863***	0.102*	0.550***	-0.535***	8 189	0.254
Greece	-1.189***	-0.161***	-0.007***	-0.000	0.315***	-0.675***	0.073	-1.065***	8 959	0.123
Ireland	-2.244***	-0.159***	-0.007***	-0.000	1.893***	0.580***	0.416***	-1.710***	5 051	0.159
Italy	-2.382***	-0.254***	-0.002	0.001**	1.954***	1.219***	0.682***	-0.409***	11 999	0.190
Luxembourg	-3.281***	-0.416***	-0.004	0.002	1.896***	1.046***	0.860***	-0.736*	756	0.267
Netherlands	-2.448***	-0.272***	0.001	0.001**	1.362***	0.297***	1.008***	-1.240***	5 985	0.215
Portugal	-0.419***	-0.107***	-0.010***	-0.001***	1.317***	0.030	0.269***	-0.828***	9 355	0.117
Spain	-2.052***	-0.161***	-0.018***	-0.001***	1.690***	0.780***	0.999***	-0.321***	10 755	0.170
Sweden	0.747***	-0.298***	-0.022***	-0.000	0.770***	0.171	-0.394***	-1.727***	1 622	0.342
UK	-0.935***	-0.275***	-0.004***	0.001**	0.328***	0.293***	0.251***	-0.275***	5 792	0.222

corresponds to the log-odds of being employed for a person aged 60, married, in good health, and with only primary education completed.

The behaviour by age agrees with the non-parametric estimates in Figure 2.2. In all countries except Greece, employment probabilities increase with schooling attainments and are significantly higher for people with tertiary education (college degree). They are also lower for people in bad health. Another common feature is the different effect of marital status on the employment probabilities of men and women: not having a spouse tends to reduce employment probabilities for men, whereas for women the effect is just the opposite except in the Nordic countries (Denmark, Finland and Sweden).

2.4.2 Exit into Retirement

The availability of only five waves of ECHP data and the substantial amount of sample attrition only enable us to analyse short-run dynamics between labour force states. Thus, we can study labour force transitions between two consecutive years but it is impossible, without strong assumptions, to reconstruct complete work careers.

Here we exploit the longitudinal nature of the ECHP to study cross-country differences in the exit rates from employment into retirement (either unemployment or inactivity) over a one-year period for individuals in the 50–69 age range as a function of sex, age and other personal characteristics.

Figure 2.3 shows exit rates from employment by sex and age estimated by pooling the available pairs of waves. The limited sample size leads to very noisy estimates of retirement rates for some countries. For most countries, nonetheless, these non-parametric estimates reveal the presence of peaks in the retirement hazards at certain ages (typically age 60 or age 65). These peaks are commonly explained as the result of Social Security rules, which induce concentration of exit at certain ages.[13] We do not show exit rates from either unemployment or inactivity into employment because in all countries, except possibly the UK, this state is absorbing, with exit rates that decline rapidly with age and become negligible for both men and women after age 55.

To control for the effect of observable individual characteristics, Table 2.4 shows the estimates of a simple logit model for the probability of leaving employment. The model, fitted separately by sex and country, is similar to the one discussed in the previous section, except that the covariate vector now contains a linear trend in age, indicators for age 60 and age 65, and indicators for educational attainments (two dummies, one for college and one for secondary education), not having a spouse and bad health. The intercept of the model corresponds to the log-odds of leaving employment for a person

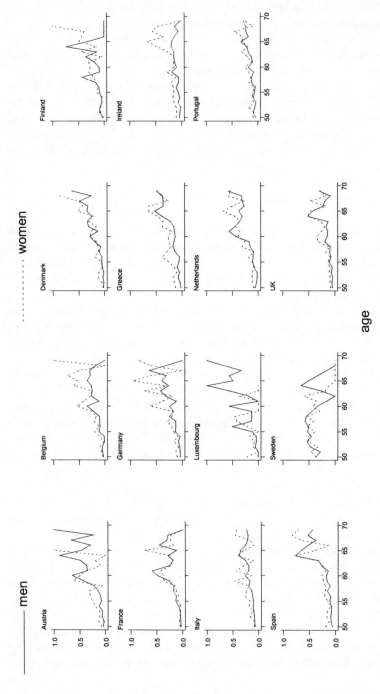

Figure 2.3 Age profiles of exit rates from employment. Pooled data 1994–98

Table 2.4 Estimated logit models for the probability of leaving employment (** denotes an observed significance level below 5%, *denotes an observed significance level between 5 and 10%).

Country	Intercept	Age	Age 60	Age 65	Tertiary	Secondary	No spouse	Bad health	n	R^2
				Men						
Austria	-2.101**	0.272**	1.437**	-0.234	-0.941*	-0.200	0.347	1.993**	1109	0.190
Belgium	-2.130***	0.160***	1.044***	0.958	-0.818***	-0.379	-0.137	0.642	1109	0.123
Denmark	-2.879***	0.222***	1.032***	-0.088	-0.328	0.094	0.239	1.245**	1413	0.196
Finland	-2.181***	0.115***	-1.001	0.196	-1.029**	-0.076	0.158	0.955***	522	0.088
France	-2.112***	0.223***	1.035**	-1.622	-0.672***	-0.053	-0.259	0.936***	2464	0.153
Germany	-2.372***	0.158***	0.413***	0.815***	-0.230	0.197	0.329**	0.840***	3337	0.096
Greece	-2.500***	0.160***	-0.175	0.647**	-0.528**	0.096	0.422*	0.520***	3493	0.116
Ireland	-2.771***	0.101***	0.281	0.452	-0.258	0.087	-0.016	1.336***	2231	0.051
Italy	-2.000**	0.107***	0.279	0.843***	-0.716***	-0.431**	0.137	0.650***	4310	0.062
Luxembourg	-2.197***	0.289***	0.673	-0.691	-0.401	-0.960	-0.609	3.089***	210	0.315
Netherlands	-2.430***	0.187***	1.520**	0.275	-0.312	-0.050	0.083	1.500***	1992	0.166
Portugal	-2.757***	0.101**	0.125	0.722***	0.169	0.263	-0.056	0.850***	3660	0.073
Spain	-2.254***	0.161***	-0.174	1.607***	-0.515***	-0.107	0.398**	1.054***	3183	0.112
UK	-2.539***	0.137***	-0.007	1.285***	0.233	-0.116	0.062	0.534***	2185	0.082

Table 2.4 (continued)

Country	Intercept	Age	Age 60	Age 65	Tertiary	Secondary	No spouse	Bad health	n	R^2
					Women					
Austria	-1.403**	0.169**	0.144		-0.189	-0.153	-0.111	1.176***	611	0.067
Belgium	-1.780***	0.182***	1.266***	-0.515	-0.307	-0.437	-0.055	1.361**	600	0.143
Denmark	-2.193***	0.165***	0.742**	0.798	-0.110	-0.097	-0.097	1.875***	1054	0.126
Finland	-2.106***	0.163***	0.331	0.728	-0.800*	0.348	-0.091	0.788	497	0.118
France	-2.105***	0.167***	0.714***	1.347**	-0.281	-0.061	-0.188	0.180	1758	0.099
Germany	-1.724***	0.183***	1.659***	1.713***	-0.194	-0.040	-0.172	0.537**	1893	0.093
Greece	-1.474***	0.104***	-0.144	0.913***	-0.324	0.247	-0.024	-0.026	1503	0.060
Ireland	-1.449***	0.097***	-0.202	1.857***	-0.910**	-0.031	-0.359	3.005***	634	0.076
Italy	-1.323***	0.115***	-0.238	-0.567	-0.588***	-0.625**	-0.177	0.072	1698	0.049
Luxembourg	-1.690***	0.151			0.604	0.314	-1.182	1.411	76	0.089
Netherlands	-1.059***	0.148***	0.439	1.639*	-0.741***	-0.264	-0.919**	0.212	899	0.108
Portugal	-1.909***	0.082***	0.078	-0.009	-0.855***	0.261	-0.146	0.366**	2286	0.036
Spain	-1.359***	0.099***	0.010	0.419	-0.974***	-0.618***	-0.337**	0.697***	1209	0.081
UK	-1.955***	0.121**	0.688**	0.780*	0.204	-0.036	-0.163	0.450**	1789	0.064

aged 55, married, in good health and with only primary education completed. We exclude Sweden because of the limited sample size.

Qualitatively, the behaviour of the estimates by sex and age agrees with the non-parametric estimates in Figure 2.3. In particular, exit rates from employment at age 55 are higher for women than for men. Retirement rates increase with age in all countries and the dummies for age 60 or 65 are positive in most countries. In most countries, retirement rates decrease with schooling attainments and are significantly lower for people with college degrees. For women, they are also lower for people without a spouse. Finally, as already found for the ECHP by Jiménez *et al.* (1999), bad health significantly increases the probability of leaving employment over a one-year period.

2.5 INCOME

In addition to changes in health status and the allocation of time to market and non-market activities, aging is associated with important changes in the level and composition of income. Standard measures of the level of income are total household income, total equivalized household income and total personal income. Equivalized household income is total household income divided by the number of 'adult equivalents' in the household, as measured by the modified OECD scale. The different age profiles of these three income measures largely reflects the impact of changes in household size and composition.

The role of household size and composition is indicated in Figure 2.4, which reports the average size (number of persons in the household) and the average number of adults (persons aged 16+) in households that contain at least one adult by the age of that person. The age profile of household size declines over the 20–30 age range, reaches a minimum at about age 30, and rises again peaking at about age 40. It then starts a prolonged decline over the remainder of the age range. In Greece, Ireland, Italy and Spain, however, the decline stops around age 70 and the average size of a household never falls below two (in Ireland, Italy and Spain it actually increases again for people aged 80+). In all other countries, the decline is instead monotone and the household size eventually falls below two (this occurs as early as age 60 in Denmark). The age profile of the average number of adults is very similar, except that both the bottom of the U-shaped portion of the profile and the subsequent peak are reached later. The difference between the two curves, which is just the average number of household members aged less than 16, becomes negligible at about age 50 in all countries.

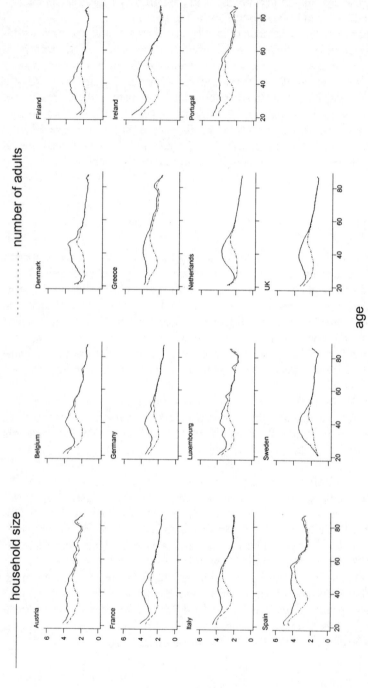

Figure 2.4 Average household size and average number of adults in households that contain at least one person aged 16+ by country and age of that person. Pooled data 1994–98

2.5.1   Level and Composition of Income

Table 2.5 presents summary statistics (the median and the interquartile range) of our three income measures.[14] The original data (in national currencies and current prices) have been converted to 1998 prices and a common scale by using purchasing power parities. All income measures refer to the year before the survey and are net of income and payroll taxes (and after item and unit imputation). The number of adult equivalents in a household is measured according to the OECD scale.

Cross-country differences in median income (top half of Table 2.5) are large at all ages. Cross-country variability of median household income tends to decline with age, but there is little evidence of cross-country convergence for the other two income measures. In all countries, however, cross-sectional median household income falls with age. At age 80, median household income is about half its level at age 50. Although this phenomenon also reflects cohort effects, most of it appears to be a genuine feature of the life cycle. In all countries, the reduction in household income is at least partly offset by the parallel reduction of household size. Thus, the median of equivalized household income falls much less, and in some countries (Italy, and Spain) hardly changes with age. Finally, the pattern of median personal income is intermediate between the one of household income and equivalized household income.

Information on the variability of income is provided by the bottom half of Table 2.5 that presents the interquartile range of our three income measures at selected ages (50, 60, 70 and 80). The variability of all income measures tends to fall with age. This decline is particularly strong for personal income. In some countries (most notably Ireland, Portugal and Spain), the drop in the variability of personal income is quite sharp and concentrated in the age range where retirement typically occurs.

Parallel to the age-related changes in the distribution by activity status described in Section 2.4, we observe substantial changes in the composition of personal income (Figure 2.5). As employment rates fall and the fraction of inactive people rises, the importance of earnings on total personal income also falls and that of pension income rises. Except for Italy, Finland and Sweden other types of transfers (mainly unemployment insurance and sickness/invalidity benefits) play an important role over the range of ages (55–65) that correspond to the transition from activity to inactivity, but become negligible afterwards (except in Belgium and Denmark). The role played by other types of income (asset income and private transfers received) is instead negligible.

Table 2.5 Median and interquartile range of income (in thousands of purchasing power parities and 1998 prices) by country and age. Pooled data 1994–98

Country	Household income				Equiv. hh income				Personal income			
	50	60	70	80	50	60	70	80	50	60	70	80
Median												
Austria	31.3	24.0	19.5	14.8	15.6	13.0	11.8	11.0	12.5	9.6	9.0	8.5
Belgium	28.2	20.7	15.0	11.2	14.6	12.8	10.9	9.4	14.2	10.3	10.1	8.7
Denmark	29.3	21.0	13.4	11.1	16.0	13.8	9.6	8.8	13.4	11.2	7.7	7.5
Finland	22.1	16.3	13.0	10.5	12.1	11.0	9.0	8.2	15.4	11.6	8.4	8.1
France	27.4	19.5	16.5	13.9	14.1	11.9	11.4	10.4	13.9	10.0	9.5	8.9
Germany	29.3	20.9	17.7	14.8	15.4	13.1	12.7	12.0	13.9	9.5	9.9	11.4
Greece	17.4	12.7	9.0	7.1	7.8	7.0	5.7	4.8	7.6	5.1	4.6	3.2
Ireland	25.6	20.4	11.4	9.6	10.3	9.9	7.6	6.6	8.4	5.7	5.4	5.3
Italy	22.2	18.3	13.2	12.2	10.3	9.8	8.9	8.5	11.1	8.0	6.5	6.7
Luxembourg	45.7	31.0	26.0	24.5	21.2	19.1	18.4	18.3	19.2	17.1	15.7	19.0
Netherlands	26.0	20.1	15.1	11.4	13.8	13.2	11.1	9.0	13.1	10.7	9.2	8.3
Portugal	17.3	12.6	8.1	5.6	7.4	6.5	5.0	4.1	6.1	3.3	3.0	2.9
Spain	20.5	16.4	12.4	11.3	8.3	8.1	7.7	7.1	6.4	4.6	6.1	5.6
Sweden	24.2	21.1	15.6	11.3	13.8	14.5	11.0	9.1	12.2	11.8	8.9	8.2
UK	30.5	23.1	14.3	10.8	16.1	14.8	10.1	8.8	13.3	10.8	7.9	7.1
Interquartile range												
Austria	23.0	19.2	17.0	16.9	8.7	7.9	6.7	8.1	15.5	11.1	8.1	7.4
Belgium	20.8	18.9	11.9	8.9	9.1	9.2	7.1	6.3	13.3	12.7	10.9	6.4
Denmark	16.0	12.5	7.3	6.4	7.3	6.5	4.6	3.6	6.4	6.4	5.3	4.0
Finland	14.2	10.8	8.2	7.3	5.9	5.8	3.9	3.7	12.3	8.4	6.2	4.5
France	19.0	16.2	13.3	12.3	11.0	9.3	7.2	7.6	15.2	12.3	9.5	8.3
Germany	20.9	18.1	11.9	13.7	9.5	9.4	7.5	8.0	14.6	12.2	10.3	9.8
Greece	14.9	13.3	9.5	10.5	6.8	6.4	5.1	4.3	13.4	10.6	6.5	4.7
Ireland	20.3	21.4	11.5	9.9	8.4	8.5	6.0	3.5	16.1	13.0	5.2	2.1
Italy	17.4	15.6	11.1	11.6	7.8	6.7	6.1	6.0	15.9	11.2	5.8	5.0
Luxembourg	30.6	27.8	24.6	17.7	13.9	13.6	11.6	10.4	37.6	24.9	18.0	12.9
Netherlands	15.1	15.2	11.5	8.5	8.0	8.6	7.3	5.1	16.8	16.6	7.8	4.7
Portugal	14.9	14.1	9.2	6.9	6.4	5.5	4.7	3.3	11.1	6.4	3.2	2.2
Spain	17.4	16.6	11.7	13.0	7.0	6.8	5.2	4.4	15.2	11.0	5.1	2.2
Sweden	15.1	12.7	9.9	7.4	6.6	6.3	5.0	3.9	6.1	6.1	4.5	3.4
UK	20.3	20.1	11.1	10.5	10.3	10.4	6.4	6.6	12.9	12.4	7.0	5.7

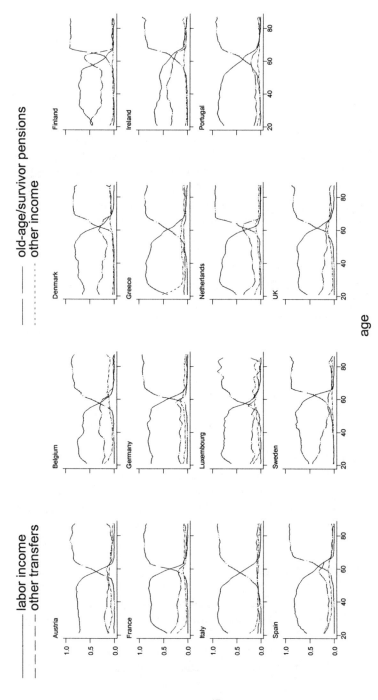

labor income
other transfers
old-age/survivor pensions
other income

age

Figure 2.5 Composition of personal income by country and age. Pooled data 1994–98

47

2.5.2 Poverty

The problem of poverty among the elderly is of great concern for public policy. The issue is controversial, however, because of the lack of agreement on how poverty should be measured. In this section we follow one of the possible approaches and define poverty in relative terms, namely as having an equivalized household income that falls below a 'poverty line' defined as a given fraction of the country-specific median equivalized household income. Even following this approach does not solve all problems, however, as there is no clear consensus on how household income should be scaled and where to draw the poverty line. As far as the first problem is concerned, we simply adopt the modified OECD scale. With regard to the second problem, we explore the sensitivity of the results to different income cut-offs.

Figure 2.6 presents the incidence of poverty by age in the countries of the EU under three alternative cut-offs, namely 40 per cent, 50 per cent and 60 per cent of median equivalized household income. The last of the three corresponds to the 'poverty line' adopted by the European Commission. For each country, median income has been computed by pooling all the available waves using the weights provided by the survey.

European countries display considerable variation both in the incidence of poverty at each age and its profile by age. In particular, the incidence of poverty declines monotonically with age in Finland, Italy, Netherlands and Sweden; it increases monotonically with age in Greece and Portugal; it is U-shaped in Denmark and the UK; and shows no recognizable pattern in all the other countries.[15] Our general conclusion is that, in most countries, poverty is a problem among younger people but not among the elderly, whereas the opposite is only true in a few countries (Denmark, Greece, Portugal and the UK).

In the remainder of this section we look at the two main income sources of the elderly, namely wage and salary earnings and old-age pensions. We present evidence on cross-country differences in the structure of these income components, that is, on differentials by sex, age, and other observable individual characteristics, and on replacement rates by sex, age and education.

2.5.3 Structure of Earnings

Table 2.6 presents the estimates of a simple median regression model for the logarithm $\ln W$ of monthly current wage and salary earnings, net of taxes and social security contributions, at constant 1998 prices and converted to a common scale by using purchasing power parities. The model specifies the conditional median of W given a vector X of observable individual

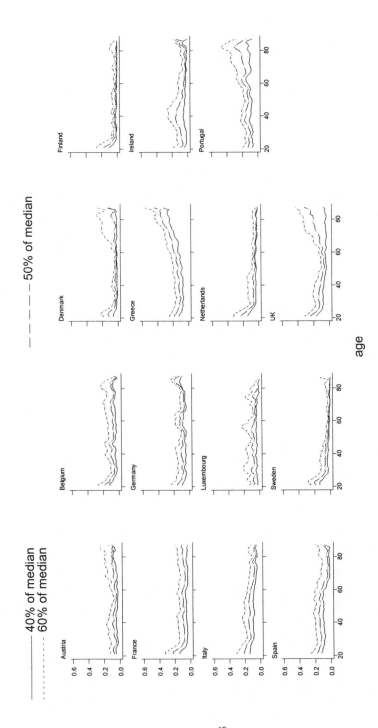

Figure 2.6 Fraction of people below the poverty line by country and age for different definitions of the poverty line. Pooled data 1994–98

Table 2.6 Estimated median regression models for the logarithm of net monthly wage and salary earnings of full-time non-agricultural employees in thousands of purchasing power parities and 1998 (** denotes an observed significance level below 5%, * denotes an observed significance level between 5 and 10%).

Country	Intercept	Age	Experience	Tertiary	Secondary	No spouse	Bad health	n	R^2
				Men					
Austria	7.078**	−0.053**	−0.006**	0.742**	0.247**	−0.036	−0.100*	1146	0.108
Belgium	7.274**	0.002	−0.000	0.372**	0.126**	−0.105**	−0.150**	1044	0.123
Denmark	7.029**	−0.006**	−0.001*	0.318**	0.050**	−0.033*	−0.080*	1460	0.119
Finland	7.377**	−0.006	−0.001	0.624**	0.167**	−0.122**	−0.083	602	0.179
France	7.105**	0.015	0.002**	0.768**	0.148**	−0.097**	−0.145**	2071	0.171
Germany	7.183**	0.010**	0.001**	0.400**	0.029*	−0.058**	−0.052**	3583	0.095
Greece	6.736**	−0.007	−0.001	0.542**	0.319**	0.052	−0.023	1471	0.141
Ireland	7.132**	−0.011**	−0.000	0.675**	0.274**	−0.286**	−0.110	1343	0.211
Italy	7.013**	−0.012**	−0.001**	0.587**	0.234**	−0.053**	−0.080**	2355	0.140
Luxembourg	7.618**	0.009	0.001	0.731**	0.466**	−0.142**	−0.206	250	0.212
Netherlands	7.347**	−0.006	−0.001	0.342**	−0.027	−0.125**	−0.093	1872	0.102
Portugal	6.501**	−0.009**	−0.000	1.191**	0.620**	−0.103**	−0.142**	2009	0.187
Spain	6.978**	−0.007*	−0.000	0.682**	0.320**	−0.029	−0.175**	2594	0.183
Sweden	6.952**	−0.006	−0.000	0.343**	0.135**	−0.081**	−0.323**	686	0.103
UK	7.019**	−0.018**	−0.001	0.313**	0.132**	−0.124**	−0.153**	1768	0.080

Table 2.6

Country	Intercept	Age	Experience	Tertiary	Secondary	No spouse	Bad health	n	R^2
					Women				
Austria	6.845**	-0.002	-0.001	0.688**	0.355**	-0.031	-0.150	386	0.107
Belgium	6.890**	-0.020**	-0.001	0.353**	0.162**	0.049**	0.063	468	0.157
Denmark	6.818**	0.006	0.000	0.283**	0.151**	0.034*	-0.126**	983	0.112
Finland	7.051**	-0.007	-0.001	0.389**	0.111**	0.052	-0.003	709	0.143
France	6.878**	-0.012	-0.000	0.524**	0.129**	-0.003	-0.113*	1250	0.114
Germany	6.837**	0.003	-0.000	0.307**	0.044	0.131**	-0.012	1647	0.050
Greece	6.408**	-0.006	0.000	0.600**	0.337**	0.004	-0.091	396	0.156
Ireland	6.797**	0.013	0.001	0.708**	0.196**	-0.014	-0.165	349	0.200
Italy	6.835**	-0.004	-0.001	0.377**	0.240**	0.024	-0.074**	785	0.127
Luxembourg	7.008**	-0.117**	-0.009**	-0.238	0.974**	-0.206	-0.089	68	0.165
Netherlands	7.013**	-0.001	-0.001	0.308**	0.001	0.070	0.230	398	0.104
Portugal	6.214**	-0.008	0.000	1.106**	0.706**	0.101**	-0.065	1100	0.189
Spain	6.668**	-0.015**	-0.002*	0.662**	0.399**	0.074**	-0.052	757	0.244
Sweden	6.720**	-0.012**	-0.001*	0.301**	0.037*	0.028	-0.252**	671	0.102
UK	6.590**	-0.008	0.000	0.529**	0.207**	-0.064*	0.003	1200	0.118

characteristics as $m(X) = \alpha + \beta' X$, where α and β are parameters to be estimated and the vector X includes age, potential labour market experience (defined as the difference between the current age and the one at which the person started her/his working life), indicators for educational attainments, not having a spouse and bad health. The use of median regression instead of the more conventional mean regression offers some protection against outliers and makes the interpretation of the results somewhat easier. Notice, in particular, that the intercept α corresponds to the logarithm of median monthly earnings for a worker aged 60, married, with 40 years of labour market experience and only primary education completed. Because the median is equivariant under increasing transformations, it then follows that the exponential of the intercept α corresponds to median monthly earnings for a worker aged 60, married, with 40 years of labour market experience and only primary education completed.

The model has been fitted separately by country and sex using the subsample of full-time non-agricultural employees aged 50–69, full-time being defined as working at least 30 hours per week. The estimated standard errors have been computed under the homoscedasticity assumption. Table 2.6 also reports a measure of goodness of fit (R^2) computed, by analogy with ordinary least squares, as the complement to 1 of the ratio between the mean absolute regression residual and the mean absolute deviation of log earnings from its median.

Most of the estimated coefficients have the expected sign. In particular, earnings increase with educational attainments (often substantially, as in Austria, France, Ireland, Portugal and Spain) and tend to decrease with age. They also tend to be lower for people in bad health and, in the case of men (but not of women), for people without a spouse. As expected, the intercept is always smaller for women than for men, although the coefficients on age, experience and the education dummies do not differ systematically between men and women. The only variable that does not seem to have the expected sign is labour market experience, whose coefficient is mostly negative.

As in the case of employment probabilities and exit rates from the labour force, cross-country differences in the estimated coefficients are very large. For example, the estimated baseline 'gender gap' ranges from a minimum of about 19 per cent in Italy to a maximum of 84 per cent in Luxembourg, whereas the variability in the size of the education dummies is even larger. What accounts for these large differences across countries, in particular the relative importance of market forces, institutional settings and measurement problems, is an open issue.

2.5.4   Structure of Pensions

Table 2.7 presents the estimates of a simple median regression model for the logarithm ln*P* of net monthly old-age pension benefits, defined as annual benefits divided by 12, at constant 1998 prices and converted to a common scale by using purchasing power parities.

The model for ln*P* is similar to the one discussed in the previous section for the logarithm of earnings except that the covariate vector now contains the number of years since retirement (defined as the difference between the current year and the year the person stopped working in the last job), the length of the work career, and indicators for educational attainments (two dummies, one for college and one for secondary education) and not having a spouse. The intercept of the model corresponds to the logarithm of median monthly benefits for a new retiree, married, with a work career of 40 years and only primary education completed. The model has been fitted separately by country and sex using the subsample of people aged 50+ who have been retired for at least one year.[16] As before, the estimated standard errors have been computed under the homoscedasticity assumption.

The coefficients on education have the same sign and magnitude as those in Table 2.6, which is exactly what one would expect if pension benefits were roughly proportional to lifetime earnings, as is the case for most of the countries considered. In particular, pension benefits increase with educational attainments and are higher for men than for women. Notice that, despite the progressive nature of most benefit formulae, the differences by education tend to be larger for pensions than for earnings. This means that, at least along the educational dimension, pre-retirement inequalities in the distribution of earnings are actually accentuated after retirement.

Also notice that the coefficient on the number of years since retirement tends to be positive for men. For the countries where this coefficient is positive and statistically significant (Finland, France, Germany and Spain), its order of magnitudes appears to be roughly consistent with indexation of outstanding pensions to real productivity growth. The only puzzling result is the tendency for the coefficient on the length of the work career to be negative.

Finally, men with a spouse tend to have higher pensions than those without a spouse, whereas the opposite tends to be true for women. Because most men without a spouse are single but most women without a spouse are widows, this is likely to reflect the fact that our definition of pension benefits includes survivor's benefits which, in most countries, can be added to the own old-age pension.

Table 2.7 Estimated median regression models for the logarithm of net monthly old-age pension benefits of people retired for at least one year in thousands of purchasing power parities and 1998 (**denotes an observed significance level below 5%, *denotes an observed significance level between 5 and 10%).

Country	Intercept	Years ret.	Career	Tertiary	Secondary	No spouse	Bad health	n	R^2
					Men				
Austria	6.746**	0.002	-0.009**	1.001**	0.291**	-0.033	-0.117**	2044	0.099
Belgium	6.851**	0.001	-0.004**	0.291**	0.197**	-0.118**	-0.059*	1818	0.069
Denmark	6.353**	-0.007**	-0.011**	0.639**	0.103**	0.099**	-0.100**	1563	0.118
Finland	5.602**	0.068**	0.021**	1.282**	0.329**	-0.064	-0.115	786	0.115
France	6.842**	0.012**	-0.029**	0.662**	0.236**	-0.163**	-0.153**	4848	0.137
Germany	6.436**	0.022**	0.003**	0.478**	0.278**	-0.014	-0.101**	3410	0.076
Greece	6.125**	0.004	-0.023**	0.801**	0.610**	-0.029	-0.124**	4072	0.174
Ireland	6.446**	0.000	-0.006**	0.773**	0.403**	-0.309**	-0.121**	2202	0.173
Italy	6.719**	-0.006**	-0.014**	0.618**	0.296**	-0.174**	-0.212**	4890	0.119
Luxembourg	7.484**	-0.000	-0.006**	0.422**	0.190**	-0.172**	-0.216**	416	0.083
Netherlands	7.175**	-0.022**	-0.006**	0.618**	0.105**	-0.038	-0.140**	2686	0.107
Portugal	6.125**	-0.014**	-0.027**	1.401**	1.097**	-0.134**	-0.187**	3382	0.163
Spain	6.592**	0.005**	-0.019**	0.775**	0.413**	-0.107**	-0.093**	5079	0.144
UK	6.352**	0.002	0.002**	0.501**	0.044	-0.207**	-0.156**	3232	0.082

Table 2.7

Country	Intercept	Years ret.	Career	Tertiary	Secondary	No spouse	Bad health	n	R^2
					Women				
Austria	6.112**	-0.004	-0.004*	0.888**	0.492**	0.067*	-0.095**	1287	0.113
Belgium	6.600**	-0.013**	-0.005*	0.409**	0.123**	0.069*	-0.090	757	0.068
Denmark	6.189**	-0.003	-0.004**	0.171**	0.016	0.195**	-0.039	1307	0.051
Finland	5.571**	0.050**	0.017**	0.608**	0.115**	-0.026	0.000	813	0.054
France	6.134**	-0.003	-0.013**	0.838**	0.480**	0.349**	-0.183**	3269	0.128
Germany	6.105**	-0.001	0.006**	0.455**	0.140**	0.102**	-0.012	2888	0.054
Greece	5.400**	-0.017**	-0.041**	1.049**	0.853**	0.063**	-0.109**	2069	0.388
Ireland	5.948**	0.010**	0.005**	0.769**	0.281**	-0.025	-0.025	578	0.143
Italy	6.088**	-0.002	-0.002**	0.924**	0.710**	0.022	-0.042*	2123	0.210
Luxembourg	6.058**	-0.033**	0.007	1.751**	0.407**	0.521**	0.322**	87	0.154
Netherlands	6.099**	-0.001	0.004**	0.626**	-0.043	0.473**	-0.102**	780	0.167
Portugal	5.466**	-0.001**	-0.001**	1.834**	1.371**	0.001	-0.012**	2280	0.135
Spain	6.143**	-0.002**	-0.001**	1.104**	0.551**	0.011**	-0.004	1309	0.194
UK	5.373**	0.002*	-0.000	0.431**	0.078**	0.624**	0.005	3188	0.198

2.5.5 Replacement Rates

The analysis of earnings and pensions in the previous sections could have been carried out by just using one or more cross-sections of the population, without any need of longitudinal data. We now exploit the longitudinal nature of the ECHP to study the extent to which pensions of retirees replace pre-retirement earnings. Replacement rates, defined as the ratio of post-retirement pension benefits to pre-retirement earnings, play a very important role in the public policy debate because they provide a simple and easily understandable measure of the income-smoothing role of pensions.

Table 2.8 shows the estimates of a median regression model for the logarithm of the replacement rate fitted separately by country. The replacement rate has been computed by using all the available waves of the ECHP and the subsample of people aged 50–69 at the time of retirement. We exploit the information on self-reported main activity status in each month to locate the time when people retire. More precisely, considering people who classify themselves as retired when last observed in the sample and looking backward to their monthly employment status between 1993 and 1997, we select those who left the labour force in any month between February 1993 and December 1997. The replacement rates of these individuals is computed as follows. For people who retired in year t (t = 1994, 1995, 1996), the replacement rate is the ratio of monthly pension benefits in year $t+1$ (annual pension income in year $t+1$ divided by 12) and monthly earnings in year $t-1$ (annual earnings divided by the number of months during which the person was employed). For people who retired in 1993, the replacement rate is the ratio between monthly pension benefits in 1994 and monthly earnings in 1993. Finally, for those who retired in 1997, the replacement rate is the ratio between monthly pension benefits in 1997 (annual pension income in 1997 divided by the number of months during which the person was retired) and monthly earnings in 1996.

Pension income only includes old-age pensions, while earnings are the sum of wage and salary earnings and self-employment income. All income amounts are net of taxes and social security contributions, and have been converted to constant prices using the consumer price indexes. The only exception is France, where both pension benefits and earnings are gross. If the ratio between net and gross earnings is equal to the ratio between net and gross pension benefits, then the replacement rate for France should not be affected by the fact the income is gross instead of net. The replacement rates for the Netherlands and Sweden are not computed because the monthly information on activity status is not available in the UDB for these two countries. For Germany and the UK we consider only the data sets obtained from the national panels, the GSOEP and the BHPS. Unfortunately, even

Table 2.8 Estimated regression models for the logarithm of the replacement rate (** denotes an observed significance level below 5%, * denotes an observed significance level between 5 and 10%).

Country	Intercept	Sex	Age	Career	No spouse	Tertiary	Secondary	Earnings	n	R^2
Austria	−0.2834**	−0.0341**	0.0101**	−0.2132**	0.1237	0.5538**	0.0808	−0.4476**	177	0.238
Belgium	−0.2132**	0.0140	0.0001	−0.0511	0.0065	0.2438*	0.0675	−0.6048**	126	0.112
Denmark	−0.0736	0.0397**	−0.0131	−0.1011	0.0436	0.1449	−0.0877	−0.8873**	171	0.198
Finland	−1.4890**	0.0780	0.0300	0.6578	0.1755	0.8065	−0.4007	−0.8322**	79	0.155
France	−0.0388	−0.0022	−0.0093**	−0.0749	0.1687**	0.3194**	0.0351	−0.3216**	384	0.128
Germany	−0.2407**	0.0328*	−0.0084	−0.2634**	0.3427**	0.5589**	0.1734	−0.8021**	307	0.117
Greece	−0.1123	−0.0275	−0.0020	−0.1615	0.0858	0.6744**	0.4826*	−0.4484**	289	0.124
Ireland	−0.1911**	−0.0074	−0.0030	−0.1910	−0.2926**	0.4061**	0.1214	−0.8694**	130	0.219
Italy	−0.0367	0.0001	0.0001	−0.0898	−0.0716	0.4116**	0.2146**	−0.8592**	533	0.157
Luxembourg	0.0977	0.0312	−0.0457	0.5495	−0.3624	0.4338	−0.1092	−0.4558**	34	0.237
Portugal	0.0681	−0.0156	0.0044	0.3451**	−0.0695	−0.0015	0.1712	−0.1672**	233	0.071
Spain	0.2006*	−0.0119	0.0038	0.0033	−0.0125	0.5943**	0.1145	−0.7041**	285	0.188
UK	−0.6188**	0.0983**	−0.0233	−0.3322*	−0.0598	0.7483**	0.5442**	−0.2602**	177	0.106

57

with five waves, the available sample sizes are quite small, ranging from a minimum of 34 observations in Luxembourg and 79 in Finland, to a maximum of 384 observations in France and 533 in Italy.

The covariates in the regression model include age and labour market experience at retirement, pre-retirement earnings,[17] and indicators for gender, educational attainments and not having a spouse. The intercept of the model corresponds to the logarithm of the median replacement rate for a married man aged 60 at the time of retirement, with a work career of 40 years, only primary education completed and pre-retirement earnings equal to the country median for a new retiree aged 50–69. The exponential of the intercept is the estimated median baseline replacement rate. It ranges between a minimum of 23 per cent in Finland and 54 per cent in the UK to over 100 per cent in Luxembourg, Portugal and Spain. Our results also show that the logarithm of the replacement rate depends negatively on the level of pre-retirement earnings, that is, in all countries pension benefits increase less than proportionally with pre-retirement earnings. Everything else equal, people with higher education tend to have higher replacement rates. On the other hand, the coefficients on age, length of the work career, sex and being without a spouse, although quite different across countries, are not statistically significant in general.

2.6   WEALTH

The changes in household and personal income described in Section 2.5 are likely to have an impact on savings and wealth holding. Unfortunately, the ECHP is not well suited for studying these aspects of aging, as it only contains some information on housing[18] and durables owned by a household, but no information on other forms of wealth, especially financial wealth, and no information whatsoever at the individual level. In this section we look at the probability of home ownership and at ownership of several types of durables for households with and without an elderly (aged 50+) member.

2.6.1   Home Ownership

Figure 2.7 shows, for each age, the fraction of people living in a home owned by the household ('homeowners'), along with the fraction of those living in a rented home and those for whom the accommodation is provided rent-free.[19] The percentage of homeowners varies widely by country. It tends to be lower in Germany and the Netherlands, and higher in Finland, Ireland and the Southern European countries. In some countries (most notably Denmark, France, Netherlands, Sweden and the UK), we observe a steady decline in

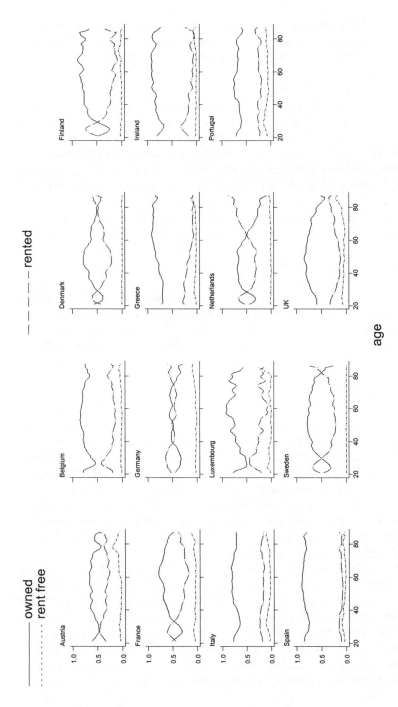

Figure 2.7 Tenure by country and age. Pooled data 1994–98

home ownership after age 50 and a parallel increase in the fraction of elderly people living in rented homes. In no country do we see a trend towards increasing home ownership with age after 50. This evidence may be viewed as lending support to the life cycle hypothesis, which predicts some form of asset decumulation at older ages.

To control for the effect of observable individual characteristics, we also consider a standard logit model for the probability of home ownership, defined in broad sense by including the case when the dwelling is provided free of rent. The covariate vector consists of age, age squared, and indicators for educational attainments, not having a spouse and bad health. The intercept of the model corresponds to the log-odds of home ownership for a person aged 60, married, in good health and with only primary education completed.

Table 2.9 reports the estimates obtained by fitting the model, separately by country and sex, to the subsample of people aged 50+. The estimates confirm the negative age trend in home ownership in Denmark, the Netherlands, Spain, Sweden and the UK. The estimated baseline age profile of home ownership has a inverse U-shape in Austria, Finland, France, Italy and Luxembourg. Not having a spouse or being in bad health negatively affects the probability of home ownership, whereas the effects of educational attainments are mixed. In Austria, Greece, Portugal and Spain home ownership is less common among people with higher education, while the opposite is true in all other countries.

2.6.2 Durables

The household questionnaire of the ECHP collects information on ownership of certain types of durables, namely car, colour TV, video recorder, microwave, dishwasher, telephone and home personal computer (PC). Figure 2.8 shows the fraction of households that own such durables. The figure, obtained by pooling all the available waves, reports ownership separately for households with and without an elderly (aged 50+) member and plots, separately by country and type of durable, the fraction of owners among the two types of household. For countries near the 45^0 line, ownership does not change much with the household type.

Ownership of a telephone, and especially of a colour TV, shows little differences across countries and household types. On the other hand, cross-country differences and differences across households are large for all other durables, in particular the micro wave, the dishwasher and especially the home PC. These three types of durables are much less common in Southern European countries and among households with an elderly member. Qualitatively, these conclusions do not change if we instead compare households with and without a member aged 70+.

Table 2.9 Estimated logit models for home ownership (** denotes an observed significance level below 5%, * denotes an observed significance level between 5 and 10%).

Country	Intercept	Age	Age^2	Tertiary	Secondary	No spouse	Hh. Income	n	R^2
					Men				
Austria	2.252**	0.014**	-0.001*	-1.377**	-1.197**	-0.702**	-0.105	5 011	0.053
Belgium	1.691**	-0.022**	0.001**	0.692**	0.418**	-1.337**	-0.496**	5 017	0.080
Denmark	1.862***	-0.033***	0.002***	0.469***	-0.351***	-1.368***	-1.084***	4 436	0.112
Finland	2.592***	0.045***	-0.002***	0.610***	0.529***	-1.374***	-0.263	2 586	0.076
France	1.592***	0.033***	-0.001***	0.363***	0.291***	-1.033***	-0.428***	10 728	0.042
Germany	-0.706***	0.020***	-0.000*	1.117***	1.080***	-0.581***	-0.267***	9 931	0.051
Greece	2.529***	0.048***	-0.000	-0.554***	-0.592***	-0.245***	-0.152	11 414	0.033
Ireland	2.944***	0.033***	0.001	3.731**	0.540***	-0.951***	-0.985***	6 820	0.072
Italy	1.857***	0.016***	-0.001**	0.646***	0.243***	-0.495***	-0.146***	15 262	0.011
Luxembourg	2.075***	0.069***	-0.003***	1.191***	1.282***	-1.792***	-0.405	987	0.167
Netherlands	0.132***	-0.068***	0.001***	1.500***	0.421***	-0.791***	-0.486***	7 467	0.104
Portugal	1.606***	0.008*	0.000	-0.161	0.067	0.027	-0.109***	11 330	0.001
Spain	2.474***	-0.016**	0.001**	-0.405**	-0.530***	-0.322***	-0.107	13 675	0.007
Sweden	1.768***	-0.017***	-0.001	-0.015	0.072	-1.199***	-0.547***	2 143	0.068
UK	1.500***	-0.024***	0.000	1.189***	0.307***	-0.800***	-0.408***	7 079	0.080

Table 2.9 (continued)

Country	Intercept	Age	Age^2	Tertiary	Secondary	No spouse	Hh. Income	n	R^2
					Women				
Austria	1.855**	0.014**	−0.001**	−1.092**	−0.746**	−0.661**	−0.363**	6 023	0.043
Belgium	1.966**	0.012**	−0.000	0.277**	0.177**	−1.424**	−0.522**	5 995	0.083
Denmark	1.562**	−0.002	−0.000	0.610**	0.369**	−1.808**	−0.659**	4 892	0.155
Finland	2.725**	0.047**	−0.002**	0.948**	0.385**	−1.468**	−0.632**	2 793	0.104
France	1.777**	0.015**	−0.001**	0.566**	0.121*	−1.113**	−0.293**	12 439	0.057
Germany	0.082**	0.017**	0.000	0.231**	0.137**	−0.657**	−0.265**	11 197	0.018
Greece	2.718**	0.035**	−0.001**	−0.156	−0.541**	−0.658**	−0.291**	13 132	0.020
Ireland	3.016**	0.028**	0.001	0.886**	1.142**	−1.385**	−0.544**	7 015	0.077
Italy	1.871**	0.003	0.000	0.887**	0.449**	−0.470**	−0.304**	16 600	0.016
Luxembourg	2.790**	0.051**	−0.003**	−0.232	0.426*	−1.322**	−0.977**	1 046	0.085
Netherlands	0.179**	−0.057**	0.001**	1.650**	0.372**	−0.898**	−0.711**	8 543	0.122
Portugal	1.628**	−0.003	0.001**	−0.075	−0.454**	−0.376**	−0.117**	13 784	0.006
Spain	2.411**	−0.017**	0.001**	−0.010	−0.246**	−0.368**	−0.185**	16 360	0.008
Sweden	1.589**	−0.019**	−0.001*	0.280*	0.000	−1.109**	−0.389**	2 408	0.086
UK	1.466**	−0.011**	−0.000	1.322**	1.027**	−0.756**	−0.221**	8 854	0.082

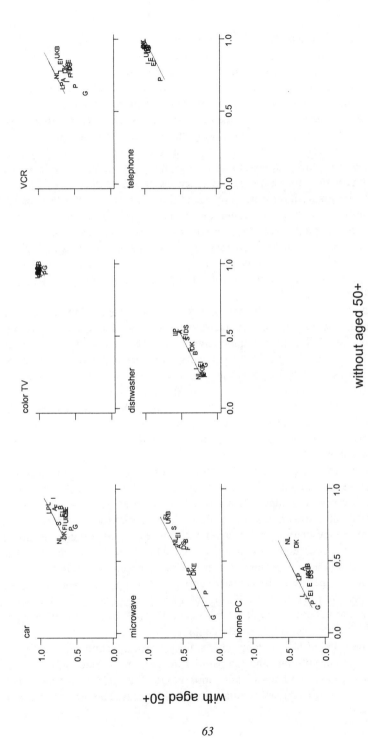

Figure 2.8 Ownership of durables by type of household and durable. Pooled data 1994–98

2.7   CONCLUSIONS

The ECHP represents an important source of information on several aspects of the aging process. The comparability of the survey across countries and waves constitutes its main advantage over other data sets. Nonetheless, there are delicate issues that must be taken into account when carrying out a cross-country study. First, the heterogeneity in the sampling design, the data collection process and the non-response behaviour, and the different importance of the imputation and weighting procedures reduce the comparability of information across countries. Second, the survey collects almost no information on work careers and lifetime earnings. For this reason, we can only study short-run labour and income dynamics, such as exit rates from the labour force over a one-year period and replacement rates for new retirees. Third, the survey provides little information on wealth, private pension coverage, intra-family transfers, and physical and mental health. Finally, the anonymization criteria limit the detail of the available information.

The analysis of the ECHP data shows that some basic relations between aging and socio-economic characteristics of the individuals and the households they live in are qualitatively the same across Europe. In all countries considered, aging is associated with a substantial reduction in the size of a household and with changes in its composition. These phenomena partly offset the observed fall of household income, causing only a modest decline in median equivalized household income. While aging increases the differences in household income with respect to people of younger ages, it does appear to reduce household income differentials within the various age groups or cohorts.

In all countries, aging is accompanied by a steady deterioration of health status, as measured by a variety of indicators. Over the age range considered, however, we see no evidence that this deterioration accelerates with age. In terms of labour market outcomes, aging is characterized by a rapid decline in labour force participation and a parallel decline of the importance of labour earnings as a source of personal income. After age 70, labour earnings become negligible and personal income is made up almost entirely by old-age or survivor pensions. In several countries, other types of social insurance benefits play an important role during the transitional period from activity to inactivity, but become negligible afterwards. The role played by other types of private income, instead, is always negligible.

Although the ECHP contains little information on wealth, the decline in home ownership with age and the parallel increase in the fraction of elderly people living in rented homes lends support to the life cycle hypothesis which predicts some form of asset decumulation at older ages. The precise nature of these trends differs across countries. This is also true for the estimated parameters of the models that describe their basic relationships with observable individual characteristics. What accounts for these large differences is an open issue. On the one hand, these differences are likely to reflect genuine differences linked to economic, social and institutional diversity across countries. On the other hand, they may also be related to non-sampling problems, such as the importance of measurement errors and survey non-response. How to separate these two sources of variation is one of the topics of our current research.

NOTES

1. The 2002 UDB was the most recent available at the time this chpater was written.
2. For a more detailed description of the ECHP and the statistical problems arising with these data see Peracchi (2002).
3. By achieved sample size we mean the number of people who returned the personal questionnaire.
4. Detailed tabulations are available from the authors upon request.
5. For more details on the computation of the weights see Eurostat (1999, 2000a, 2000b).
6. We refer to Little and Rubin (1987) and Schafer (1997) for a description of estimation with incomplete data using the EM algorithm.
7. For further details see Raghunatan *et al.* (1999) and Eurostat (2000a).
8. See for example Sickles and Taubman (1986). For a discussion of the reverse causality running from economic variables to health status, see Deaton (2003).
9. The ECHP also asks whether the person suffers of any chronical physical or mental health problem, illness or disability, but this question is affected by severe problems of non-response in almost all countries (Finland is the only exception), with non-response rates ranging between 33 per cent and 45 per cent for people aged 50+.
10. Our definition of employment includes those currently working less than 15 hours per week.
11. On the arbitrariness and ambiguity of this definition see Jones and Riddell (1999).
12. Sample frequencies are computed by pooling all the available waves and using the cross-sectional personal weights.
13. See Gruber and Wise (1999) for details.
14. Sample percentiles are computed by pooling all the available waves and using the cross-sectional personal weights.
15. For simplicity, we do not distinguish between men and women. Results available from the authors upon request show that, in most countries, age profiles by gender differ little until about age 70. After that age, the incidence of poverty tends to be higher for women. The main exception is the UK, where the incidence of poverty is always higher for women.
16. No result is available for Sweden because of the lack of information on the number of years since retirement and the length of the work career.
17. Pre-retirement earnings enter the model as the ratio to median pre-retirement earnings for the estimation subsample.
18. In particular, the survey provides information on home ownership (including possession of a second home) and tenure, along with information on the characteristics of the dwelling and the area where it is located.
19. Sample frequencies are computed by pooling all the available waves and using the cross-sectional personal weights.

REFERENCES

Deaton, A. (2003), 'Health, inequality and economic development', *Journal of Economic Literature*, **41**, 113–158.

Eurostat (1998), 'Weighting for wave 3: technical specifications', PAN 109/98, Eurostat, Luxembourg.

Eurostat (2000a), 'Imputation of income in the ECHP', PAN 164/00, Eurostat, Luxembourg.

Eurostat (2000b), 'Construction of the weights in the ECHP', PAN 165/00, Eurostat, Luxembourg.

Flinn, C.J. and J.J. Heckman. (1983), 'Are unemployment and out of the labour force behaviourally distinct labour force states', *Journal of Labour Economics*, **1**, 26–42.

Gruber, J. and D.A. Wise (1999), *Social Security and Retirement Around the World*, Chicago: University of Chicago Press.

Horowitz, J.L. and C.F. Manski (1998), 'Censoring of outcomes and regressors due to survey non-response: Identification and estimation using weights and imputation', *Journal of Econometrics*, **84**, 37–58.

Jiménez, S., J.M. Labeaga and M. Martnez (1999), 'Health status and retirement decisions for older European couples', IRISS Working Paper 1999–01.

Jones, S.R.G. and W.C. Riddell (1999), 'The Measurement of Unemployment: An Empirical Approach', *Econometrica*, **67**, 147–62.

Little, J.A. and D.B. Rubin (1987), *Statistical Analysis with Missing Data*, New York: Wiley.

Nicoletti, C. and F. Peracchi (2001), 'Aging in Europe: What can we learn from the Europanel?', in T. Boeri, A. Börsch-Supan, A. Brugiavini, R. Disney, A. Kapteyn and F. Peracchi (eds), *Pensions: More Information, Less Ideology. Assessing the Long-Term Sustainability of European Pension Systems: Data Requirements, Analysis and Evaluations*, Dordrecht: Kluwer.

Peracchi, F. (2002), 'The European Community Household Panel: A review', *Empirical Economics*, **27**, 63–90.

Raghunathan, T.E., P.W. Solenberger and J.V. Hoewyk (1999), *IVEware: Imputation and Variance Estimation Software. Installation Instructions and User Guide. Survey Methodology Program*, Survey Research Center, Institute for Social Research, University of Michigan.

Schafer, J.L. (1997), *Analysis of Incomplete Multivariate Data*, London: Chapman and Hall.

Sickles, R.C. and P. Taubman (1986), 'An analysis of the health and retirement status of the elderly', *Econometrica*, **54**, 1339–56.

3. Labour taxes and unemployment: A survey of the aggregate evidence

Francesco Daveri[*]

3.1 INTRODUCTION

The bulk of the rise in Government revenues in industrial countries over the last 30 years originated from the increased taxation of wage incomes.[1] The definite increase in labour taxation has often been contrasted to the parallel rise of European unemployment since the second half of the 1970s. Yet providing robust evidence of a positive relation between labour taxes and unemployment has proved a tricky undertaking.

This chapter surveys the findings and the unresolved issues faced in the strand of literature which has employed aggregate data to study the relation between labour taxes and unemployment.

In Section 3.2, trends in labour taxation, wages and unemployment in the US and the five largest EU countries are described. There is evidence of a positive, but noisy, relation between labour taxes and unemployment. This is more evident over time than across countries. Pairwise correlation also reveals a timing issue: taxes and wages rose well before unemployment started rising.

Section 3.3 sums up what theory says. A textbook partial equilibrium model of the labour market posits a close relation between labour costs and unemployment, as well as between labour taxes and labour costs, as long as some conditions are met. The close link between labour costs and unemployment breaks down, however, when abandoning a static representation of the functioning of the labour market.

* This chapter draws on joint work with Marco Maffezzoli and Guido Tabellini, to whom I am indebted for many helpful discussions. This research project was funded by the CNR (Consiglio Nazionale delle Ricerche; project 'Riforme fiscali e mercato del lavoro in Europa', #99.03504.ST74).

Section 3.4 surveys the aggregate evidence, emphasizing that recent research has overall strengthened the case for a positive relation between labour taxes and unemployment. Yet attributing a causal meaning to the findings from the macroeconometric literature remains hard to swallow for most scholars. In Section 3.5, the prospects from alternative methods of analysis (micro data and simulation techniques) are briefly evaluated. Section 3.6 concludes.

3.2　LABOUR TAXATION, WAGES AND EMPLOYMENT ACROSS COUNTRIES AND OVER TIME

Table 3.1 presents summary data on labour taxes, unemployment and real wages in the United States and the five largest EU countries in 1965–99. It thus provides first-hand evidence on the pattern of correlation across countries and over time between the main variables of interest here.

3.2.1　Labour Taxes

In Table 3.1, labour taxes are defined as average effective tax rates on labour incomes, in the same fashion as in Mendoza *et al.* (1994). They include social security contributions and an imputation of income taxes; consumption taxes are not included. The data reported here are updates of the data in Daveri and Tabellini (2000) to 1999.

Table 3.1 shows that cross-country differences in labour tax rates are large. In 1999, the latest available year, labour taxes equaled 45–50 per cent of labour incomes – about one third of GDP – in France, Germany and Italy. Much lower values were observed in Spain, the US and the UK, with tax rates ranging between 25 and 30 per cent of labour incomes, equivalent to 16–20 per cent of GDP.

Labour taxes went up in all countries in 1965–99. This is more evident in countries in Continental Europe, where average effective tax rates rose by a minimum of 16 (Germany) to a maximum of 25 percentage points (France), with Italy and Spain in between. In Anglo-Saxon countries, the increase was more moderate (+11 percentage points in the US, + 6 percentage points in the UK).

Such increases in labour taxation did not uniformly spread over time. In five countries, most of the increase in labour taxation took place in 1965–80. In the US, the UK and Spain, labour taxes barely rose in 1980–99 (+1.5–2.0 percentage points in about 20 years). In Italy, the only exception to this rule, taxes on labour incomes went up by 9 percentage points in the 1960s and the 1970s and by nearly 13 points in the 1980s and the 1990s.

Table 3.1 Labour taxes, unemployment and real wages

	USA	UK	Germany	France	Italy	Spain
	Average effective labour tax rates					
1965	17.5	20.4	29.0	25.4	24.8	13.3
1970	22.6	24.7	31.5	32.6	27.3	17.5
1975	24.6	27.4	36.4	34.5	30.1	22.9
1980	27.6	25.0	38.3	40.2	33.8	29.8
1985	28.3	26.8	40.4	44.2	38.2	34.2
1990	29.1	24.5	40.2	45.8	42.2	36.9
1995	27.4	25.4	43.5	49.3	47.1	31.5
1999	29.2	26.4	45.1	50.9	46.5	31.7
1965–99	**+11.7**	**+6.0**	**+16.1**	**+25.5**	**+21.7**	**+18.4**
1965–80	**+10.1**	**+4.6**	**+9.3**	**+14.8**	**+9.0**	**+16.5**
1980–99	**+1.6**	**+1.4**	**+6.8**	**+10.7**	**+12.7**	**+1.9**
	Unemployment rates					
1965	4.4	2.0	0.3	1.5	5.3	2.6
1970	4.8	3.0	0.8	2.5	5.3	2.4
1975	8.3	4.3	3.6	4.0	5.8	3.6
1980	7.0	6.4	2.9	6.2	7.5	11.1
1985	7.1	11.2	7.1	10.2	9.6	21.1
1990	5.4	6.8	4.8	8.9	10.3	15.9
1995	5.5	8.7	8.2	11.6	11.6	22.7
1999	4.2	6.1	8.8	11.3	11.3	15.9
1965–99	**–0.2**	**+4.1**	**+8.5**	**+9.8**	**+6.0**	**+13.3**
1965–80	**+2.6**	**+4.4**	**+2.6**	**+4.7**	**+2.2**	**+8.5**
1980–99	**–2.8**	**–0.3**	**+5.9**	**+5.1**	**+3.8**	**+4.8**
	Cumulated real wage growth					
1965–99	+32.2	+62.1	+53.0	+47.7	+54.2	+58.0
1965–80	+14.8	+28.8	+40.5	+37.5	+44.6	+49.6
1980–99	+17.4	+33.2	+12.5	+10.2	+9.6	+8.4
	Cumulated TFP growth					
1965–99	+25.2	+46.1	+44.3	+58.1	+50.3	+52.8
1965–80	+8.4	+20.4	+30.1	+30.9	+33.2	+28.7
1980–99	+16.8	+25.7	+14.2	+27.2	+17.1	+24.1
	Cumulated (wage-TFP) growth					
1965–99	**+7.0**	**+16.0**	**+8.7**	**–10.4**	**+3.9**	**+5.2**
1965–80	**+6.4**	**+8.4**	**+10.4**	**+6.6**	**+11.4**	**+20.9**
1980–99	**+0.6**	**+7.5**	**–1.7**	**–17.0**	**–7.5**	**–15.7**

3.2.2 Unemployment Rates

The behaviour of unemployment rates in these countries is well-known and documented, both along the cross-section and the time series dimension. In 1999, Spain featured the highest unemployment rate in the sample (about 16 per cent of the labour force). In the other countries in Continental Europe (France, Italy and Germany), unemployment rates ranged around 10 per cent of their labour force. Unemployment was instead lower in the UK (about 6 per cent) and the US (about 4 per cent).

Table 3.1 also shows that, notably, the US has not always been an 'employment miracle'. In the 1960s and the 1970s, the unemployment rate was lower in Europe than in the US. Back in 1965, the rate of unemployment was as low as 0.3 per cent in Germany, and did not go above 3 per cent in France, the UK and Spain. In Europe, just Italy had a higher unemployment rate (5.3 per cent) than the US.

Unemployment rates went up considerably in Europe, particularly in Continental Europe, in the 1980s and the first half of the 1990s. Within Europe, unemployment reached its maximum at different times in the various countries: 1985 in the UK, 1995 in France, Italy and Spain, 1999 in Germany. The UK since 1985 and Spain since 1995 clearly reversed the previous upward trend.

Between 1965 and 1999, the unemployment rate remained instead roughly constant close to 4.5 per cent in the US. After reaching a maximum of 8.3 per cent in 1975, the US share of unemployed people fell gradually to about 5.5 per cent in 1990 and further down to about 4 per cent in the 1990s.

3.2.3 Real Wages

Table 3.1 also presents summary evidence as to the cumulated growth rates of real wages, gross and net of total factor productivity growth. The textbook model of the functioning of the labour market would point to changes in labour costs as a necessary transmission mechanism of a labour tax shock onto unemployment (see the next section). This suggests looking at what happened to real wages net of TFP growth as a potential cause of unemployment.

Table 3.1 bears two clear implications. First, there is evidence of an overall 'wage push' in five of the six countries in the sample. In 1965–99, real wages grew faster than TFP in all countries, but France. Hence, there was a wage push, but not specific to Europe or Continental Europe.

Second, the 'wage push' was largely over by 1980. In particular, in 1980–99, cumulative TFP growth was higher than cumulative real wage growth by more than 15 percentage points in Spain and France, about 7 percentage points in Italy and less than 2 percentage points in Germany. Real wage and TFP growth roughly offset each other in the US in the last 20 years. Somehow unexpectedly, the only country where real wage growth systematically outpaced TFP growth was the UK, both before and after 1980.

3.2.4 Summing up

Altogether, data in Table 3.1 suggest four main conclusions.

1. There is evidence of a positive, but noisy, pairwise correlation between labour taxes and unemployment, on one side, and between labour taxes and wages, on the other. This makes thinking about it worthwhile.
2. The cross-country correlation between labour taxes and unemployment is not a close one. Unemployment is not necessarily high/low in countries where labour tax rates are high/low. In addition to labour taxes, other structural, i.e. time invariant, determinants of unemployment must be sought.
3. The within-country time correlation between labour taxes and unemployment is stronger for some countries (such as Germany, France, Italy, Spain) than for others (the US, the UK).
4. The within-country time correlation between labour taxes and unemployment hides a 'timing mismatch'. The rise of unemployment in Europe took place five to ten years after the occurrence of the tax and wage hikes. A theory linking labour taxes and unemployment should also provide a solution to this puzzle.

Conclusions 1–4 provide useful guidance as to the list of plausible theoretical and empirical models to be employed when looking at the relation between labour taxes and unemployment.

3.3   WHAT THEORY SAYS

A partial equilibrium competitive model of the labour market shows that labour taxes raise labour costs and gross wages, negatively affecting equilibrium employment, as long as:

(a) labour demand is not too elastic and labour supply is not too inelastic;[2]
(b) the tax-financed benefit accruing to the worker is not fully internalized by the worker himself;
(c) the worker's outside option is taxed at a lower rate than wage income and is not fully indexed to the net real wage.

Condition (a) is a standard tax-incidence argument. It can be found in any Economics I textbook. Condition (b) – first discussed by Summers (1989) with reference to the effects of mandated benefits – says that if workers internalize individual benefits arising from a tax on labour, their labour supply schedule would shift rightwards, keeping employment roughly constant. Condition (c) predicts that, for a tax on labour to affect employment, the relative convenience of being employed vs. unemployed must change. Some variants of condition (c) were discussed by Pissarides (1998).[3]

To summarize: condition (a) establishes a close link between labour costs and the employment effects of a labour tax, while conditions (b) and (c) are necessary and sufficient conditions for a labour tax to affect labour costs.

The tight link between labour costs and employment implied by the partial equilibrium competitive framework does not carry over to more complicated settings, however. Here I briefly discuss what happens when allowing for capital accumulation. Suppose, under conditions (a) – (c), that some increase in the gross real wage occurs as a result of the increase in labour taxation. This feeds on impact into a rise in the capital-labour ratio, possibly through an employment decline for a given capital stock. In turn, this reduces the rate of return on investment and hence investment. By this channel, the capital-labour ratio is gradually driven down back (or close, depending on technological assumptions) to its initial level. Note however that, as long as the downward revision in the outside income is incomplete, employment keeps falling alongside with real wages. This is potentially important on empirical grounds, for it suggests that we may observe a decline in the real wage – as a result of a past shock to capital accumulation – in the absence of an employment recovery.

Appending capital accumulation to a static representation of the labour market is thus important to make sense of the puzzle emphasized in conclusion (4) of par. 3.2.4. There are other reasons for the link between labour costs and unemployment to break down (see for example the recent paper by Blanchard and Giavazzi, 2001). Their implications are not explored here.

3.4   AGGREGATE EVIDENCE

In principle, employing aggregate data involves dealing with aggregation problems. They have two main dimensions. Suppose labour homogeneous first. Even in this case, the conditions for meaningfully extracting unbiased estimates of deep parameters (i.e. demand and supply elasticity) from aggregate data are stringent. The problem – first emphasized by Theil (1954) and summarized by Hamermesh (1993) – is one of linearly aggregating non-linear relationships and can be exemplified as follows. If all the establishments in the economy have identical CES technologies – a heroic assumption indeed – this gives rise to the following labour demand functions at the establishment level: $\ln L_i = \delta - \sigma \ln W_i + \ln Y_i$ (with δ = distribution parameter; σ = constant elasticity of substitution between capital and labour, W = wage and Y = output). Unfortunately, there is no reason to expect that estimating the aggregate relation $\ln L = \delta' - \sigma' \ln W + \theta \ln Y$ ($A = \sum_i A_i; A = L, W, Y$) would deliver $\sigma = \sigma'$ or $\theta = 1$. Moreover, the direction of the bias is unknown, unless specific assumptions as to the distribution of the W_i or Y_i are made.

The other dimension of the aggregation problem has to do with the heterogeneity of workers. Obviously no worker is exactly the same as another one, but estimating separate demand functions for each worker in the labour force is not feasible. A theoretically acceptable compromise would be to aggregate workers according to the respective degree of substitutability. Yet the evidence on the extent of the elasticity of substitution between different types of workers is controversial as well.

Hence, although partial equilibrium analysis suggests that demand and supply elasticities crucially determine the impact of labour taxes on wages and employment, early and recent studies employing aggregate data mostly left the estimates of deep parameters and aggregation problems aside.

3.4.1 The Early Aggregate Evidence

The early aggregate evidence on taxes and unemployment, surveyed in Bean (1994, 589–90), found little or no evidence of distorting effects of taxes on unemployment. Moreover, the numerical estimates of the tax shifting onto wages varied so much as to be practically devoid of economic meaning. Not by chance, a list of the causes of European unemployment compiled in the mid-1990s include labour market regulation, unemployment subsidies, terms of trade shocks, skill-biased technical change and anti-inflationary aggregate demand policies but not labour taxes.

Leuthold (1975) and Beach and Balfour (1983) evaluated the impact of payroll taxes on labour demand in, respectively, the US private sector and the UK manufacturing sector, by replacing the wage W with $W(1 + t_w)$ in the first order condition of firm's profit maximization. As pointed out by Feldstein (1972), however, this procedure does not produce an estimate of the equilibrium shift of wage and employment.

Studying the role of taxation as a possible source of high unemployment rates in an 'elasticity-free' framework was the focus of Layard *et al.* (1991). In the words of Blanchard and Katz (1997, p.67):

The effort was judged only partially successful at the time (Bean, Layard and Nickell, 1986), and has not withstood the test of time well. The cross-sectional evidence within Europe does not reveal much correlation between tax rates and unemployment rates, nor between changes in tax rates and changes in unemployment rates. In the recent study by Jackman, Layard and Nickell (1996), taxes no longer appear in the equation used to explain time series and cross-section movements in unemployment.

Within this strand of early studies, a few also provided evidence on the coefficient of payroll taxes in reduced-form wage equations. Hamermesh (1979), Holmlund (1983), Bean *et al.* (1986) and others quoted in Hamermesh (1993, Table 5.1, p.171) estimated Phillips-curve-type equations with a payroll tax term appended. The estimates of the tax shift on wages are usually – not always ! – positive and within the admissible zero-one range. No consensus emerged, however, either about the likely size of the tax shift or about the likely causes of the estimated differences. Newell and Symons (1987) report estimates in the error correction form, where the change, and not the level, of the tax wedge is found significant, implying only a transient effect of permanent tax shocks.

3.4.2 The Recent Aggregate Evidence

Recent research employing aggregate data has led to conclusions somewhat different from the past. Recent macroeconometric studies have estimated reduced-form employment (or more often, unemployment) and wage regressions, inclusive of shifters of labour supply (replacement rates, benefit duration) and labour demand (TFP growth, measures of strictness of employment protection and other labour and goods market imperfections). The inclusion of such supply and demand shifters serves identification purposes. It is also meant to address the potential bias due to variable omission, emphasized, for example, in Hamermesh (1993).

Results
All of the recent studies have found statistically significant labour tax coefficients, although the size of the estimated coefficients greatly differs. The view that labour taxation exerts little employment effect has been forcefully reasserted by Blanchard and Wolfers (2000). Most other studies, such as Alesina and Perotti (1997), Elmeskov *et al.* (1998), Nickell and Layard (1999), and Daveri and Tabellini (2000), have found evidence of (1) medium-sized to large effects of labour taxes on unemployment; and: (2) positive but incomplete forward shifting of labour taxation onto labour costs and gross wages. These findings hold in particular for countries in Continental Europe, and much less elsewhere.

The precise boundaries of the disagreement across the different studies are as follows. Blanchard and Wolfers (BW, from now onwards) found a β of about 0.02. The upper bound of the recent estimates is $\beta = 0.30$ obtained by Daveri and Tabellini (DT), with Nickell and Layard (NL)'s 0.22[4] and Elmeskov *et al.*'s 0.15 lying in between.

The polar cases within this small cross-section of estimates bear very different numerical implications. The rise in labour taxation documented in Section 3.2 may be taken to have increased the German unemployment rate by 0.3 percentage points if Blanchard and Wolfers are right, or by 4.8 percentage points if Daveri and Tabellini are right. These figures compare with an overall rise of German unemployment of about 8.5 percentage points. Differences are even sharper if we take data for France, Italy and Spain.

In the light of this more recent evidence, Nickell and Layard conclude that '... there is evidence that overall labour tax rates do influence labour costs in the long run and hence raise unemployment' [Nickell and Layard, 1999, end of Section 5, p.44]. The important methodological question to be addressed is how studies using roughly similar data can get so wildly different answers to the deceptively simple question: does a tax on labour raise unemployment?

Why such differences?
At first sight, the various studies differ in many respects: within-equation restrictions, methods of estimation, time periods and number of countries. It may thus look complicated to reconcile the different results or – a more modest goal – understand the source of the differences.

The typical unemployment regression estimated in recent multi-country time series studies has the form:

$$U_{it} = CONSTANT_i + \beta * TAX_{it} + \gamma * X_{it} + e_{it} \tag{3.1}$$

where i is the country index; t is the time index, often referred to period (typically: five-year) averages; U is the unemployment rate (sometimes in log form), TAX is the average tax rate on labour income (payroll and imputation of direct taxes to labour incomes) or the total tax wedge (inclusive of payroll, direct and consumption taxes), and X is a vector of control variables, typically inclusive of variables measuring each country's labour market institutions.

The list of the X variables varies across studies, but often includes replacement rates, benefit duration, density and coverage of trade unions, the GDP share of government spending in active labour market policies (ALMP), indices of employment protection legislation (EPL), the extent of bargaining coordination and centralization for employers and employees. Such variables are deemed to change very slowly over time. Available information is often insufficient, however, to evaluate this claim, for only a handful of observations (typically in the late 1980s or early 1990s) is available.

The main specification problems plaguing these regressions are the potential biases arising from the exclusion of unobservable explanatory variables and the endogeneity of some included regressors. Different treatments of these issues may be at the root of diverse regression results.

Omitted variables bias

The omitted variables bias is potentially more serious for DT than for the other studies, for a somewhat smaller number of control variables is included in DT than NL and BW. In particular, DT never includes the whole list of X variables, but only a few of them at a time. Both NL and BW usually have all of them at once. It may thus be the case that DT's β is high due to the exclusion of some potentially important variables, otherwise included in other studies.

This brings out a very important issue, concerning the nature of the X variables. Most of the Xs are qualitative and/or subjective indices. Such variables are often the result of an aggregation of individual labour market features, whose extent has been evaluated by experts well aware of labour market circumstances of each country. The rationale for aggregating – often merely adding them up – such diverse things as hiring and firing rules and other legislative features into a single figure remains somehow obscure. In general, the subjective and qualitative nature of such summary indices makes them prone to endogeneity and measurement error, and somehow hard to update over time. Appending many of them to the right-hand side of a regression is thus not necessarily a good idea.

BW also makes the X vector interact with fixed time effects. One may wonder why the potentially valuable available information on the time variation of some of the X variables (such as tax rates and replacement rates)[5] is not exploited instead. One commonly shared opinion is that the X variables (mostly the qualitative ones) are rather crude proxies, which only imprecisely capture the role of labour market institutions. Taking average values over the entire period of analysis (1960–96) would lessen this problem. Yet, as mentioned above, most available indices of labour market institutions are not long-run estimates, but rather point-wise values calculated at a specific date in the late 1980s or the early 1990s.

Moreover, by interacting institutions with time-fixed effects, a specific correlation structure is superimposed over the data. By construction, above-average values of the tax impact unemployment to the same extent in each country. This is at variance with the DT finding that the estimated tax coefficients differ across country groups (identified from both coverage and density data, based on Table 3.2) and may contribute to explain why BW finds a much smaller coefficient than DT. If the DT regressions are run without distinguishing the groups, the estimated coefficient gets smaller, although the estimated β does not fall to the BW coefficient of 0.02.

Table 3.2 Features of labour bargaining in industrial countries*

Country	Coverage		Density		Coordination	
	1980	1990	1976–81	1986–91	Union	Employer
ANGLO						
Canada	37	38	26	32	1	1
Japan	28	23	31	26	2	2
USA	26	18	23	15	1	1
United Kingdom	70	47	48	39	1	1
EUCON						
Australia	88	80	46	44	2	1
Belgium	90	90	55	54	2	2
France	85	92	19	12	2	2
Germany	91	90	35	31	2	3
Italy	85	83	45	34	2	2
Netherlands	76	71	35	23	2	2
Spain	68	68	25	11	2	1
NORDIC						
Finland	95	95	69	71	2	3
Norway	75	75	52	54	3	3
Sweden	83	83	76	83	3	3

Notes:
*'Coverage' measures the extent to which contracts signed by organized unions extend to the rest of the labour force.
'Density' measures the rates of net union density, i.e. the number of union members net of pensioners divided by the labour force.
'Coordination' measures the extent of contracting coordination within different union and employer organizations in 1989–94. The index provides a qualitative ranking of countries: '1' means 'Low', '2' is for 'Medium', '3' is for 'High'.

Source: Daveri and Tabellini (2000).

Endogeneity bias
It may be the case that the estimated β in all of the studies surveyed here simply reflects reverse causation from unemployment to labour taxes. Suppose that some exogenous shocks other than labour taxation has pushed up the unemployment rate. This, in the face of an unchanged level of

government spending, may have translated into higher taxes levied on the employed. As a result it may well be that the higher unemployment rates, induced by such exogenous shocks, drive effective taxes on labour high, and not the opposite. Note that the same line of reasoning applies to proxies for labour market institutions, especially considering that they are measured in the late 1980s or in the early 1990s.

This is a serious issue for all of the studies surveyed here, and possibly for all regressions employing aggregate data. The overall issue is the long-standing problem of finding reliably exogenous instruments at yearly or five-year frequencies. DT, in line with the applied growth regression literature, employ lagged variables of the tax rates as instruments for current tax rates. Yet this does not fully tackle the bias problem, as long as taxes are generated by an AR process. It is only fair to say that solutions to the endogeneity issue are hard to come by within this strand of literature. In Section 3.5 the potential for solving this problem through other methods of analysis is briefly evaluated.

Wage equations

It remains to test whether the channel of transmission from labour taxes to unemployment goes through wages, as it should based on static partial equilibrium analysis. Compared with the earlier attempts discussed above, the range of the available estimates appears smaller. DT (2000, Table 11, p.83) estimated a reduced-form wage regression of the form:

$$g_{w_{it}} = cons\tan t + \delta_1 \Delta \tau_{it}^w + \delta_2 \Delta x_{it} + e_{it}^w \qquad (3.2)$$

where g_w is the growth rate of gross real wages, $\Delta \tau^w$ is the change in the tax rate on labour, and Δx is a set of control variables in first differences, inclusive of shifters of the wage setting function (such as the replacement rates and the past unemployment rate) and of the labour demand (TFP growth rate or the instrumented per-capita GDP growth rate).

Their estimate of δ_1 is 0.4 for countries in Continental Europe, about 0.2 for Nordic countries (but imprecisely measured) and statistically zero for the US, Japan and Canada. These results are very similar to the results in Alesina and Perotti (1997, Table 7, column 4), where the same idea of estimating different coefficients between countries with similar labour market institutions was implemented first.[6] Alesina and Perotti found a positive relation between labour taxes and unit labour costs in manufacturing in a sample of annual data from 14 OECD countries (the same as Daveri and Tabellini), except that they have Denmark instead of Spain. Their estimated coefficients were again 0.4 for countries in Continental Europe, 0.3 for other EU countries and zero for the US and Canada.

Summing up
While the evidence provided in the early studies unanimously rejected it, recent research with aggregate data has overall strengthened the case for an empirical link between labour taxes and unemployment. Whether the pattern of detected partial correlation is to be interpreted in a causal sense remains highly controversial, however.

3.5 ALTERNATIVE METHODS OF ANALYSIS

3.5.1 Micro Data

Studies based on micro data, as long as carried out in quasi-natural experiment settings, are well-equipped to tackle the difficulty of isolating the really exogenous component of a policy change by finding reliable instruments for right-hand side variables. Moreover, the policy change under study and its differential effects on various groups of workers can be precisely captured. Scope exists for classifying policies depending on whether they affect demand or supply of labour, or if they are general or tailored to some group. These conditions are not easily met when working with aggregate data.[7]

Labour economists working micro data have seemingly reached an overall consensus on the long-run neutrality of labour taxes on labour costs and employment. The bulk of the evidence surveyed in Gruber (1998, Table 8, 75–76) finds nearly full backward shifting of exogenous changes in employer-provided insurance costs and maternity benefits on net wages only, and cannot thus be literally taken to imply zero employment effect of labour taxes as well. A few micro studies look at wages and employment or hours simultaneously, though. Gruber (1997) finds that the dramatic reduction in payroll taxation, associated with the 1981 Chilean pension reform, fed into higher net wages in the manufacturing sector, with little or no employment effects. Gruber and Krueger (1991), Gruber (1994) and Anderson and Meyer (2000) had also obtained similar results when studying the impact of government-mandated employer-provided benefits in the US (insurance for workplace injuries, childbirth coverage, unemployment insurance), where the mandated cost was different across states at a point in time and within each state over time.

As appropriately pointed out by Gruber (1997, S79), however, it remains unclear whether the results obtained for a specific benefit programme in Chile and specific states of the US can be readily extended to other programmes and country-specific institutions. Moreover, natural experiments do not occur often, which somehow constrains the scope for extending the application of studies on micro data.

Finally, sudden changes may be slow in producing effects. Hence, even in the absence of a long-run employment effect of taxes, the transition to the long run may last long enough to be relevant for most policy-makers, even in countries where the long-run neutrality result is found to hold.

3.5.2 Simulation

Irrespective of the aggregate evidence previously surveyed, the view that taxes have no employment effects finds its ultimate roots in the timing mismatch between the 'wage push' in the 1960s and the 1970s, and the rise in unemployment in the 1980s and the 1990s. When unemployment went up, it is argued, the wage push was largely gone. Unless a transmission mechanism to explain the delayed effects of the wage push of the 1970s is postulated,[8] this timing mismatch weakens the tax-push-based explanation of the rise in unemployment in Europe. If labour taxes have important distorting effects, why did unemployment rates start their rise so much later than labour costs? If there is such a close connection between wages and unemployment (as posited by the static labour market model), why did unemployment stay up well after the decline in real wages? The macroeconometric literature has not addressed these questions yet. It may even never succeed doing so, for the exogenous shocks to taxes – sometimes luckily available when working with micro data – are not easily identified in the aggregate data.

A possible way out of this dilemma draws on numerical simulation. In recent work, Daveri and Maffezzoli (2001), building on Daveri and Tabellini (2000), have pursued this idea further. A dynamic general equilibrium model with a labour market imperfection and exogenous growth is calibrated to replicate the functioning of EU artificial economies, constructed by plugging actual data onto the steady state representation of the theoretical model. In this framework, the dynamic effects of the wage push on capital accumulation and wage aspirations can be studied along a transitional dynamics path.

Their numerical analysis shows that wages predictably fall after the initial tax shock (or their growth rate falls short of TFP growth), but this is not beneficial to employment. The initial employment fall is even magnified over time, as long as aspirations take time to adjust. When the adjustment is complete, real wages are eventually back to where they were at the beginning, while employment never does recover. The slowdown of real wage growth with still high unemployment rates in Europe – a symptom of 'hysteresis' according to Blanchard and Summers (1986) – may then be given a neoclassical rationale and interpreted as the backlog of the adjustment process of the economy in the aftermath of the tax shock.

This paves the way to solving the mismatch puzzle mentioned above.

Moreover, the endogeneity problem which plagues the macroeconometric literature is solved by construction in simulation studies.

Numerical simulation also allows one to carefully assess the importance of alternative methods of financing tax reduction. Carraro *et al.* (1996) explore the 'double dividend hypothesis' asking whether a reduction in labour taxes financed through a 'green tax' (such as a tax on CO_2 emissions) would bring substantial gains from employment. In the paper quoted above, Daveri and Maffezzoli evaluate the effects of alternative fiscal policy measures on employment and growth. Both papers conclude that employment is unlikely to be markedly affected by labour tax reductions when this simply reallocates the deadweight loss elsewhere (e.g. from labour to capital). Daveri and Maffezzoli also find that sizable employment gains arise instead if fiscal reform comes about as a result of a plan aimed at shrinking overall government size. Based on these findings, one may conclude that a large effect of labour taxation on unemployment is more likely observed when government size expands in parallel, as has been the case since the mid-1970s. This also suggests that we should not expect much employment gain from reductions in labour taxation when the overall tax burden stays unchanged. In other words, as also emphasized in Mendoza *et al.* (1997), the structure of taxation does not appear to matter very much.

3.6   CONCLUSIONS

Charlie Bean ended his 1994 survey on the causes of European unemployment stating:

> There needs to be a more deliberate attempt to compare results across studies and to identify the extent to which apparent differences in fit are due to different variable definitions and different conditioning assumptions [Bean, 1994, p. 616].

In this chapter, I took his statement seriously and put together the results from different studies trying to make sense of differences and similarities. In general, the applied literature on labour taxes and unemployment has attracted a lot of attention for its policy relevance, and has been the object of careful empirical scrutiny. Whether these studies have substantially furthered our understanding of the causes of unemployment in the OECD remains perhaps debatable. Undeniably, however, a broad pattern of partial correlation between labour market outcomes (unemployment, employment, wages) and proxies for institutions and policies has been explored at length and brought to public attention.

In conclusion, although the labour market effects of labour taxes have been extensively analysed in macroeconometric, microeconometric and simulation studies, we still don't know whether labour taxes have statistically significant and economically important effects on labour costs and employment. My reading of the empirical literature is that the three strands of analysis have not just been distinct but outright separate. A contribution of this chapter is to show that scope for comparison across methods and studies does exist and may be fruitful for future research.

NOTES

1. Taxes on wage incomes may include imputations to labour incomes of income and consumption taxes, plus social security contributions and other payroll taxes. The statement in the main text holds irrespective of how 'taxation of wage incomes' is defined.
2. Here I use 'labour demand' and 'labour supply' as handy shortcuts to the more precise and general concepts of 'price-employment' and 'wage setting' schedules, which apply to both competitive and non-competitive settings.
3. Pissarides' 1998 paper also studies other important issues disregarded here, such as the role of progressive taxation.
4. The estimated coefficient of the tax variable (the overall tax wedge on labour, thus including payroll, income and consumption taxes) in the most recent unemployment regressions (in logs) estimated by Nickell and Layard (1999, Table 15) was 0.027. Once multiplied by 7.9 per cent (the average unemployment rate in the sample over the years 1985–94) to get rid of the semi-log form, this gives a point-wise estimate of the β in (3.1) roughly equal to 0.22.
5. Both variables are now regularly updated once a year (taxes) and every other year (replacement rates) in the OECD Revenue Statistics and the Social Expenditure Database.
6. Note however that, as is often the case in this literature, the classification of countries marginally differs in some cases. Alesina and Perotti followed the qualitative classification suggested by Calmfors and Driffill (1988), instead of relying directly on coverage and density data as criteria for separating countries as Daveri and Tabellini did.
7. Contini (2000) effectively surveyed the main methodological issues confronting users of micro data.
8. There is indeed a long list of potential candidates as transmission mechanisms. Blanchard and Summers (1986) proposed a theory of hysteresis in unemployment due to insider-outsider mechanisms. Bentolila and Bertola (1990) modelled asymmetric firing costs. Phelps (1972) and others mentioned skill deterioration of the unemployed as an obstacle to their re-entry in the labour market. Dreze and Bean (1990) collected a few papers where the idea of capital shortages as a factor contributing to the persistence of unemployment was explored. My, perhaps biased, reading of Bean's 1994 survey (Section 5) is that all of these mechanisms were usually regarded as theoretical curiosa, establishing possibilities rather than necessities.

REFERENCES

Alesina, A. and R. Perotti, (1997), 'The Welfare State and competitiveness', *American Economic Review*, **87**, 921–39.

Anderson, P.M. and B.D. Meyer (2000), 'The effects of unemployment insurance payroll tax on wages, employment, claims and denials', *Journal of Public Economics*, **78**, 81–106.

Beach, C. and F. Balfour (1983), 'Estimated payroll tax incidence and aggregate demand for labour in the United Kingdom', *Economica*, **50**, 35–48.

Bean, C. (1994), 'European unemployment: a survey', *Journal of Economic Literature*, **32**, 573–619.

Bean, C., R. Layard and S. Nickell (1986), 'The rise in unemployment: a multi-country study', *Economica*, **53**, S1–S22.

Bentolila, S., and G. Bertola (1990), 'Firing costs and labour demand: how bad is Eurosclerosis?', *Review of Economic Studies*, **57**, 381–402.

Blanchard, O.J. and F. Giavazzi (2001), 'Macroeconomic effects of regulation and deregulation in goods and labour markets', NBER Working Paper #8120, February.

Blanchard, O.J. and L.F. Katz (1997), 'What we know and do not know about the natural rate of unemployment', *Journal of Economic Perspectives*, **11**, 51–72.

Blanchard, O.J. and L. Summers (1986), 'Hysteresis and the European unemployment problem', *NBER Macroeconomics Annual*, 15–78.

Blanchard, O.J. and J. Wolfers (2000), 'The role of shocks and institutions in the rise of European unemployment: the aggregate evidence', *Economic Journal*, **110**, 1–33.

Calmfors. L. and J. Driffill (1988), 'Bargaining structure, corporativism and macroeconomic performance', *Economic Policy*, **6**, 13–61.

Carraro, C., M. Galeotti and M. Gallo (1996), 'Environmental taxation and unemployment: some evidence on the "double dividend hypothesis" in Europe', *Journal of Public Economics*, **62**, 141–81.

Contini, B. (2000), 'Introduction to the Workshop *Lowering payroll taxes: does it help to improve employment opportunities?*', Turin, mimeo.

Daveri, F. and M. Maffezzoli (2001), 'Employment and output effects of reducing labour taxes in Europe: a numerical approach', IGIER, Università Bocconi, May, mimeo.

Daveri, F. and G. Tabellini (2000), 'Unemployment, growth and taxation in Industrial Countries', *Economic Policy*, April, 47–104.

Drèze, J. and C. Bean (1990), 'European unemployment: lessons from a multi-country econometric study', *Scandinavian Journal of Economics*, **92**, 135–65.

Elmeskov, J., J.P. Martin and S. Scarpetta (1998), 'Key lessons for labour market reforms: evidence from OECD countries' experiences', *Swedish Economic Policy Review*, **5**, 205–52.

Feldstein, M. (1972), 'The incidence of the payroll tax: a comment', *American Economic Review*, **62**, 735–8.

Gruber, J. (1994), 'The incidence of State-mandated maternity benefits', *American Economic Review*, **84**, 622–41.

Gruber, J. (1997), 'The incidence of payroll taxation: evidence from Chile', *Journal of Labour Economics*, **15**, S72–S101.

Gruber, J. (1998), 'Health insurance and the labour market', NBER Working Paper #6762, October.

Gruber, J. and A. Kruger (1991), 'The incidence of mandated employer-provided insurance: lessons from workers' compensation insurance', in D. Bradford (ed.), *Tax Policy and the Economy*, **5**, Cambridge, Mass., MIT Press.

Hamermesh, D.S. (1979), 'New estimates of the incidence of the payroll tax', *Southern Economic Journal*, **45**, 1208–19.

Hamermesh, D.S. (1993), *Labour demand*, Princeton, NJ: Princeton University Press.

Holmlund, B. (1983), 'Payroll taxes and wage inflation: the Swedish experience', *Scandinavian Journal of Economics*, **85**, 1–15.

Layard, R., S. Nickell and R. Jackman (1991), *Unemployment: Macroeconomic performance and the labour market*, Oxford, Oxford University Press.

Leuthold, J. (1975), 'The incidence of the payroll tax in the United States', *Public Finance Quarterly*, **3** , 3–13.

Mendoza, E., G. Milesi-Ferretti and P. Asea (1997), 'On the ineffectiveness of tax policy in altering long-run growth: Harberger's superneutrality conjecture', *Journal of Public Economics*, **66** , 99–126.

Mendoza, E., A. Razin and L. Tesar (1994), 'Effective tax rates in macroeconomics: cross-country estimates of tax rates on factor incomes and consumption', *Journal of Monetary Economics*, **34** , 297–323.

Newell, A. and J. Symmons (1987), 'Corporatism, laissez-faire and the rise in unemployment', *European Economic Review*, **31**, 567–601.

Nickell, S. and R. Layard (1999), 'Labour market institutions and economic performance', in O. Ashenfelter and D. Card (eds), *Handbook of Labour Economics*, vol. III, Amsterdam: North Holland.

Padoa Schioppa, F. (1990), 'Union wage setting and taxation', *Oxford Bulletin of Economics and Statistics*, **52,** 143–66.

Phelps, E.S. (1972), *Inflation policy and unemployment theory*, London: Macmillan.

Phelps, E.S. (1994), *Structural slumps: the modern equilibrium theory of unemployment, interest and assets*, Cambridge, Mass.: Harvard University Press.

Pissarides, C. (1998), 'The impact of employment tax cuts on unemployment and wages; the role of unemployment benefits and tax structure', *European Economic Review*, **42**, 155–83.

Summers, L. (1989), 'Some simple economics of mandated benefits', *American Economic Review*, **79**, 177–83.

Summers, L., J. Gruber and R. Vergara (1993), 'Taxation and the structure of labour markets: the case of corporatism', *Quarterly Journal of Economics*, **108**, 385–411.

Theil, H. (1954), *Linear aggregation of econometric relations*, Amsterdam: North-Holland.

4. Measuring the impact of the Italian CFL programme on job opportunities for young people[*]

Bruno Contini, Francesca Cornaglia, Claudio Malpede and Enrico Rettore

4.1 INTRODUCTION

The Italian 'Contratto di Formazione e Lavoro' (CFL, working and training contract) started operating in 1985 to improve labour-market opportunities for young workers. Eligible people are workers younger than 30 (with some minor changes over the years and across areas).

The programme provides employers willing to hire eligible workers with two key benefits:

- a (roughly) 30 per cent rebate on the labour cost via a reduction in Social Security taxes
- a full exemption from firing costs.

In principle, the programme should also feature an off-the-job training component. In fact, it seems that most times it has not been implemented.

Over the years several reforms of the programme took place. Since June 1988 the rebate on the SS fee has been reduced to (roughly) 0.15. Since January 1991 the rebate on the SS fee has been further reduced in the Centre-North of Italy to (roughly) 0.07. Moreover, an eligibility rule has been introduced on the employer side in that an employer is allowed to hire new CFL workers during year t only if at least 50 per cent of the CFL workers

[*] We thank David Card, Luciano Forlani, Andrea Gavosto, Paolo Sestito and participants at the CeRP conference, Turin, 22 June 2001, and at the AIEL annual conference, Firenze, 4–5 October 2001, for helpful discussions on previous versions of the chapter. The usual disclaimer applies.

completing their employment spell during years t-1 and t-2 have been kept with the firm on a permanent basis.

To properly measure the CFL programme impact one has to take into account the interaction of the programme with other incentive schemes. Among these, the main one provides firms operating in the South with a ten-year long 100 per cent rebate on the SS fee for each worker newly hired on a permanent basis irrespective of the age of the hired worker. As a result, to hire a new worker any firm operating in the South chooses between the following options:

(a) hiring a young worker with the package (SS rebate = 100 per cent, fixed term contract)
(b) hiring any worker with the package (SS rebate = 100 per cent, permanent basis contract).

As a matter of fact, alternative (b) has been chosen since there have been very few CLF workers in the South up to December 1991 when the alternative incentive scheme was withdrawn for new hires.

In this chapter we measure the marginal effect of changing the cost of hiring a young worker relative to an older one on job opportunities for young people during their eligibility period. Following Blundell *et al.* (1998), to measure this marginal effect we exploit the variation over time and across geographical areas of the cost of hiring a young worker relative to an older one due to reforms and interactions between alternative benefit schemes. Secondly, we check whether the possibly longer work experience gained by young people during their eligibility period as an impact of the CFL programme raised the probability of employment after the eligibility period has elapsed. Finally, we check whether a substitution effect emerges as a result of the likely incentive on employers to replace their no longer eligible employees by younger still eligible workers.

Data we use are from the Social Security files. We track 40 year-of-birth/geographical area cohorts over the time window 1986 to 96 and over their age window 19 to 34 assessing whether the variability over time and across areas in the cost of hiring eligible workers relative to non-eligible ones bears any consequence on the stock of employees.

In Section 4.2 we present the institutional context and the main features of the CFL programme. In Section 4.3 we formalize the analysis and develop the econometric model. In Section 4.4 we deal with some empirical problems raised by the data set we use to obtain our estimates. In Section 4.5 we present the result of our estimation. Final remarks follow.

4.2 THE INSTITUTIONAL CONTEXT AND THE MAIN FEATURES OF THE CFL PROGRAMME

Since the 1980s several reforms have changed the rules of the Italian labour market, bringing about effects on the 'natural' labour mobility and on net job creation. As years went by, the focus of the debate on the labour market has moved from employment protection to business back-up measures: those that were once tools of labour policies (i.e., labour cost regulation and flexibility) have become the objectives to pursue, assuming their positive effect on employment. The main result of twenty years of reforms has been that of improving possible matches between workers and firms. The 'normal' open-ended contract continues to be the main method of hiring but it is not any longer the only one. The year 1984 was a remarkable one for the reform process of the Italian labour market: binding obligations on hirings were reduced, diminishing the monopolistic role of employment agencies; part-time work legislation was introduced as well as the *Contratti di Formazione e Lavoro* (CFL).

The CFL is a multi-purpose tool: it defines a target group that is intended to gain from it – young people 15 to 29 years old – hiring whom firms obtain both a rebate on welfare contribution and greater flexibility. It is indeed a fixed-term contract, with a predetermined duration that cannot be shorter than 18 months nor longer than 24. Compared with the already existing fixed-term contract, introduced in 1962, the field of action of the former has widened: in fact the latter allowed firms to hire on a fixed-term basis only to replace employees temporarily unable to work or to carry out seasonal activities. At the lapse of the contract the firm has the right, but not the obligation, to turn the CFL contract into an open-ended one, taking advantage of favourable tax treatment over a further year.

The other classical tool to hire on a fixed-term basis, the so-called apprenticeship, introduced in 1959, has a narrower target, young people less than 19 years old, provides for a minimum of five years' duration and is directed at getting a professional degree certificate.

The CFL, right from the start, aims higher: it cannot be used to acquire elementary professional experience and provides for a certain amount of hours devoted to off-the-job training.

As years passed by, provisions ruling CFL have gone through many changes that reduced both its advantages concerning taxation and those concerning flexibility. Benefits to the firms coming with the CFL programme made this type of contract a competitive tool in comparison with other recruitment procedures – primarily, the classic open-ended contract – particularly in the Centre-North of Italy. Indeed, in the Northern part of Italy significant back-up measures for business activities did not exist before, either from the fiscal point of view (labour costs) or in terms of flexibility. Therefore, the CFL – jointly with the part-time work legislation introduced at the same time – provided a good opportunity for employers as well as an incentive for hiring young people.

Table 4.1 Social Security fee for CFL employees over time, across geographical areas and industries

Period	Main legal reference	South	Centre-North, craftsmen	Centre-North, sales and tourism	Centre-North, others
1/5/84–31/5/88	L. 19.12.84, nr.863	Social Security fee on a fix quota basis as for apprentices			
1/6/88–23/11/90	L. 26.7.88, nr.291	Social Security fee on a fix quota basis as for apprentices		Rebate on Social Security fee = 50%	
24/11/90–31/12/90	DL. 22.11.90, nr.337			Rebate on Social Security fee = 50%	Rebate on Social Security fee = 25%
1/1/91–31/3/95	L. 29.12.90, nr.407			Rebate on Social Security fee = 40%	
1/4/95–	L. 19.7.94 nr. 451				

Table 4.2 Target population of the CFL programme and maximum duration of a CFL spell

Period	Target population, Centre-North	Target population, South	Maximum duration of a CFL spell
1/5/84–4/4/91	15–29 years old		Maximum time length 24 months not renewable
5/4/91–19/11/93	15–29 years old	15–32 years old	Maximum time length 24 months not renewable
Since 20/11/93	16–32 years old	A regional authority can extend the age limit above 32 years (only up to the end of 1997)	Two types of contracts: (a) max 24 months – intermediate skills; (b) max 12 month – professional settling

By comparison, firms operating in the South of Italy have not made much use of the CFL. A straightforward explanation for this is that up to 1991

Southern employers were entitled to a ten-year tax relief on the total amount of SS contributions for each new employee hired on a permanent basis,[1] whereas the share due to the national health-care system was covered by exemption from Social Security taxes.[2]

Such a system could explain the lack of interest in CFL shown in the South, at least until 1991, when the reform of the tax break for Southern regions started. This reform entails the progressive reduction of tax relief and exemption rates as well as the reduction of the total allowance for the new employees, that goes from being on a ten-year basis to an annual one.

Figure 4.1 shows the tax rates trend over time (allowing for tax cuts and tax exemptions) in the North and in the South (distinguishing between newly employed and employed workers). It should be noted that as time goes by, starting from the tax relief reform, the tax rates in the two macro regions progressively converge.

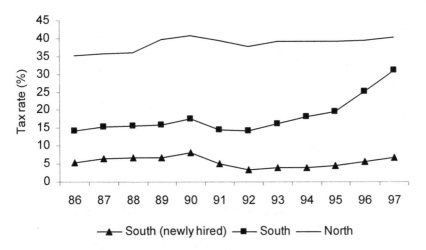

Figure 4.1 The pattern of the Social Security fee rate (Manufacture) over the years and across geographical areas

To evaluate the relative advantage from hiring an employee on the CFL scheme as compared to hiring him on a permanent basis contract we need to introduce a little notation. Let w be the worker yearly wage and:

$$r = f(t, \text{macro-region, industry, worker status, firm size})$$

be the Social Security (SS) fee tax varying over time, across geographical areas and industries as well as with the worker status and the firm size. In the absence of any rebate on the SS fee the per year cost from hiring a worker is

$w(1+r)$. Exploiting the rebates made available to the employers by the existing incentive schemes results in a per year cost equal to $w(1+r(1-reb))$ where:

$$reb = f(t, \text{macro-region, industry})$$

is the rebate on the SS fee rate, varying over time, across geographical areas and industries available to the employer. It is the one provided by the CFL programme in the Centre-North of Italy. As for the South, as we explained, up to 1991 most firms did not exploit the benefits from CFL. Rather, they exploited the alternative scheme which is not targeted to a specific age group.

As a result, in the Centre-North the relative labour cost from hiring a young employee becomes:

$$rlc = (1+r(1-reb))/(1+r)$$

a function of time, geographical area, firm industry and size and worker status. Instead, in the South it is basically equal to 1 up to 1991 just because both young and older workers are eligible for the rebate provided by the alternative scheme.

We evaluated a weighted mean of rlc by geographical area and over time using as weights the proportion of employees by firm industry and size and worker status in each year and geographical area. Figure 4.2 shows the pattern of rlc over time for the two macro-regions.

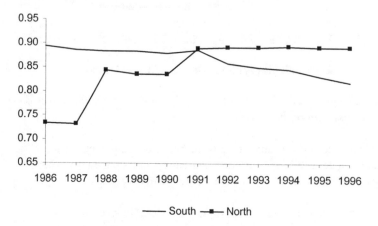

Figure 4.2 Labour cost for an eligible worker as a proportion of the labour cost for a non-eligible worker

As for the duration of a CFL employment spell, up to 1994 it could not last more than 24 months. In 1994 a reform introduced two types of CFL contracts:

- type A, with an off-the-job training component aimed at acquiring 'intermediate skills' and with a maximum duration of 24 months;
- type B, with a limited training component, aimed at fostering the settling in of new young employees by means of work experience, with a maximum duration of 12 months. This is mainly intended as a tool to adapt professional skills to the production environment and organisational structure.

As for the conversion of a CFL contract into an open-ended one, the turning point is January 1991. Up to then firms did not face restrictive clauses regarding the replacement of expiring CFL contracts with new young employees. Employers were allowed to freely hire new CFL employees no matter what the proportion of CFL employees kept with the firm on a permanent basis as the CFL contract expired.

On January 1991 things changed. The new rule stipulates the following:

> Starting from 1 January 1991 the right to hire by means of CFL cannot be asserted by employers that, while calling for new CFL hiring, are not proved to have hired at least 50 per cent of those workers whose CFL contract has expired in the previous 24 months. Starting from 19 November 1993 this percentage is raised to 60 per cent. Discarded workers, fairly dismissed ones and those who refused at the end of the CFL spell to be hired on an open ended contract are not included in the percentage.

The reason for the change seems to be that of discouraging the use of CFL by firms that were mainly interested in tax cuts and convenience in firing, rewarding instead those employers that by means of selecting and training young people use this tool to have in the upcoming future more skilled labour. Figure 4.3 shows the pattern of CFL hiring over the total hiring for the period 1986–96.

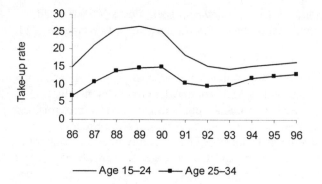

Figure 4.3 Take-up rate for the CFL programme by age (nr. of newly hired CFL workers in the specified age window/total nr. of newly hired workers, as a percentage)

4.3 MODEL SPECIFICATION

4.3.1 Formalizing the Benefit Scheme

In this section we go through the details of the CFL programme as reviewed in Section 4.2 to formalize them in a way suitable for the econometric analysis. The main step we take here is to convert the degree of flexibility allowed by the various type of labour contracts into expected firing costs as seen from the time period in which a hiring takes place.

As before, w is the worker yearly wage and r the Social Security (SS) fee rate. The per year cost to an employer from hiring a worker non-eligible for the CFL programme is $w(1+r)$. Let p be the probability that the employer eventually fires that worker, fc the firing costs and d the number of years the matching to that particular employee is expected to hold before firing as perceived at the time of hiring. Then the expected per year total labour cost of a non-eligible worker is:

$$tlc_{ne} = w(1+r) + p\,fc/d \qquad (4.1)$$

As from the time the CFL programme is introduced, an employer hiring an eligible worker enjoys a rebate on the SS fee as well as a full exemption from firing costs at the end of the CFL spell. As a result, the per year total labour cost of an eligible worker is:

$$tlc_{e} = w(1 + r(1 - reb_{1})) \qquad (4.2)$$

where reb_{1} is the rebate on the SS fee at that time.

The reform in operation since June 1988 reduces the rebate on SS fee. Let $reb_2 < reb_1$ be the new rebate. Then, the per year total labour cost of an eligible worker is straightforwardly obtained by modifying (4.2).

A further reform has been in operation since January 1991. It introduces both a new rebate on the SS fee lower than the previous one, $reb_3 < reb_2$ say, and an eligibility rule on the employer side. According to this eligibility rule, an employer is allowed to hire new workers on the CFL scheme only if at least 50 per cent of his CFL employees concluding their CFL spell over the previous two years have been kept on a permanent basis.

Let t_o be the current calendar year. The employer decides whether or not to hire a CFL worker; $t_o + 2$ is the calendar year in which the CFL employment spell would end.[3] As seen from t_o the eligibility rule on the employer side induces a firing cost. To see this, note that on hiring a CFL worker in t_o the employer exposes himself to the risk of bearing a higher per year total labour cost on the employees to be (possibly) hired in $t_o + 2$. For this risk to materialize in $t_o + 2$ three events need to take place:

1. as the CFL employment spell ends the employer is unwilling to keep the CFL employee with him on a permanent basis,
2. the decision to fire the CFL employee makes the employer lose eligibility,
3. the employer needs to hire a new employee which because of (2) cannot be a CFL one.

Let q be the joint probability of these events. As seen from t_o the expected cost of firing the CFL employee is $(tlc_{ne} - tlc_e)q$, namely the additional cost of hiring in $t_o + 2$ a non-eligible employee instead of an eligible one times the joint probability of the events $1 - 3$. Hence, from 1991 onward the per year expected total labour cost of a CFL employee becomes:

$$tlc_{ne} = w(1 + r(1 - reb_3)) + (tlc_{ne} - tlc_e)q.$$

Solving for tlc_e one gets:

$$tlc_e = w(1 + r(1 - reb_3))(1 - \theta) + tlc_{ne}\theta \qquad (4.3a)$$

$$\theta = q/(1 + q). \qquad (4.3b)$$

Apparently, as a result of the 1991 reform tlc_e becomes a weighted mean of what it would be in the absence of the newly introduced eligibility rule on the employer side, namely the worker wage plus the reduced SS fee, and of the expected per year total labour cost of a non-eligible worker. In particular, note that the employer starts bearing a fraction of tlc_{ne} even during the two CFL years of his eligible employee.

The weight θ increases with q, rising from 0 to 0.5 as q rises from 0 to 1, meaning that the fraction of tlc_{ne} the employer incurs by hiring a CFL worker increases with the joint probability of the events $1 - 3$. Note that before January 1991 q (hence θ) is zero because the probability of the event 2) is zero.

Finally, as explained in Section 4.2, we need to account for an alternative targeted wage subsidy programme operating in the South of Italy up to 1991 whose benefits cannot be cumulated to the CFL ones. According to this scheme firms operating in the South enjoy a ten-year long full exemption from SS fees on each new employee hired on a permanent basis no matter what the employee's age.[4] As an implication, on hiring a new employee a firm operating in the South chooses between hiring an employee whose expected per year labour cost is:

$$tlc = w + p\,fc\,/\,d \qquad (4.4)$$

no matter what his age – ten-year full exemption from SS fees – and hiring an employee eligible for the CFL programme whose per year labour cost is:

$$tlc_e = w(1 + r(1 - reb)) \qquad (4.5)$$

– full exemption from firing costs – with $reb = reb_1$ up to May 1988, $reb = reb_2$ from June 1988 to December 1990 and $reb = reb_3$ from January 1991 onward.

As a matter of fact, firms in the South made very little use of the CFL programme up to December 1991 suggesting that even for a worker eligible for CFL the labour cost in (4.5) is larger than the one in (4.4). In other words, up to 1991 in the South of Italy there has been no actual incentive to hire young people since the benefits to the employers coming with the CFL programme are outperformed by the benefits coming with the alternative scheme which is not targeted to a specific sub-population.

In the econometric model we shall work with the ratio tlc_e / tlc_{ne}, the expected per year total labour cost from hiring an eligible worker as a fraction of the corresponding cost of hiring a non-eligible worker. Let

$$\psi = w(1 + r) / \left[w(1 + r) + p\,fc\,/\,d\right] \qquad (4.6)$$

be the reduction in the labour cost resulting from the exemption from firing costs as a proportion of the expected per year total labour cost of a non-eligible worker. Let

$$rlc = w(1+r(1-reb))/w(1+r) = (1+r(1-reb))/(1+r) \qquad (4.7)$$

be the further reduction in the labour cost resulting from the rebate on the SS fee. Then, the following identity holds:

$$tlc_e / tlc_{ne} = \psi \, rlc . \qquad (4.8)$$

This identity highlights how the two components of the programme – exemption from firing costs and rebate on SS fee – cumulate to yield the total reduction in the labour cost the firm obtains from hiring an eligible worker as compared to hiring a non-eligible one.

In the Centre-North the ratio tlc_e / tlc_{ne} is as in (4.8) up to December 1990, then it switches to

$$(1-\theta)\psi \, rlc + \theta \qquad (4.9)$$

(see equations (4.3a) and (4.3b)) with $reb = reb_1$ up to May 1998, $reb = reb_2$ from June 1998 to December 1990 and $reb = reb_3$ from January 1991 onward.

As for the South, the ratio tlc_e / tlc_{ne} is slightly less than 1^5 up to December 1991. Then, it becomes the same as in (4.9) but with reb very close to reb_2 in 1992 and then slightly decreasing over time.

4.3.2 The Econometric Model

To measure the impact of the CFL programme on job opportunities for young people we elaborate on the standard binary-outcome fixed-effect model:

$$y_{it}^* = \alpha x_{it} + u_i + \varepsilon_{it} \qquad (4.10)$$

with the observable $y_{it} = 1/0$ – meaning that the i-th subject is at work/not at work in period t – depending on the sign of the latent variable y_{it}^*; x_{it} are the explanatory variables relevant to the chance of being at work and u_i represents the time-invariant unobserved heterogeneity.

Specifically, we want to measure the marginal effect of changing the cost of hiring a young worker relative to an older one. Following Blundell *et al.* (1998), to measure this marginal effect we exploit the variation over time and across geographical areas of the cost of hiring a young worker relative to an older one due to reforms and interactions between alternative benefit schemes.

To keep things simple, in the following we develop the analysis maintaining that both ψ as defined in (4.6) and θ as defined in (4.3b) are constant across subjects and over time — that is we treat them as parameters to be estimated.

The main explanatory variable entering the rhs of (4.10) is the ratio tlc_e / tlc_{ne}. Given the assumption we just made about ψ and θ, the variability tlc_e / tlc_{ne} is due to rlc, the relative labour cost as defined in Section 4.2. Since conditional on the geographical area and on the time period both r and reb vary across firms and across workers we evaluate the mean value of $(1+r(1-reb))/(1+r)$ as explained in Section 4.2. Let rlc_{it} be the resulting mean ratio. It varies over time — due to the reforms illustrated above — and across areas — due to the interaction with the alternative targeted wage subsidy scheme, but it is common to all subjects living in a specific geographical area in a given time period.

As explained in Section 4.3.1, tlc_e / tlc_{ne} is a function of the unknown parameters ψ and θ and of the observable variable rlc_{it}. Let $g(rlc_{it}, \psi, \theta)$ be this function which as a result of (4.8) and (4.9) is linear with respect to rlc_{it}. Inserting it as an explanatory variable in (4.10) yields:

$$y_{it}^{*} = \alpha_1 g(rlc_{it}, \psi, \theta) + u_i + \varepsilon_{it} \qquad (4.11)$$

where α_1 is the marginal effect of tlc_e / tlc_{ne} we are looking for whose expected sign is negative.

We modify this model:

1. to identify the lasting effects of the programme
2. to identify substitution effects

As for the lasting effects of the programme, following Bell *et al.* (1999), we design the analysis to identify the programme impact on the eligibles during their eligibility period as well as the lasting effect of the programme led by the role played by work experience.

By including among the explanatory variable the work experience $exp_{it} = \sum_{j=t_o}^{t-1} y_{ij}$ — namely, the number of years at work before period t — we can test whether the possibly longer work experience obtained by young people during their eligibility period as an impact of the CFL programme yields a higher chance of working after the eligibility period. If it were not the case, then it is not clear whether the programme is worthwhile even in the presence of an impact during the eligibility period.

By including work experience, model (4.11) becomes:

$$y_{it}^{*} = \alpha_1 g(rlc_{it}, \psi, \theta) + \alpha_2 \, exp_{it} + u_i + \varepsilon_{it}. \qquad (4.12)$$

Note that being affected by the entire previous history of the disturbance ε_{is}, $s < t$, exp_{it} is predetermined in the model which we need to account for in the estimation of the parameters.

To identify the parameter associated with the experience we need to take into account that during the age window in which individuals are eligible for CFL they might get post-compulsory education. To keep things easy let the schooling choice take place the following way. t_{0i} is the time period in which the i-th unit completes compulsory schooling and chooses further schooling. Let E_i be the chosen years of further schooling which we assume is not revised after t_{0i}. Then, from t_{0i} to $t_{0i} + E_i$ the i-th individual is (mainly) studying (with possible minor employment spells). From $t_{0i} + E_i + 1$ onward the individual participates in the labour market.[6]

We model this process by including a dummy S_{it} equal to 1 if the i-th subject is still attending school at time t and equal to 0 otherwise. Moreover, to control for the level of education of people participating at work, we include the variable $(1 - S_{it})E_i$ where E_i is the final level of formal education attained by the i-th subject. The overall model becomes:

$$y_{it}^* = \alpha_1 g(rlc_{it}, \psi, \theta) + \alpha_2 exp_{it} + \alpha_4 S_{it} + \alpha_5 (1 - S_{it}) E_i + u_i + \varepsilon_{it} \quad (4.13)$$

with an expected negative and positive sign, respectively, for α_4 and α_5. Given the way we are assuming subjects choose their level of formal education both S_{it} and E_i might be correlated to u_i but they are uncorrelated with ε_{it}. Also, since they are very likely to be correlated to exp_{it} omitting them would result in an inconsistent estimate of α_2.

As for the substitution effects of the programme, consider an eligible worker born in the calendar year c. As he/she completes the eligibility period he/she becomes at risk of being substituted out by the workers born in the calendar year $c + 1$ who are still eligible for CFL. This is because presumably the composition of the cohort c, with respect to all the characteristics relevant to being hired, is very close to the corresponding composition of the cohort $c + 1$ except for how much they cost a potential employer: hiring a worker from the still eligible cohort $c + 1$ is cheaper than hiring one from the no longer eligible cohort c.

To account for this potential substitution effect we interact the ratio tlc_e / tlc_{ne} with a dummy variable, I_{it}, indexing whether the i-th subject at time t is eligible for CFL. Model (4.12) becomes:

$$y_{it}^* = \alpha_1 g(rlc_{it}, \psi, \theta) I_{it} + \alpha_2 \exp_{it} + \alpha_3 g(rlc_{it}, \psi, \theta)(1 - I_{it}) + \alpha_4 S_{it}$$
$$+ \alpha_5 (1 - S_{it}) E_i + u_i + \varepsilon_{it} \quad (4.14)$$

with a positive expected sign for α_3.

Note that the substitution effect we are dealing with is a peculiar one. In the common usage of the word, a programme is said to have a substitution effect when the intended effect on the eligible subjects comes at the price of harming subjects who are not eligible for the programme itself. In the CFL case more precisely we should say that the programme impact on subject i is twofold. As the subject enters the labour market he/she benefits from the programme because of the higher chance of being hired during the eligibility period. As the subject exits from eligibility he/she is harmed by the very same programme he/she got benefits from because there are other subjects around still eligible for CFL. The overall impact depends on the relative size of the two parameters α_1 and α_3.

4.4   INFERENCE

Preliminarily, a major problem we need to solve is that information on education and school attendance is not available in the Social Security archive we draw our data from. As a result we miss both S_{it} and E_i.

The solution to the problem rests on grouping subjects according to their year of birth and to the geographical area they live in. The aggregated counterpart of equation (4.14) is as follows:

$$y_{(c)t} = \alpha_1 g\left(rlc_{(c)t}, \psi, \theta\right) I_{(c)t} + \alpha_2 \exp_{(c)t} + \alpha_3 g\left(rlc_{(c)t}, \psi, \theta\right)(1 - I_{(c)t})$$
$$+ \alpha_4 S_{(c)t} + \alpha_5 \left[(1 - S)E\right]_{(c)t} + u_{(c)} + \varepsilon_{(c)t} \qquad (4.15)$$

where $y_{(c)t}$ is the number of subjects belonging to the cohort c at work at time t; $I_{(c)t}$ is a dummy variable defined the same way as I_{it}; $\exp_{(c)t}$ is the total number of years at work at the beginning of time t for the subjects belonging to the cohort c; $S_{(c)t}$ is the number of subjects still at school and $\left[(1 - S)E\right]_{(c)t}$ is the aggregate level of education for those who have already completed their schooling. Note that the aggregation leaves unmodified the variable rlc_{it} since it is common to all subjects living in a specific geographical area (we rewrite it as $rlc_{(c)t}$ for convenience). Also, note that there is an abuse of notation in (4.15) since, because of the non-linearity of the micro model (4.14), the parameters in (4.15) cannot be equal to those in (4.14). To avoid introducing a new set of symbols we go on with the old ones. The missing data problem disappears at the cohort level since both $S_{(c)t}$ and $\left[(1 - S)E\right]_{(c)t}$ can be recovered from other data sources.

There is an apparent analogy between what we do with our data and the literature on pseudo-panel modelling (see Deaton, 1985; Verbeek, 1996). In fact, in both cases the analysis is eventually based on data aggregated by cohort. The difference between our case and the standard pseudo-panel problem is that in the latter truly longitudinal data are not available and the longitudinal dimension is recovered by resorting to a time series of cross-sectional data, while in the former the raw data are truly longitudinal and the aggregation by cohort is introduced only to solve a missing-regressor problem.

As one switches from the micro model (4.14) to its aggregated counterpart (4.15) the unobserved heterogeneity is integrated out so that one might wonder why we leave the cohort-specific time-invariant component $u_{(c)}$ in the model. The main reason to leave it is that the size of the year-of-birth cohorts we are considering is rather heterogeneous, increasing over time up to the year of birth 1965 and then sharply decreasing. As a consequence, members of the cohorts born around the mid-1960s might find it *ceteris paribus* more difficult than members of the older and younger cohorts to find a job when they enter the labour market because of the number of peers they have to compete with. Since the size of the cohorts – which *prima facie* approximates the number of peers competing for a given stock of available jobs – is time-invariant it is suitably accounted for by a cohort-specific time-invariant component.

A further problem with model (4.15) is that due to the time window our data refer to – 1986 to 1996 – the work experience is not observable for the cohorts entering the labour market before 1986. To avoid loosing all the observations on the older cohorts – which are exactly those cohorts allowing us to identify possible substitution effects – we work with the first-differenced model:

$$\Delta y_{(c)t} = \alpha_1 \Delta g\left(rlc_{(c)t}, \psi, \theta\right) I_{(c)t} + \alpha_2 y_{(c)t-1} + \alpha_3 \Delta g\left(rlc_{(c)t}, \psi, \theta\right)(1 - I_{(c)t})$$
$$+ \alpha_4 \Delta S_{(c)t} + \alpha_5 \Delta\left[(1-S)E\right]_{(c)t} + \Delta\varepsilon_{(c)t} \tag{4.16}$$

exploiting the identity $\Delta\exp_{(c)t} = y_{(c)t-1}$. This way we only lose one degree of freedom for each cohort. In this equation the dependent variable is the yearly variation of the stock of employees belonging to the $c-th$ cohort.

Note that differencing as in (4.16) also sweeps the unobserved heterogeneity $u_{(c)}$ away but as a result the explanatory variable $y_{(c)t-1}$ turns out to be correlated to the disturbance $(\varepsilon_{(c)t} - \varepsilon_{(c)t-1})$. To solve the endogeneity problem we use $y_{(c)t-2}$ as an IV for $y_{(c)t-1}$.

4.5   EMPIRICAL RESULTS

4.5.1   Data

The estimates we obtain exploit a 1:90 random sample from the Social Security files over the time window 1986-96. The reference population of the SS archive is slightly reduced with respect to programme one since it does not include agriculture and civil service employees (ISTAT codes 0 and 911, respectively). Unfortunately, due to the unreliability of the information from the archive previous to 1986 it is not possible to exploit in the analysis the 1985 break introduced by the CFL programme.

The dependent variable at the micro level is $y_{it} = 1$ if the i-th subject is at work during May of year t and $y_{it} = 0$ otherwise. We chose May since it is a 'normal' month with respect to the pattern of seasonality.

Aggregation by year of birth and geographical area (Centre-North and South) cohorts took place the way we explained in Section 4.4. The cohorts we include were born over the time window 1958–77 (see Table 4.3). We track them over the age window 19–34. The lower age limit has been set at 19 because there is nearly no CFL hiring below this age (most people younger than 19 are hired on an apprenticeship contract). On the other hand the upper age limit has been set at 34 to have some evidence on the post-eligibility work history of young people.

Table 4.3 Cohorts included in the analysis

Year of birth	Calendar years of observation	Age window of observation	Calendar years in which the cohort is eligible for CFL
1958	1986–1992	28–34	1986–1987
1959	1986–1993	27–34	1986–1988
1960	1986–1994	26–34	1986–1989
1961	1986–1995	25–34	1986–1990
1962	1986–1996	24–34	1986–91, 1994
1963	1986–1996	23–33	1986–92, 1994–95
1964	1986–1996	22–32	1986–1996
1965	1986–1996	21–31	1986–1996
1966	1986–1996	20–30	1986–1996
1967	1986–1996	19–29	1986–1996
1968	1987–1996	19–28	1987–1996
1969	1988–1996	19–27	1988–1996
1970	1989–1996	19–26	1989–1996
1971	1990–1996	19–25	1990–1996
1972	1991–1996	19–24	1991–1996
1973	1992–1996	19–23	1992–1996
1974	1993–1996	19–22	1993–1996
1975	1994–1996	19–21	1994–1996
1976	1995–1996	19–20	1995–1996
1977	1996–1996	19–19	1996–1996

Note that the time window over which we could obtain data is such that only few cohorts (year of births 1958 to 1963) are observed after their eligibility period. Finally, note that as a result of the time window and of the age window we set the number of available observations varies across cohorts (total number of observations is 310).

4.5.2 Estimation

The model we estimate is a simplified version of (4.16). The simplification we introduce is to overcome the lack of precision in the estimation of the structural parameters α_1, α_3, ψ and θ we found in some preliminary estimation exercise.

We did some experimentation setting ψ and θ to alternative likely values and found that at the selected values and as a result of its actual variability over time and across areas $tlc_e / tlc_{ne} = g(rlc_{(c)t}, \psi, \theta)$ displays a fairly large positive correlation to $rlc_{(c)t}$. Table 4.4 reports a sample of our results. In other words, $rlc_{(c)t}$ is a fairly good proxy for tlc_e / tlc_{ne}.

Table 4.4 Correlation between rlc and tlc$_e$/tlc$_{ne}$ at selected values for θ and ψ (values of q implied by θ are reported; see equations (4.3a)–(4.3b), (4.6)–(4.9))

| ψ | θ | 0.05 | 0.1 | 0.2 |
	q	0.11	0.22	0.5
0.5		0.76	0.69	0.58
0.7		0.79	0.76	0.69
0.9		0.80	0.79	0.76

Thus, instead of dealing with equation (4.16) we use the much simpler model:

$$\Delta y_{(c)t} = \alpha_1^* \Delta rlc_{(c)t} I_{(c)t} + \alpha_2 y_{(c)t-1} + \alpha_3^* \Delta rlc_{(c)t} (1 - I_{(c)t}) + \alpha_4 \Delta S_{(c)t} + \alpha_5 \Delta \left[(1-S)E \right]_{(c)t} + \Delta \varepsilon_{(c)t} \qquad (4.17)$$

where α_1^* and α_3^* measure the combined marginal effect of the rebate on the SS fee and of introducing/withdrawing a firing costs component into the programme. In other words, we do not identify the separate marginal impacts of reducing the SS fee and of reducing the firing costs. Instead, we identify an overall marginal programme impact. Finally, the results presented here do not exploit information on schooling attendance nor on education from the auxiliary data source. The approximate solution we propose also exploits the aggregation by cohort.

Specification 1

We approximate $\alpha_4 \Delta S_{(c)t} + \alpha_1 \Delta\left[(1-S)E\right]_{(c)t}$ in (4.17) by a polynomial in the cohort age. After some experimentation we chose a second degree polynomial. In this specification we account for the business cycle by including the *GDP* yearly growth rate, $\left(GDP - GDP_{-1}\right)/GDP_{-1}$, separately evaluated for the Centre-North and the South.

Table 4.5 reports the result of the IV estimation of equation (4.17) using $y_{(c)t-2}$ as the instrument for $y_{(c)t-1}$. The estimation procedure properly accounts for the non-invertible MA(1) structure of the disturbance.

Table 4.5 IV estimates of Specification 1 (accounting for the non-invertible MA(1) disturbance)

	Estimate	t-stat.
Intercept	3628.6	14.4
Age	−249.0	−13.2
Age^2	4.167	12.1
$rlc_{ct}\, I_{ct}$	−194.6	1.07
$rlc_{ct}\,(1 - I_{ct})$	−198.9	1.08
Exp_{ct}	0.02960	7.17
GDP	641.5	1.36

The main result emerging is that the programme does not have any impact on the young people's chance of obtaining a job during the eligibility period. The estimated marginal effect is both very small in absolute value[7] and statistically zero. Consistently, it does not harm them as they exit from eligibility. Work experience turns out statistically significant: an additional year at work in the past implies a three percentage points higher probability of being at work.

Specification 2

In the second specification instead of approximating the missing variables by a polynomial we get rid of them by taking the *across-cohorts* first difference $\Delta y_{(c)t} - \Delta y_{(c-1)t-1}$. The rationale of this differencing is that adjacent cohorts are presumably alike with respect to their schooling decision. As a consequence $\Delta S_{(c)t} = \Delta S_{(c-1)t-1}$ and $\Delta\left[(1-S)E\right]_{(c)t} = \Delta\left[(1-S)E\right]_{(c-1)t-1}$. In words, by comparing two adjacent cohorts at the same age we expect to observe the same proportion of subjects still attending school as well as the same mean level of education for subjects who have already completed their schooling.

By applying this differencing to model (4.17) we get:

$$\Delta y_{(c)t} - \Delta y_{(c-1)t-1} = \alpha_1^* \left(\Delta rlc_{(c)t} I_{(c)t} - \Delta rlc_{(c-1)t-1} I_{(c-1)t-1} \right) + \alpha_2 \left(y_{(c)t-1} - y_{(c-1)t-2} \right)$$
$$+ \alpha_3^* \left(\Delta rlc_{(c)t} (1 - I_{(c)t}) - \Delta rlc_{(c-1)t-1} (1 - I_{(c-1)t-1}) \right) + \left(\Delta \varepsilon_{(c)t} - \Delta \varepsilon_{(c-1)t-1} \right). \quad (4.18)$$

Finally, note that double differencing as in (4.18) also sweeps out the business cycle provided it evolves over time along a quadratic local polynomial. This allows us to avoid including the GDP yearly growth rate in the regression.

Table 4.6 reports the result of the IV estimation of model (4.18) using $\left(y_{(c)t-2} - y_{(c-1)t-3} \right)$ as the instrument for $\left(y_{(c)t-1} - y_{(c-1)t-2} \right)$. The estimation procedure properly accounts for the autocorrelation structure of the disturbance resulting from double differencing. Results are very much the same as in table 4.5. No programme impact emerges while the effect of work experience turns out statistically significant albeit somewhat larger than in the previous specification.

Table 4.6 IV estimates of Specification 2 (accounting for the autocorrelation structure of the disturbance)

	Estimate	t-stat.
Intercept	−9.316	−9.27
$rlc_{ct} I_{ct}$	−118.4	1.24
$rlc_{ct} (1 - I_{ct})$	−87.30	0.90
Exp_{ct}	0.03855	3.98

4.6   FINAL REMARKS

The CFL programme was introduced in 1985 to improve young people's occupational chances. It provides the employers with some incentive to recruit young workers by reducing both the labour and the firing costs relative to those they would bear by recruiting older workers.

Following the literature, we argue that the expected impact of the programme is twofold: it should increase the eligibles' chance of working during the eligibility period thanks to the reduction in the labour and firing costs as well as their chance of working after the eligibility period thanks to the longer work experience obtained during the eligibility period. There is also some room for a substitution effect since as subjects exit from eligibility employers might find it convenient to replace them by still younger eligible workers.

To measure the impact of the programme we exploit the variation over time and across geographical areas of the labour and firing costs for an eligible worker relative to a non-eligible one induced by several reforms of the programme as well as its interaction with other incentive schemes.

In fact, our main result is that during the eligibility period young people's opportunities to work do not react to variation of the relative labour and firing costs. Consistently, no substitution effect emerges. We identify a positive statistically significant effect of work experience which in the presence of an impact during the eligibility period would yield also an impact on the long-run work history of formerly eligible subjects.

NOTES

1. In principle, to be eligible for the benefit the employer should prove that the new employee is an additional one. In practice, the eligibility rule has been enforced in a way particularly favourable to the firms.
2. For workers already employed, firms faced, however, special provisions allowing them to have the same amount of fiscal exemption and a number of tax cuts. On the whole they paid labour costs equal to ¼ of those that comparable firms located in the North would have had to face.
3. The typical length of a CFL employment spell is two years.
4. Strictly speaking, there are some firms operating in the South which are not eligible for this scheme but their relative weight in terms of employees is rather small. See the details in Section 4.2.
5. It is not just 1 because of the presence of the firms we mentioned in the previous footnote which did use the CFL programme (more on this below).
6. Potentially, there might be an impact of the programme on the schooling choices in that, due to the availability of better occupational chances, there might be subjects revising their schooling plans and leaving school to enter the labour market. We do not deal with this further problem here and leave it for future research.
7. The reported figure means that a ten percentage points reduction of the relative labour cost yields an increase of the number of employees in a specific cohort as large as 1746 (19.4 times 90, the sampling rate). Since the cohort's size is approximately 300 000 in the South and 500 000 in the Centre-North the marginal effect we estimate is apparently negligible.

REFERENCES

Bell, B., R. Blundell and J. Van Reenen, (1999), 'Getting the Unemployed back to Work: the Role of Targeted Wage Subsidies', Institute for Fiscal Studies, London, Working Paper no. W99.12.
Blundell R., A. Duncan and C. Meghir (1998), 'Estimating labour supply responses using tax reforms', *Econometrica*, **66**.
Deaton, A. (1985), 'Panel data from time series of cross-sections', *Journal of Econometrics*, **30.**
Verbeek, M. (1996), 'Pseudo-panel data', in Matyas L. and P. Sevestre (eds), *The Econometrics of Panel Data: A Handbook of the Theory with Applications*, Dordrecht: Kluwer.

5. Are we retiring too early?[*]

Pierre Pestieau

5.1 INTRODUCTION

Like most good questions, the one raised by the title of this chapter leads to a number of other questions, namely is this really the case? Are we really retiring so early? If so, what is the problem with retiring early and is there such a thing as an optimal age for retiring? If early retirement is indeed a problem, why not just increase the retirement age? Finally, are we not confusing the people who wish to retire early with those who are simply unable to work any longer?

The purpose of this chapter is to try to answer these questions on the basis of recent work on a subject that lately has been drawing the attention of scholars, policy makers and the media. But before developing these answers at length, let us first sketch them.

Early retirement is currently being observed in most but not all European countries. The average labour participation in the age group 55–64 ranges from 24 per cent in Belgium, to 88 per cent in Iceland, with the bulk of countries closer to Belgium than to Iceland. Early retirement *per se* is a blessing for society rather than a problem, provided that it does not represent a drain. However, as generational accounts show, even though the bulk of the bill for the current generation of retirees is being financed by the retirees themselves within an incentive structure that makes it attractive, the fact is that it is future generations who are paying for the balance.

[*] This chapter presents an overview of a joint research with H. Cremer, J.-M. Lozachmeur, Ph. Michel, G. Casamatta, A. Jousten, S. Perelman, R. Desmet and B. Lipzyck. See in particular Cremer *et al.* (2001) and Casamatta *et al.* (2001). Earlier versions of this paper were presented at the CESIfo Workshop on Public Pensions, Munich, May 3–4, 2001 and at the Bordeaux Atelier Retraites, 29 March 2001. I am grateful to the referee for helpful comments. Financial support from the Belgian Research Foundation (FRFC) is acknowledged.

One can speak of an optimal retirement age that varies across individual features such as wealth, productivity and health, but which also depends on the setting: *laissez-faire*, first-best and second-best optimum. In both the *laissez-faire* and the first-best optimum setting, people retire when the marginal utility of inactivity is equal to their marginal productivity at work. People in poor health and with low productivity will retire earlier than people in good health and with high productivity.

For obvious reasons early retirement puts pressure on the financing of health care and pension schemes. This problem is made worse by growing longevity. In the European Union life expectancy at age 65 has increased by more than one year per decade since 1950. As a consequence, instead of 45–50 years of work and 5–10 years of retirement of half a century ago, a young worker can now expect to work for 30–35 years and retire for 15–20 years.

Since increased longevity is accompanied by better health, the obvious solution would seem to be to reverse the trend towards early retirement by reducing the subsidies inducing it, and increasing the statutory retirement age. Yet, as it turns out, it is difficult to conduct such a reform. The political power of individuals close to retirement, and of those already retired make it so.

When considering reforms aimed at reversing the trend towards early retirement, it is important to take into account the wide variability in the capacity to work – a variability that is widening as life expectancy increases. The practical issue is how to care for elderly workers who are in poor health without, on the other hand, opening the door of retirement to those who would like to stop working but are quite capable of continuing.

In fact, a reform of social security ought to include a close connection between pensions systems and the system of insurance for the sick, as well as the determination of a more flexible retirement age together with actuarial adjustment of yearly benefits. The ideal outcome would then be to have early retirees because of poor health receive relatively generous benefits while early retirees unwilling to continue working would receive actuarially low pensions.

I will develop these points in the rest of this chapter, guided by the following outline:

- Retirement and longevity: facts and causes;
- Optimal retirement ages;
- The politics of early retirement;
- Desire for leisure versus disability.

A point of terminology is in order. In this chapter, 'retirement age' is most generally endogenous, even though it is indirectly controlled by the social security tax-benefit package. Where there is a direct control of retirement age, it is explicitly mentioned. Retirement age is thus the age at which workers retire and claim benefits. In the reality, however, the concept is much more confusing and it is used in a variety of ways that are sometimes inconsistent. For example, it is possible to claim benefits, partial or full, without retiring, or to retire without claiming benefits right away.

5.2 RETIREMENT AND LONGEVITY

5.2.1 A Few Facts

The aging of the population is a general phenomenon in industrialized countries. It results from a drop in fertility, but mainly from a steady increase in longevity. In the European Union the proportion of individuals above 50, 70, 90 was, respectively, 0.32, 0.11, 0.005 in 1995. In 2050 it will be 0.46, 0.22 and 0.17. Table 5.1 provides detailed data on this for seven countries.

Table 5.1 Fraction of people aged 50, 60, 70, 80, 90 in 1995 and 2050

	1995					2050				
	Fraction of people at least aged									
Countries	50	60	70	80	90	50	60	70	80	90
Germany	34.6	20.7	10.5	4.1	0.4	47.9	35.0	21.7	10.6	1.5
Spain	31.0	20.6	10.2	3.3	0.4	48.8	37.1	24.7	10.4	1.7
France	29.7	20.0	10.3	4.2	0.6	44.8	33.0	21.0	10.1	2.1
Ireland	24.4	15.3	8.0	2.5	0.3	46.1	33.0	19.9	8.1	1.3
Italy	34.4	22.2	11.1	4.0	0.4	50.7	38.3	26.0	12.0	1.9
UK	31.2	20.5	11.2	4.0	0.5	44.5	31.7	19.6	9.5	1.7
Sweden	33.6	22.1	12.9	4.6	0.6	41.8	29.1	18.1	8.5	1.5
EU 15	32.2	20.6	10.6	3.9	0.5	46.3	33.9	21.7	10.1	1.7

Source: Calot and Sardon (1999).

From these figures, and on the assumption that people retire at 60 or 65, one derives the expected evolution of the dependency ratio which in some countries doubles in less than four decades. Roughly speaking, what this means for the social security system is that, everything being equal, the average contribution rate has to double as well, or that the average replacement ratio has to be cut by one half. Why not then consider an increase in the age of retirement? Is it not strange to use the same age of 60 or 65 to measure the dependency ratio when the average life expectancy was 64 in 1950 and is expected to be 84 in 2050 for French men (69 and 90 for French women)? What is even stranger is to observe that whereas life expectancy is rising, the effective age of retirement has been steadily decreasing over the last 50 years. Table 5.2 gives the effective retirement age for 1960 and 1995.

Table 5.2 Longevity and retirement age in the European Union (1960–95)

	Men				Women			
	Life expectancy		Retirement age		Life expectancy		Retirement age	
	1960–65	1995–2000	1960	1995	1960–65	1995–2000	1960	1995
Belgium	67.9	73.8	63.3	57.6	73.9	80.6	60.8	54.1
France	67.6	74.2	64.5	59.2	74.5	82.0	65.8	58.3
Germany	67.4	73.9	65.2	60.5	72.9	80.2	62.3	58.4
Ireland	68.4	73.6	68.1	63.4	72.3	79.2	70.8	60.1
Italy	67.4	75.0	64.5	60.6	72.6	81.2	62.0	57.2
Spain	67.9	74.5	67.9	61.4	72.7	81.5	68.0	58.9
Sweden	71.6	76.3	66.0	63.3	75.6	80.8	63.4	62.1
UK	67.9	74.5	66.2	62.7	73.8	79.8	62.7	59.7

Source: United Nations Population Division, World Population Prospects, 1998. Blondal and Scarpetta (1998).

From the figures just discussed, we present in Table 5.3 a range of dependency ratios that use different benchmarks: (I) age 60, which in France is the statutory age of retirement; (II) the current effective age of retirement; (III) hypothetical age of retirement based on a linear trend extrapolating from the past; (IV) another hypothetical age of retirement based on the idea that from now on the expected length of retirement is kept constant. Not surprisingly, one obtains quite contrasting profiles. Alternative (I) is the standard one based on age 60; alternative (II) is clearly unrealistic as it shows what would happen if the trend towards early retirement were kept unchanged. Clearly, the more reassuring scenario is the one wherein the current expected length of retirement is kept constant. As we can observe, the problem seems to be more acute for women than for men.[1]

Table 5.3 Alternative ratios of dependency

		Belgian men: 1970–2050		
	I	II	III	IV
	Ratio 60	Ratio based on effective retirement extrapolated after 1995	Ratio based on effective retirement kept at 58 after 1995	Ratio keeping length of retirement constant (17 years)
1970	32.3	24.3	24.3	–
1980	27.7	25.6	25.6	–
1995	32.5	37.6	37.6	37.6
2025	50.1	78.2	58.6	46.1
2050	58.6	105.8	67.4	41.2

		Belgian women: 1970–2050		
	Ratio 60	Ratio based on effective retirement extrapolated after 1995	Ratio based on effective retirement kept at 58 after 1995	Ratio keeping length of retirement constant (27 years)
1970	43.5	47.1	47.1	–
1980	37.5	47.4	47.4	–
1995	45.7	65.9	65.9	65.9
2025	63.8	130.3	95.6	78.6
2050	78.0	184.5	108.0	70.5

Source: Lannoy and Lipszyc (2000).

5.2.2 Incentive to Early Retirement

There is no doubt that social security and subsidized health have contributed to the rise in longevity. Yet the main explanatory factors seem to be economic growth. International comparisons also indicate that environmental and dietetic characteristics explain longevity differences much better than health care spending.

The trends towards early retirement has different causes. It can be explained by economic growth – after all, leisure is a normal good – and by change in preferences. However, part of the explanation seems to rest on the incentive structure implied by social protection programs aimed at elderly workers: unemployment insurance, disability insurance, early retirement schemes, pension plans.

Throughout this chapter, we use the two-overlapping-generations model wherein each individual i has productivity w_i, works the first period of his life with length normalized to 1. He also works a fraction z_i, of the second period (also of length 1) and retires for a period $h - z_i$, where $h \leq 1$ denotes his life expectancy. His life thus lasts $1 + h$ and his active life $1 + z < 1 + h \leq 2$. In the first period, he consumes c_i and in the second d_i. His lifetime utility is given by:

$$u_i = u(c_i, d_i, z_i) \tag{5.1}$$

or, with the budget constraint,

$$u_i = u(w_i - s_i, wz_i + Rs_i, z_i) \tag{5.2}$$

where s_i is savings and R a financial interest factor. For the sake of simplicity, we will use a separable form with a quadratic disutility of work:

$$u_i = u(c_i) + \beta u(d_i - \gamma z_i^2) \tag{5.3}$$

where $u(\cdot)$ is strictly concave, β is a time preference factor and γ measures the intensity of work disutility. Note that z_i cannot exceed $\bar{z}$ (even when $\gamma = 0$); by assumption $z_i < \bar{z} < h$.

In a *laissez-faire* setting each individual chooses z_i, such that:

$$\frac{\partial u}{\partial d_i} w_i = -\frac{\partial u}{\partial z_i} \tag{5.4}$$

or with our particular function:

$$z_i = \frac{w_i}{2\gamma}. \qquad (5.5)$$

As it will appear below, this is also the optimal condition for the retirement age. The more productive the worker, the later he retires. Given the particular nature of our utility function, one notes that there is no income or wealth effect in the choice of z. With a more general utility, one would expect z_i to decrease with a wealth gain such as that arising from intergenerational transfers.

Let us now introduce a PAYG pension scheme: a payroll tax of rate τ and a benefit p which may depend on z and w. Again, to make things easier, we assume that pension benefits are partially related to contributions and partially flat. We then write:

$$p_i = \tau \left[\alpha \left(w_i \left(1+n+z_i\right)\right) + (1-\alpha)\left(\overline{w} \left(1+n\right)+\overline{wz}\right)\right] \qquad (5.6)$$

where α is the contributory share and n is the population growth rate as well as the return to a PAYG system. The upper bar is used for the expected value across productivity levels. We can now write the utility of an individual of productivity w_i:

$$u_i = u\left(w_i \left(1-\tau\right)-s_i\right) + \beta u\left(Rs_i + w_i \left(1-\tau\right)z_i - \gamma z_i^2 + p_i\right). \qquad (5.7)$$

The equilibrium age of retirement is thus equal to:

$$z_i = w_i \left(1-\tau(1-\alpha)\right)/2\gamma. \qquad (5.8)$$

In other words, the lower the contributory share and the higher the tax rate, the earlier the retirement. We have here one of the sources of tax distortion, namely the fact that part of the contribution is not perceived as coming back to the worker at retirement. There are two other sources of distortion that do not appear in the above formula: a wealth effect where the system is not mature enough or where it is redistributive with additional incentives to retire early. One can easily calculate the net social security wealth of a worker of productivity i as:

$$\begin{aligned}
\theta_i &= -\tau\left(w_i + \frac{w_i z_i}{R}\right) + \frac{p_i}{R} \\
&= \tau w_i \left(\frac{1+n}{R}-1\right) \quad \text{if } \alpha=1 \qquad (5.9)
\end{aligned}$$

$$= \frac{\tau}{R}\left[\left(\overline{w}\,(1+n) - w_i R\right) + \left(\overline{w^2} - w_i^2\right)\frac{1-\tau}{2\gamma} \right] \quad \text{if } \alpha = 0.$$

Where the system is not mature, one writes $R < 1 + n$ and there is a clear wealth effect: part of the pension is paid by future generations and this induces early retirement. Where the system matures, there is a negative wealth effect (the service of the implicit debt) that ought to induce later retirement. The redistributive effect is more ambiguous: it induces high wage earners to retire later and low wage earners to retire earlier.

The distortion just analysed arises from the payroll tax. It is clear that if elderly workers could be exempted from it – only the young workers contribute – there would be no incentive for early retirement. In most countries, elderly workers are not only subject to the payroll tax, but by working one more year they often forgo some available social benefits: unemployment or disability compensation or pensions from an early retirement scheme. To put it another way, working one more year does not increase their replacement ratio.

Up to now, p_i was defined as the aggregate benefit obtained during the second period of life, and thus independent of retirement length $(1 - z_i)$. Suppose now that p_i decreases with z_i. Then the choice of z_i in the case of flat benefit is given by:

$$-\frac{\partial u_i}{\partial z_i} = \left[w_i\,(1-\tau) + \frac{\partial p}{\partial z_i} \right]\frac{\partial u_i}{\partial d_i}, \qquad (5.10)$$

where $\frac{\partial p_i}{\partial z_i} < 0$. In the quadratic example, one has $z_i = \dfrac{w_i\,(1-\tau) + \dfrac{\partial p_i}{\partial z_i}}{2\gamma}$.

The choice of prolonged activity is thus subject to a double burden: the payroll tax and the forgone pension benefit. The importance of these two burdens varies quite a lot across countries and this variation explains why effective retirement shows such a wide range among the OECD countries. It would be simplistic to only blame governments for these burdens. In general, unions and firms agree to use them, at the workers' expense, as a way of cutting the work force down to the lowest possible cost to firms. We come back to this in the concluding section.

There now exists a number of studies that provide measurements of these burdens, or what is often called the implicit tax that elderly workers face in case of early retirement. These measurements are more refined than the one defined in our simple model; they depend on various characteristics: age, sex, education, family structures, etc. for each worker. Such studies present strong evidence that these implicit taxes induce most workers to retire at the earliest possible stage.

We consider two such studies, both conducted within the NBER aging group. The first is an international comparison of implicit taxes and retirement behaviour by Gruber and Wise (1999) and the second, which is posterior, is a microeconometric study of retirement in Belgium by Dellis *et al.* (2001).

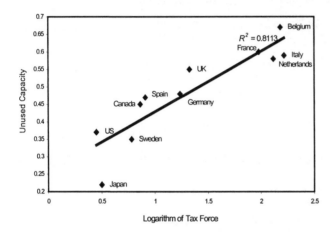

Figure 5.1 Retirement and implicit taxation – international comparison

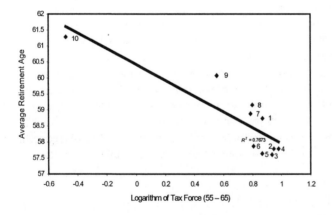

Figure 5.2 Retirement and implicit taxation – Belgian men per income deciles

Both figures present a relation between labour force participation among elderly workers and an indicator of implicit taxation on postponing retirement. This indicator, named tax force, is the sum of the implicit taxes an elderly worker faces at each age during the relevant period (55–65 in Belgium). For the international comparison, the labour participation indicator is actually one minus overall participation between 55 and 65; for the Belgian study, we use the average retirement age. As to the comparison units in the Belgian study, we use income deciles. As it appears clearly, both high implicit tax and low income levels explain early retirement.

Using the above formula:

$$z_i = \frac{w_i - \tau w_i + \dfrac{\partial p_i}{\partial z_i}}{2\gamma}, \tag{5.11}$$

w_i is the indicator for income, $\tau w_i - \dfrac{\partial p_i}{\partial z_i}$, the tax force and γ reflects the taste parameter that can vary across countries. Actually γ can also be seen as a health status parameter.

5.3   OPTIMAL RETIREMENT AGES

In the previous section we saw that most existing social security packages tend to distort the choice of retirement age downwards. In other words, the actual age of retirement is generally lower than its *laissez-faire* level which happens to be also the socially optimal level, as we now show.

To obtain optimal levels we now derive the first-best optimality conditions. Keeping the presentation simple, we drop the first period in the above problem. Each individual with productivity w_i works a fraction z_i of a lifetime normalized to 1. This can be viewed as a reduced form of a continuous time problem with instantaneous utility $u(c, \ell)$ where ℓ is equal to either 1 or 0 and the disutility for ℓ increases over time. The objective of the social planner is utilitarian, and his problem is to maximize the following Lagrangean:

$$\pounds = \sum n_i U\left[c_i - \gamma z_i^2\right] + \mu \sum n_i \left[c_i - z_i w_i\right], \tag{5.12}$$

where $U(u)$ is a social utility, u is a quasi linear individual utility and μ is the multiplier associated with the resource constraint. The optimality conditions are simply:

$$z_i^* = \frac{w_i}{2\gamma} \quad \text{and} \quad c_i - \frac{w_i^2}{4\gamma} = u^* \text{ (equal for all } i\text{)}. \qquad (5.13)$$

With 2 types and $n_1 = n_2$, $c_1 = \frac{1}{4\gamma}\left(w_1^2 + \frac{w_2^2}{2}\right)$ and $c_2 = \frac{1}{4\gamma}\left(w_2^2 + \frac{w_1^2}{2}\right)$.

Note that z_i^* is also the *laissez-faire* solution.

We could decentralize these optimal conditions if we had non-distortionary instruments. In this particular example it is pretty easy, as the government observes z_i. Even if it does not observe w_i, it can offer each individual a transfer $x_i = c_i^*$, impose a retirement age $\bar{z}_i = z_i^*$ and take away earnings. This solution is incentive-compatible.

In general, however, for either administrative or informational reasons, decentralization of this sort is not feasible. Assume, for example, that the government is constrained to use a flat-rate payroll tax with uniform benefit p. The problem can be expressed in the following Lagrangean:

$$\pounds = \sum n_i \, u\left[(1-t)\,w_i\,z_i + p - \gamma\,z_i^2\right] + \mu \sum n_i\left[t\,w_i\,z_i - p\right]. \quad (5.14)$$

If the government could not observe z_i, we would have the standard optimal linear income tax with an efficiency term $\left[\sum n_i \, w_i \dfrac{\partial z_i}{\partial t}\right]$ and an equity term $\left[\mathrm{cov}\left(\dfrac{\partial u}{\partial c_i}, \, w_i z_i\right)\right]$. In fact the government observes z_i but can only impose a minimum retirement age that constrains the lower-productivity individuals, namely those with the lower notional supply of z_i as

$$z_i = \frac{w_i(1-t)}{2\gamma}.$$

Keeping the two-types case, this means that the lower-productivity individual will be subject to a lower distortion than the higher-productivity individual. In general, we see the opposite result: no distortion at the top and downward distortion for less productive workers.

Suppose that workers face two decisions concerning labour: how long is the weekly work, ℓ, and how long is the work career measured in number of weeks, z. Again, we adopt a reduced form of the utility function with constant consumption c_i, weekly labour supply ℓ_i and length of active life z_i.

$$U_i = U(c_i - v(\ell_i) R(z_i)).\tag{5.15}$$

With this new specification [both $v(\cdot)$ and $R(\cdot)$ are strictly convex functions], the first-best optimality problem is given by maximizing:

$$\pounds = \sum n_i U(c_i - v(\ell_i) R(z_i)) + \mu \sum n_i (c_i - z_i \ell_i w_i)\tag{5.16}$$

which gives: $U'(u_i) = \mu$; $v'(\ell_i) R(z_i) = z_i w_i$ and $v(\ell_i) R'(z_i) = \ell_i w_i$. As a consequence $\dfrac{dz_i}{d\ell_i} = \dfrac{v'(\ell_i) R(z_i)}{R'(z_i) v(\ell_i)} = \dfrac{z_i}{\ell_i}$. Here too, the optimal choice of z_i and ℓ_i is the same as the market choice. With two choice variables, ℓ_i and z_i, and given that w_i and ℓ_i are not observable – $y_i = w_i \ell_i$ and z_i are common knowledge – the first-best optimum cannot be decentralized.

One can show that a non-linear tax $T(z_i, w_i \ell_i)$ can be designed. It is clearly superior to any linear policy and has the following features for the two types: there is no distortion at the top: $z_2 = z_2^*$ and $\ell_2 = \ell_2^*$. For the less productive there is a downward distortion of ℓ_1 and z_1 relative to c_1, and of ℓ_1 relative to z_1.[2] The fact that z_i is observable and that ℓ_i is not makes the distortion on the first smaller than that on the second. But the main conclusion is that asymmetric information implies some downward distortion on retirement, although lower than with a linear scheme.

5.4   THE POLITICS OF EARLY RETIREMENT

Why has it turned out so difficult to increase the statutory retirement age and to reduce subsidies to early retirement, even though such reforms would seem to be a natural outcome of higher longevity? Similarly, why have we reached a point where increased life expectancy is regarded as a problem rather than a blessing for society?

To understand this, one needs to think within a dynamic setting. When social security was first designed, there were no entitlements. We can reasonably state that the key parameters: contributions rates, replacement rates and statutory retirement age were chosen behind the veil of ignorance. At that time only the young generation was concerned; the older generation didn't have a clear idea of the free lunch it was going to receive. The joint evolution of increased longevity and early retirement came later. Quite possibly the younger generation left alone would have been ready to reform the system and reverse the pattern of retirement. But such reform was then and still is opposed by the political power of individuals at retirement or close to retirement who are ready to defend what they consider to be their legitimate entitlement.

A number of models exist that provide a political economy determination of the level of social security benefits. The first generation models assume identical individuals except for age. The retirement age is given and, in the canonical version, the level of benefits chosen is the level most preferred by the median-age voter. The outcome is a level of benefit higher than the optimal one that would be chosen at the start of the working life. The introduction of liquidity constraints, or of uncertainty, does not modify this conclusion. The second generation models assume individuals who differ not only in age but also in productivity or in altruism. Again, the dominant conclusion is that of relatively generous social security benefits.[3]

All these models assume a fixed retirement age. If we drop this assumption and let the retirement age vary then one can look at the issue of voting on such an age either directly or indirectly. In the first case, individuals vote for a mandatory retirement age and possibly other parameters of the social security system.[4] In the second case, individuals vote on the size of the payroll tax knowing that it affects the age at which they eventually retire.[5]

Without going into too many details, we use the two period model given above for $\alpha = 0$ (namely, a pure Beveridgean system). The problem for each individual is to pick his most preferred tax rate, τ_i^*, that maximizes:

$$u_i(\tau) = u((1-\tau)w_i - s_i^*) + \beta u\left(Rs_i^* + \frac{w_i^2(1-\tau)^2}{4\gamma} + \tau\left((1+n)\overline{w} + \frac{(1-\tau)\overline{w^2}}{2\gamma}\right)\right) \qquad (5.17)$$

where $s_i^* \geq 0$ is the optimal choice of saving. For low income individuals one expects savings to be equal to zero (liquidity constraint). There are three reasons for voting for a low level of τ:

- the PAYG system yields a low return: $R > 1+n$,
- the redistribution is harmful (this concerns high-income individuals),
- the level of consumption in the second period would outsize the one in the first period (this concerns low-productivity workers).

On some plausible assumptions, one obtains a profile of τ_i^* for a distribution of w_i with support (w_-, w_+). This is represented in Figure 5.3.

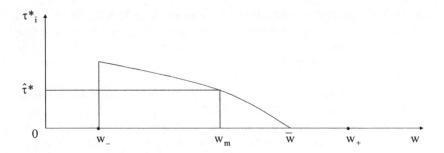

Figure 5.3   Preferred payroll tax rate

From Figure 5.3, it is clear that we have a majority in favor of $\hat{\tau}^*$. The worker with median wage, w_m, is decisive.[6]

We have assumed that such a vote occurred at one point and that only the working generation was concerned by it. If n falls a lot relative to r (and also if there is little redistribution (α is high)), it can be shown that a majority in the working generation will be in favour of reducing $\hat{\tau}^*$ and consequently of increasing the retirement age. But now the retired generation does not remain passive since it expects benefits based on $\hat{\tau}^*$.

In what way and for how long will the retired generation be able to stall reforms? First, the way. It can be stalled through the regular process of representative democracy in which lobbying by interest groups plays an important role. As regards how long, this depends on the power of these interest groups and of their selfishness. A little bit of intergenerational altruism would suffice for the retired generation to realize that such a reform could be beneficial for their children and grandchildren.

As regards reform, European countries behave in differing ways. Some countries, such as Sweden, have introduced a major restructuring of their social security with clear implications concerning retirement age. Other countries, such as the UK, do not need much reform because their social security system does not face major cost escalation problems. The majority of countries however seems to have a hard time moving towards reforms despite an abundance of national and international expert reports indicating the necessity to move quickly, particularly as regards raising the pension age. France is not unique; in fact it is quite typical of a society where the mere suggestion of raising the retirement age can be fatal for a politician, not unlike what a confession of having taken drugs in college can do for politicians in some other countries.

The surveys on this subject are quite interesting. Over years they show a majority in favour of the *status quo*. In almost all European countries, respondents oppose any restrictions of their existing social security, even though these imply tax cuts. In one ten-year-old survey (Eurobarometer) there was an interesting question about continuing the existing system even at the cost of higher contribution or contracting the welfare state with respect to a limited number of essential benefits. The 'continuists' clearly outnumbered the 'contractionists' in all the European countries (EC12), as commented by Ferrera (1993). And he concluded that 'the legitimacy of social protection in its current format remains robust within the EC as a whole'.

On the questions about the option to reform the pension system because of aging, hardly a third of the respondents thought that raising the retirement age was a likely policy option. In fact Germany (45 per cent), France (42 per cent) and the Netherlands (48 per cent) seemed more convinced than the others about the wisdom of raising the pension age.

In a recent survey conducted in Belgium, more precisely in the Flemish community, people were asked about their preferred retirement age. The majority of respondents cited the age of 57, which is also the effective retirement age, and well below the statutory age of 65 known not to be sustainable [see Schokkaert *et al.* (2000)]. In France, a recent survey (see Assous, 2001) also indicates that regardless of age workers are in favour of an age of retirement close to the actual one. The survey makes a difference between the 'ideal' and the 'expected' age of retirement, the latter being quite higher that the former (six years).

Finally, there is the survey by Boeri *et al.* (2001) conducted in Germany, France, Italy and Spain on the welfare state. It paints the same picture as the earlier Eurobarometer: a majority of the citizens do not want any rolling back of their welfare state, which does not mean that they are happy with the existing programs. Fortunately, the door is not completely closed to reform. A majority of respondents are also in favour of some sort of flexibility in the way social security in organized.

5.5 DESIRE FOR LEISURE AND DISABILITY

Up to now we have focused on individual differences in productivity. In reality, workers can be differentiated not just according to productivity but also to their health at work. Because of personal characteristics, or because of the painful nature of the job, some workers are worn out earlier than others. Clearly, this should play a role in their decision to retire, as well as in the way retirement policy ought to be designed.

In our setting, the differential capacity to work can concern weekly labour supply, ℓ_i, or the length of the working life, z_i. We focus on the latter and take the case where individuals have different productivity, say w_1 and w_2

$(w_2 > w_1)$ and different disutility for z_i, $R_i(z_i)$ $(i = 1, 2)$ such that $R_1(z) >$ $R_2(z)$ and $\dfrac{zR_1'}{R_1(z)} \geq \dfrac{zR_2'}{R_2(z)}$ for any z.

If we have three types of individuals characterized by (R_1, w_1), (R_2, w_1) and (R_2, w_2) respectively, we know that in the *laissez-faire* as well as in the first-best $\ell_1 \leq \ell_2 \leq \ell_3$ and $z_1 \leq z_2 \leq z_3$ under some normality conditions. It is however not clear that in a second-best setting we keep this ranking of the ℓ's and of the z's.

We recall that the government observes $w_i \ell_i$ and z_i but not w_i and R_i. There will be no distortion at the top: individual 3 will choose the first-best levels of ℓ_3 and z_3. Individual 2 will be subject to a positive marginal tax with respect to ℓ_2 and z_2, but the downward distortion on ℓ_2 is higher than that on z_2. This makes sense as z_2 is directly controlled, and ℓ_2 only indirectly. Finally, individual 3 will also be subject to a positive marginal tax on ℓ_3 and z_3, but now in relative term, z_3 is more distorted than ℓ_3, which is expected: as compared to type 2 individual type 3 has the same productivity w_1 but more disutility for z_1. To put it otherwise, the social planner observes ℓ_2 but not $R_2(z_2)$.

In conclusion, with asymmetric information one cannot avoid some sort of downward distortion for the retirement age of less productive and above all less healthy individuals. In other terms, the existence of implicit taxes evoked in the introduction, particularly for the disabled and low productivity workers, makes some sense.

The key question is how sensitive is this second-best pattern of retirement to increase longevity. Basically, within the simple framework adopted so far, increased longevity (h) implies a higher demand for consumption. We have to modify the above problem in two ways: first, we drop the quasi-linearity assumption which implies that longevity has no effect on c and we introduce as argument of $R_i(\cdot)$ z/h the fraction of lifetime devoted to work. The problem for each individual facing a tax function $T(w_i, \ell_i, z_i)$ is now:

$$Max \; hu\left[\frac{w_i \ell_i z_i - T(w_i \ell_i z_i)}{h}\right] - v(\ell_i) \, R_i\left(\frac{z_i}{h}\right). \tag{5.18}$$

At first sight, one would expect an increase of ℓ_i and z_i, the relative importance of which depends on the second derivatives of u, v and R_i. It is realistic to expect that for 'healthy' workers the adjustment will entail postponing retirement rather than lengthening the work week. For unhealthy individuals there can be a maximum value for z. When z_1 reaches this value $R''(z_i / h)$ tends to infinity. In other words, working one more year is unbearable. In that case, the only adjustments have to be a higher ℓ_1 and a lower c_1.

As a consequence, increased longevity could imply a wider range of retirement ages. At the top, type 3 individuals would work longer without distortion and at the bottom type 1 individuals would have a relatively shorter work career but at the expense of lower consumption and a longer work week.

5.6 CONCLUSION

Before concluding there are a couple of restrictions to the above presentation which are worth being discussed. They mainly pertain to the supply side of the labour market. A number of early retirees do not voluntarily choose to stop working but are forced to do so, for example, because of the closure of their firm or because they are too expensive in comparison with their time productivity. From their perspective they seem to retire 'too early', not as a result of their own decision. However, it is very likely that the benefits package they receive at retirement is sufficiently generous to obtain the agreement of labour unions and avoid social unrest. In other words, their retirement decision might not be individually rational but it is collectively so.

There are two reasons why employers decide to dismiss old workers with the support of public authorities. One is a consequence of the 'Lazear effect':[7] for incentive reasons, wage contract moves away from spot-market equilibrium and implies wages below productivity in the beginning and above productivity at the end of the career. There is thus a strong motivation for the firm to dismiss employees before the term of the contract.

Another reason is when governments facing politically sensitive unemployment problem in declining sectors implement early retirement plans to reduce labour supply. Quite often these soft-landing plans were supported by the hope that they would free positions for young or low-wage unemployed. Note in this respect that there is no evidence that early retirement of older workers causes a reduction of unemployment among younger workers (Boeri *et al.*, 2001).

It is clear that our analysis would benefit from taking into account the demand side of the labour market. We however believe that collectively most cases of early retirement are pretty voluntary. Let us now summarize the main findings of this chapter.

During the last few decades many European countries have expanded their social security systems in ways which have discouraged labour market participation in old age and thus induced retirement. This tendency coupled with a steadily increasing longevity, threatens the financial viability of PAYG pension systems.

In a first-best world one would clearly aim at later retirement, particularly for productive and healthy workers. In a second-best world, wherein both productivity and capacity are not observable, the trend towards early retirement is partially unavoidable. More importantly, long due reforms are effectively opposed by particular interest groups more concerned with their own entitlements than with public interest.

The type of reforms that are called for, and which have been conducted in countries such as Sweden, scale down the non-contributory part of the public pension system. Even though they can be shown to be Pareto improving in the steady-state, they involve less redistribution and lower utility for the poor workers in the transition period.

NOTES

1. It is important to note that the increased length of retirement we are discussing here is partially offset by the rising female participation in the labour market.
2. See Cremer *et al.* (2002).
3. Casamatta *et al.* (2000).
4. Lacombe and Lagos (1999).
5. Casamatta *et al.*(2001), Conde-Ruiz and Galasso (2000).
6. In Figure 5.3, the most preferred tax rate declines with w ($w < \overline{w}$). This occurs with enough substitutability between c and d. When there is no such substitutability, the most preferred tax rate increases with w and the equilibrium is such that 50 per cent of the population, that is both low incomes and high incomes, would vote for less while 50 per cent, or middle incomes, would vote for more. This is what Epple and Romano (1996) call 'ends against the middle'.
7. Lazear (1979).

REFERENCES

Assous, L. (2001), 'Les opinions des Français au début 2000 en matière d'âge de départ à la retraite', *Etudes et Résultats*, **150**, Ministère de l'Emploi, Paris.
Blondal, S. and S. Scarpetta (1998a), *Falling participation rates among older workers in the OECD countries*, OECD, Paris.
Blondal, S. and S. Scarpetta (1998b), 'The retirement decision in OECD countries', OECD-EDWP 202.
Boeri, T., A. Börsch-Supan and G. Tabellini (2000), 'Would you like to shrink the welfare state?', *Economic Policy*, **32**, 7–50.
Boeri, T., A. Börsch-Supan, A. Brugavini, R. Disney and F. Perrachi (2001), *Pensions: More Information, Less Ideology*, Dordrecht: Kluwer.
Calot, G. and J.-P. Sardon (1999), 'Vieillissement démographique et protection sociale', *Futuribles*, July–August, 19–45.
Casamatta, G., H. Cremer and P. Pestieau (2000), 'The political economy of social security', *Scandinavian Journal of Economics*, **102**, 503–22.

Casamatta, G., H. Cremer and P. Pestieau (2001), 'Voting on pensions with endogenous retirement age', unpublished.

Conde-Ruiz, J. I. and V. Galasso (2000), 'Early retirement', unpublished.

Cremer, H. and P. Pestieau (2000), 'Reforming our pension systems: is it a demographic, financial or political problem?', *European Economic Review*, **44**, 974–83.

Cremer, H., J. M. Lozachmeur and P. Pestieau (2002), 'Social security and variable retirement schemes. An optimal income taxation approach', unpublished.

Dellis, A., R. Desmet, A. Jousten and S. Perelman (2001), 'Micro-modelling of retirement in Belgium', unpublished.

Diamond, P. (1999), *Social Security Reforms*, Lindhal Lectures.

Diamond, P. and J. Mirrlees (1986), 'Payroll tax financed social insurance with variable retirement', *Scandinavian Journal of Economics*, **88**, 25–50.

Epple, D. and R. Romano (1996), 'Public provision of private goods', *Journal of Political Economy*, **104**, 57–84.

Fabel, D. (1994), *The Economics of Pension and Variable Retirement Schemes*, New York: J. Wiley.

Fehr, H.,W. I. Sterkelry and O. Thorgosen (2000), 'Social security reforms and early retirement', unpublished.

Ferrera, M. (1993), *EC Citizens and Social Protection. Main Results from a Eurobarometer Survey*, EC. Div V/E/2, Brussels.

Gruber, G. and D. Wise (1999), *Social Security and Retirement around the World*, Chicago: The Chicago University Press.

Lacombe, J. A. and F.M. Lagos (1999), 'Social security and political election on retirement age', unpublished.

Lannoy, F. and B. Lipszyc (2000), *Le vieillissement en Belgique: données démographiques et implications économiques*, in P. Pestieau *et al.*, 11–36.

Lazear, E.P. (1979), Why is there mandatory retirement?, *Journal of Political Economy*, **87**, 1261–84.

Lumsdaire, R.L. and D. Mitchell (1999), 'New developments in the economic analysis of retirement', in O. Ashenfelter and D. Card *Handbook of Labour Economics*, vol. 3, Amsterdam: North Holland.

Michel, Ph. and P. Pestieau (2000), 'Optimal taxation of capital and labour income with social security and variable retirement age', unpublished.

Pestieau, P., L. Gevers, V. Ginsburgh, E. Schokkaert and B. Cantillon (2000), *Réflexions sur l'avenir de nos retraites*, Garant, Leuven.

Schokkaert, E., M. Verhue and G. Pepermans, (2000), Les Flamands et leur système de retraite, in Pestieau *et al.*, 59–80.

PART 2

Taxation and pensions

6.   Saving incentives in the US[*]

Surachai Khitatrakun and John Karl Scholz

6.1   INTRODUCTION

The metaphor used to describe retirement preparation in the United States is the 'three-legged stool'. The seat of the stool is retirement security, which is supported by three legs: employer-provided pensions, public pensions (Social Security and, for disabled or indigent elderly, Supplemental Security Income), and private saving. Low rates of household and national saving in the US, both in comparison to previous US experience and relative to saving rates in other countries, have generated considerable interest in increasing saving by US policy makers.

Tax incentives have been the primary way that policy makers have sought to stimulate household saving. The resulting set of incentives – individual retirement accounts (IRAs), Roth IRAs, 401(k)s, SEP IRAs, Simple IRAs, Keoghs and a variety of education- and medical-related incentives that are also saving vehicles (education IRAs, qualified state tuition plans, and medical saving accounts) – require specific rules, which contributes to tax complexity, and, since affluent taxpayers are more likely than others to take advantage of the provisions, they contribute to income and wealth inequality. A central question is whether these provisions increase household and national saving.

This chapter begins with a brief discussion of US saving rates over time and policies designed to increase household and national saving. A central issue when evaluating the merits of tax incentives for saving is the degree to which families are preparing adequately for retirement. The literature comes to mixed conclusions.

We then present new descriptive information using data from the Health and Retirement Survey (HRS) on the efficacy of the largest tax incentives for

---

[*] We are grateful to the participants to the CeRP conference "Pension Policy Harmonization in an Integrating Europe" for helpful reactions.

private savings, 401(k)s. Our strategy is twofold. If 401(k)s increase private wealth, 401(k)-eligible households ought to have 'better' retirements than those without (assuming that after conditioning on covariates, 401(k) eligibility is exogenously determined). We examine this intuition using subjective questions about retirement satisfaction and worries in the HRS. Our second, more standard approach is to examine the relationship between 401(k)s and wealth in the HRS.

We find mixed evidence about the efficacy of 401(k)s. 401(k) eligibility is strongly correlated with worrying less about income in retirement. However, in cross-sectional data (and in pooled cross-sectional HRS data across waves), there is no evidence that 401(k)s are positively associated with wealth. We speculate that the frequent reporting of 401(k) balances and relative simplicity of program rules help people better appreciate the resources they have to draw on in retirement, and hence they help reduce worry. But at the same time, they also allow people to make economic or financial adjustments in other aspects of their labor supply or household portfolios, so 401(k)s do not increase private wealth.

The chapter concludes with a brief discussion of issues related to social security, employer-provided pensions, and tax incentives for private saving.

6.2   SAVING RATES IN THE UNITED STATES

Figure 6.1 plots a time series of US household (personal) saving rates as a percentage of disposable personal income from the National Income and Product Accounts (NIPA) and the Flow of Funds. Between 1950 and 1993, personal saving rates as a percentage of disposable income (as measured by the NIPA) ranged between 6.9 per cent and 10.9 per cent. Personal saving rates began falling in the mid-1980s and then fell sharply beginning in 1993, reaching –0.1 per cent of disposable income in 2000. The Flow of Funds personal saving rate, which account for purchases of consumer durables as saving, show a similar pattern, with sharp reductions starting in the mid-1980s.

The apparent striking decline in personal saving raises the concern that American households are not preparing adequately for retirement. Gale and Sabelhaus (1999), however, note that these saving measures do not account appropriately for the effects of inflation on interest flows, do not count consumer durables accumulation as investment, and do not treat contributions to retirement programs on a consistent basis. Moreover, the distinction between household and corporate saving is blurry. If adjustments are made to address these concerns, the apparent decline in saving over the last two decades is much smaller. If unrealized capital gains are included in saving

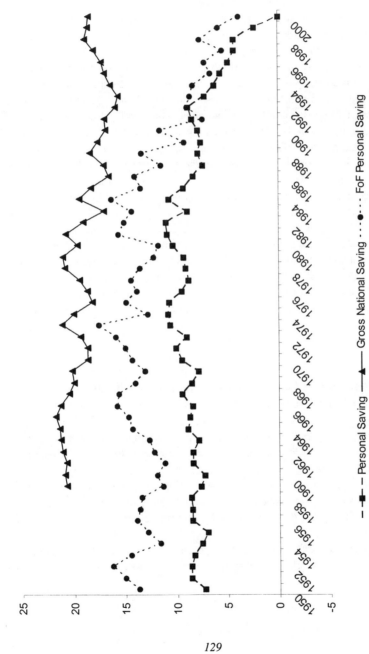

Figure 6.1 Personal saving as a percentage of disposable personal income, and national saving as a percentage of GDP

measures (and as income), saving rates in 1998 were at 40-year highs.[1] Adjusting saving series for asset revaluations raises thorny issues having to do with the factors driving asset price increases, but when assessing retirement security, it probably makes sense to do so.

Two distinct questions arise with the NIPA and Flow of Funds saving series and potential adjustments of them. First, what do they tell us about retirement preparation and national saving? Gale and Sabelhaus (1999) conclusively show that aggregate series on household saving do not prove that households are preparing less aggressively for retirement than they had done in the past. Even without the Gale and Sabelhaus adjustments, Figure 6.1 shows that gross national saving rates remain only slightly lower than historical averages in the 1990s, reflecting primarily the sharp improvements in the federal budget deficit over this period.

Second, how do policy makers respond to changes in the household and national saving series? The pairing of two results, that the most well publicized series on household saving was negative in 2000 and that the US is a low-saving country internationally,[2] leads to considerable ongoing political interest in saving-promotion policies. The tax bill signed by the President in June 2001, creates a new account in 2006 called the Roth 401(k), which has a $15 000 annual contribution limit; it increases contribution limits for IRAs (to $5000 in 2008) and 401(k)s, 403(b)s and 457 plans (up to $15 000 by 2006); it raises contribution limits for workers over 50 on IRAs, 401(k)s, 403(b)s and 457 plans; and it creates a new tax credit (providing a 50 per cent match on saving up to $2000) for low-income families (with incomes under $30 000) to save from 2002 to 2005.

6.3   THE EVOLUTION OF POLICY RELATED TO HOUSEHOLD SAVING

Most economists and policy makers believe national saving rates are an important long-term determinant of economic growth (see, for example, Aaron and Shoven, 1999). As discussed in more detail below, however, there is mixed evidence that Americans are failing to prepare adequately for retirement and that tax incentives have significantly increased private saving. Nevertheless, the US continues to enact policies to expand tax incentives for saving.

The key building blocks for increasing saving are public pensions, employer-provided pensions, and non-pension net worth. We briefly discuss each of these.

6.3.1 Public Pensions (Social Security)

Social security was founded in 1935 as one of President Franklin Roosevelt's New Deal programs and was designed to meet the unmet social need of older workers leaving the workforce without sufficient post-retirement income to be self-supporting.[3] Over the years it has been referred to as 'the third rail of American politics,' meaning that any politician that dares to reduce (or 'touch') social security would not be reelected (which is 'death' for a politician). Benefits have steadily increased over the years, to the point where replacement rates (the percentage of final-year earnings accounted for by social security) are estimated to be 53 per cent for retirees who first receive benefits at age 65 in 2000 and who earned 45 per cent of the average covered wage over their complete working lives (in 1997 this would be $12 342). Replacement rates are 40 per cent, 32 per cent and 24 per cent for workers earning the average covered wage ($27 426 in 1997), 160 per cent of the average covered wage ($43 882), and the maximum ($65 400) respectively, over their working lives.

For some time social security has been collecting more in taxes than it spends in benefit payments, hence the program has been accumulating a surplus. The surplus is expected to increase over time, until 2016 when benefits are expected to exceed taxes for the first time. With the aging of the baby boom generation, the social security surplus is expected to last until 2029.[4] Rhetoric from politicians of both parties suggest social security will be preserved, but debates will continue over the best way to ensure the system's long-run solvency (see, for example, Aaron and Shoven, 1999).

6.3.2. Employer-provided Pensions

Rules governing employer-provided pensions were largely set in place by the 1974 Employee's Retirement Income Security Act, though pension arrangements in the US have changed sharply since then. In 1975, 70.8 per cent of the 38.4 million active participants in pensions (and 71.5 per cent of the total pension assets) were in defined benefit (DB) plans, where pension benefits typically depend on length of service and compensation patterns, but have little to do with the investment returns of pension assets. By 1995 only 35.5 per cent (and 51.5 per cent of the assets) of the 66.2 million active participants were in DB plans.[5] The rest were in defined contribution (DC) plans, where the size of the pension benefit depends directly on the investment performance of the assets held in the pension. In roughly 85 per cent of these DC plans, workers control investment choices, given a specific set of employer-designated options (Mitchell, 2000).

Employers bear the risk of market fluctuations under DB pension arrangements, while this risk is borne by individuals under DC pensions. The costs of job changes are likely lower with DC pensions, where benefits are portable upon vesting. Benefits are also more transparent under DC pensions, where participants typically receive quarterly benefit statements. DB pension formulas generally depend on years of service and earnings trajectories and are back-loaded, which may influence job change decisions. These differences may result in different behavioral responses to the alternative pension arrangements.

A particularly popular form of DC pension over the past twenty years is the 401(k). Employers may decide to offer a 401(k) plan to their workers (nonprofit employers can offer 403(b) plans and state and local governments can offer 457 plans). Employers frequently match employee contributions up to a specific threshold (for example, 10 per cent of salary or $5000). Workers then choose whether or not to participate. In 2001, contributions up to $11 000 are exempt from tax. Moreover, earnings on the contributions accumulate tax free. Withdrawals on the 401(k) are taxed as ordinary income.

The budgetary cost of the net exclusion of pension contributions and earnings from employer plans is estimated to be $89.1 billion in 2001 (IRAs are another $15.2 billion and Keoghs are another $5.5 billion).[6] This tax expenditure is designed to increase private and national saving and enhance retirement income security. If people fully substitute pension and financial wealth, however, the pension tax expenditure will not increase private saving. The revenue loss from the tax expenditure could lower national (the sum of public and private) saving, and do nothing more than provide a large incentive for employers to offer compensation in the form of pensions, which in turn disproportionately benefits high-wage workers and their employers (since the probability of pension coverage increases with earnings). Alternatively, if there is little offset, pension subsidies may be a cost-effective way to increase private and national saving.

If employer-provided pensions increase household saving, 'non-discrimination rules' are likely to be an important reason. These rules limit the amount of benefits received by highly-compensated employees in a company relative to the benefits received by other employees. Thus, a company is not able to provide overly generous amounts of untaxed fringe benefits to executives without providing the same (or similar) benefits to the lowest-paid workers. Perhaps as a consequence of non-discrimination rules, firms that offer voluntary pension arrangements, such as 401(k)s, often provide generous match rates in order to ensure a high enough degree of participation by less well-compensated employees. It is likely that non-pension wealth offsets are lower for families with few assets in non-pension form than they are for high net worth families.

6.3.3   Tax Incentive for Private Savings

At any given time, roughly half of all workers are not covered by employer-provided pension plans (roughly one-third of all workers reach retirement with no benefits from employer-provided pension plans). Policy makers have designed a variety of tax incentives to promote (non-pension) private saving. These are justified, in part, as provisions to enhance the retirement income security of pensionless workers.

An individual retirement account (IRA) is available to those under age 70½ who have earned income. Earnings grow tax-deferred until withdrawal. Contributions are deductible for all taxpayers not covered by an employer-provided pension. For those that are covered, full deductibility is restricted to households with incomes below specific income thresholds.[7]

Roth (or 'backloaded') IRAs differ from regular IRAs in that contributions to the account are not deductible, but withdrawals from the account are not taxable. Like regular IRAs, earnings on the account are typically not taxable. Penalty-free withdrawals can be taken after the taxpayer reaches age 59½ or becomes disabled or buys a home for the first time. There are also income limits on Roth IRAs.[8]

Optimal investment planning is made even more difficult by IRA-like saving incentives designed for educational expenses. Education IRAs are similar to Roth IRAs in that there is no up-front deduction, but deposits and earnings may be withdrawn tax-free if used to pay for the costs of higher education. If accumulations are not used for educational expenses, a 10 per cent excise tax is imposed. Relative to some forms of taxable saving, even if the investor pays the non-education excise tax, education IRAs would be good investments. But education IRAs are not the only and, in some cases, not the best college saving plan.

Qualified state tuition plans (QSTPs, or 529 plans) are investments operated by a state to help families save for future college costs. Plans vary across states, some provide tuition at in-state universities and others operate like a mutual fund. Some states offer a state income tax deduction for contributions (up to a ceiling) to the QSTP, and investments can be directed into a S&P500 index fund. Like other saving incentives, QSTPs provide tax-free accumulation, but have contribution limits as high as $100 000 per beneficiary. If the account is not used for educational expenses, most states collect a penalty of 10 per cent of the earnings portion of a 'non-qualified' withdrawal (meaning, an investor would recover 100 per cent of the principal and 90 per cent of the earnings from the investment).

Two concerns arise from the patchwork of retirement and education saving incentives. First, it is hard for people to figure out the best investment choices given various plan features. While the financial consequences of suboptimal choices for an individual may not be large, they nevertheless may contribute to the feeling that somebody smarter, better connected or better informed is not facing commensurate tax responsibilities, given their circumstances. Second, participation in tax incentives is positively correlated with income and wealth, and hence they contribute to the erosion of tax progressivity and the striking increase in US income inequality.[9]

The case for tax incentives for saving rests with two issues. First, are Americans under-saving for retirement? If they are, it may make sense to try to encourage saving through tax incentives. However, even if there is evidence of under-saving, tax incentives may not be a sensible policy response unless they stimulate additional private and national saving. So the second critical question is whether or not tax incentives stimulate private and national saving at a reasonable cost. We provide a brief review of work examining the first issue in the next section. Following that we present new work on the relationship of 401(k)s on retirement wealth and subjective retirement expectations.

6.4   THE ADEQUACY OF RETIREMENT PREPARATION

The following quotation from the *Wall Street Journal* captures a popular view of US consumption patterns.

> A long time ago, New England was known for its thrifty Yankees. But that was before the baby boomers came along. These days, many New Englanders in their 30s and 40s, and indeed their counterparts all over America, have a different style: they are spending heavily and have sunk knee-deep in debt. ... A recent study sponsored by Merrill Lynch & Co. showed that the average middle-aged American had about $2,600 in net financial assets. Another survey by the financial-services giant showed that boomers earning $100,000 will need $653,000 in today's dollars by age 65 to retire in comfort – but were saving only 31 per cent of the amount needed. In other words, saving rate will have to triple. Experts say the failure to build a nest egg will come to haunt the baby boomers, forcing them to drastically lower standards of living in their later years or to work for longer, perhaps into their '70s.[10]

The academic (as opposed to journalistic) evidence on this issue is mixed. Several academic papers that focus on consumption changes around retirement find results consistent with inadequate retirement preparation.[11] Recent papers identify what has been termed 'the retirement-savings puzzle', where consumption falls upon retirement by more than would be anticipated by a life-cycle model where households are equating the marginal utility of consumption across time, subject to an uncertain environment. Banks *et al.* (1998) estimate a model of changes in log consumption using cohort data from 25 years of the British Family Expenditure Survey. The model accounts for changes in the number of people in the household, the increase in mortality risk as households age, expected retirement and unemployment. While the model closely tracks consumption growth for cohorts prior to retirement, it systematically understates the decline in consumption in the first two years around retirement. The economic magnitude of the discrepancy is not large – they find the anticipated fall in consumption growth, after accounting for household demographics and labor force status, is around 2 per cent while the actual consumption growth around retirement falls by as much as 3 per cent. Nevertheless, they interpret their results as suggesting there are unanticipated (negative) shocks occurring around the time of retirement.

Bernheim *et al.* (2001) also examine changes in consumption around retirement. Using data from the Panel Study of Income Dynamics (PSID) they find the mean (median) drop in average consumption in the two years following retirement for American households is 13.1 per cent (11.3 per cent). After conditioning on similar factors as Banks *et al.*, they report that 31 per cent of the sample of American households reduce their consumption by at least 35 per cent. While the PSID only contains information on a few expenditure categories, the decline in consumption occurs with food consumed at home, with food consumed away from home, and is consistent with sensitivity analysis using budget share data from the Consumer Expenditure Survey. While one might expect some drop in consumption following retirement, particularly for work-related expenses, finding that consumption drops by a much larger amount than found by Banks *et al.* and that it drops across several distinct consumption categories is provocative. Bernheim *et al.* argue their results are difficult to reconcile with the life-cycle model and that they are more likely to be the result of household behavior not governed by rational, farsighted optimization.

Moore and Mitchell (1998) also conclude Americans are not preparing adequately for retirement.[12] They calculate the annuity value of old age wealth and compare this to observed income in the Health and Retirement Study. They translate shortfalls in usual replacement rates into the amount of income one would need to save approaching retirement. They find the median household would need to save 16 per cent of annual earnings between 1992 and the time of retirement (at 62) to have a replacement rate of 69 per cent. Delaying retirement age to 65 would require saving of 7 per cent, and lead to a replacement rate of 78 per cent. Moore and Mitchell conclude, '... despite seemingly large accumulations of total retirement wealth, the majority of older households will not be able to maintain current levels of consumption into retirement without additional saving'.

In contrast, Engen *et al.* (1999) conclude that married American couples where the husband works full time are saving adequately for retirement.[13] They present optimal wealth to income ratios calculated from a dynamic, stochastic life-cycle simulation model, and then compare these to actual ratios calculated from the HRS and Surveys of Consumer Finances (SCFs). They find a wide distribution of optimal simulated ratios within the population due to realizations of earnings uncertainty, so they argue that empirical work that focuses on discrepancies of actual wealth relative to a median (or mean) target wealth-income ratio does not provide compelling evidence of under- or over-saving. They then show that actual wealth distributions from the HRS and SCF closely match (or are larger than) the simulated optimal distributions.

A skeptic could look at the work suggesting that retirement preparation is inadequate and note (1) the Banks *et al.* results imply an economically insubstantial retirement saving puzzle; and (2) the Moore and Mitchell results are not necessarily indicative of inadequate saving since households should not be expected to fully accumulate retirement resources until the time of their retirement.[14] Bernheim *et al.* (2001) document an economically substantial change in consumption around retirement. This result, however, is not *prima facie* evidence of inadequate retirement preparation. Both food consumed at home and away from home could clearly fall upon retirement as retired households replace expensive convenience foods with food made from scratch. Without further evidence on leisure-consumption complementarities, it is not fully clear how to interpret their results.

A skeptic might also raise concerns about the evidence showing American families are preparing adequately for retirement. Gustman and Steinmeier (1999a) explicitly acknowledge that they do not offer a standard for assessing adequacy, but rather simply note that HRS households have accumulated considerable wealth relative to their lifetime incomes. Engen *et al.* (1999) focus only on married couples where the husband works at least 20 hours per week, excluding, for example, more than 30 per cent of the HRS sample that is single-person households. Even for households they do consider, the standard they impose for assessing adequacy, while a significant contribution to the literature, is modest. Remember, they compare distributions of wealth-income ratios in the HRS and SCFs with simulated optimal distributions. Variation in the optimal targets arise, for example, if households have positive or negative income shocks late in life. But specific households in the HRS (and SCFs) receive income shocks and there is no good reason to think that those who have negative (positive) income shocks late in life are necessarily those who have low (high) wealth-income ratios. Put differently, each HRS household has an optimal wealth income ratio given the Engen *et al.* model, but the fact that distributions match does not necessarily imply that each household is achieving its target. The result on distributions in their paper (assuming the distributions match perfectly, which they do not) only ensures that at least half the households exceed their targets.

We are left without a strong conclusion about the findings of existing work on the adequacy of retirement preparation in the US. Additional work on this topic that helped resolve discrepancies would be worthwhile. But even if the weight of the evidence was consistent with the idea that Americans are not preparing adequately for retirement, it does not necessarily follow that tax incentives for saving, like IRAs and 401(k)s, are sensible policy initiatives. For this to be true they must, at a minimum, increase private saving. More generally, holding all else constant, tax incentives will only increase national saving if the increase in household saving is larger than the reduction in government saving associated with the tax preference.

6.5   THE EFFICACY OF TAX INCENTIVES TO ENHANCE RETIREMENT SECURITY

Tax preferences for household saving have been widely available since 1981, when eligibility for Individual Retirement Accounts was made universal (eligibility was restricted in 1986, but the popularity of 401(k) plans has increased steadily since the early 1980s). Despite the widespread availability and popularity of tax preferences for saving, measures of private, household saving have declined sharply over this period, as shown in Figure 6.1. Of course, household saving might have been even lower in the absence of the tax preferences.

A number of authors have tried to systematically evaluate the effects of tax incentives for saving. Engen *et al.* (1996) present new work and examine the older papers and conclude there is little compelling evidence that tax incentives have significantly increased private, and particularly national saving. Poterba *et al.* (1996) examine the same data and conclude the opposite. Papers examining the effects of 401(k)s on saving typically either treat 401(k) eligibility as being exogenous, and hence rely on simple regression-adjusted comparisons of the wealth of households eligible and households ineligible for 401(k)s, or rely on the intuition that if 401(k)s increase household saving, asset accumulation should increase with the period of 'exposure' to 401(k)s. Scholars continue to reach different conclusions because of disagreements about whether or not 401(k) eligibility is in fact exogenous, and how the composition of 401(k) eligible groups changes over time.

A nice, recent contribution is Engen and Gale (forthcoming). They use over time variation (using data from the 1987 and 1991 Surveys of Program Participation) to identify the effects of 401(k)s on wealth, and allow these effects to vary by income group. They assume, therefore, that within an income class after conditioning on other characteristics, that 401(k)-eligible households would have similar wealth accumulation patterns as 401(k)-ineligible households in the absence of 401(k)s. They only find positive effects of 401(k)s on wealth for low income groups, and conclude that between 0 and 30 per cent of 401(k) contributions between 1987 and 1991 represented net additions to private saving. Since 401(k)s generate a substantial tax preference, the effects on national saving would be considerably smaller.

Engelhardt (2000) uses the 1992 wave of the HRS to show that 401(k) eligibility is positively, significantly associated with net worth, but the effect is sharply reduced if the empirical specification incorporates pension wealth. The intuition for this result is that 401(k)s may substitute for other forms of pension wealth, so excluding other pensions from the analysis excludes an important wealth component for 401(k)-ineligible households.

In this section we explore the relationship between 401(k)s and retirement security. We do this in two ways. First, we present correlations between 401(k) eligibility and subjective views about retirement. If 401(k)s increase retirement wealth, we expect to see households eligible for 401(k)s to feel better about retirement than observationally equivalent households without 401(k)s. Second, we examine the correlation between 401(k) eligibility and wealth to see if these correlations are consistent with the evidence on subjective expectations.

6.5.1 The Health and Retirement Study[15]

The Health and Retirement Study is a national panel study with an initial sample (in 1992) of 12 652 persons and 7702 households.[16] It oversamples blacks, Hispanics and residents of Florida. The baseline 1992 study consisted of in-home, face-to-face interviews of the 1931–41 birth cohort, and their spouses, if married. Follow-up interviews were given by telephone in 1994, 1996, 1998 and 2000. The 2000 HRS is currently preliminary.

The survey covers a wide range of topics, including batteries of questions on health and cognitive conditions and status; retirement plans and perspectives; attitudes, preferences, expectations and subjective probabilities; family structure and transfers; employment status and job history; job demands and requirements; disability; demographic background; housing; income and net worth; and health insurance and pension plans.

Table 6.1 provides summary information on the sample used for the analysis. Households eligible for 401(k)s have greater educational attainment than others. This is reflected by their greater mean expected lifetime earnings, $2.1 million, relative to the mean expected lifetime earnings of those not

Table 6.1 Means of characteristics of the HRS households: Wave I [1]

	401(k) ineligible	401(k) eligible	**Total**
Demographics (Mean)			
Age	56.60	55.80	**56.34**
Fraction Male	0.69	0.79	**0.72**
Fraction Couple	0.61	0.79	**0.67**
Race			
White	0.83	0.88	**0.85**
Black	0.13	0.08	**0.11**
Hispanic	0.01	0.00	**0.01**
Other	0.03	0.03	**0.03**
Education			
School Years	12.13	13.37	**12.53**
Not Complete High School	0.29	0.15	**0.24**
High School Graduate	0.53	0.58	**0.54**
College Graduate	0.10	0.16	**0.12**
Post-College Graduation	0.08	0.12	**0.09**
Fraction Working	0.67	0.86	**0.73**
Fraction Self-employed	0.21	0.08	**0.16**
Fraction Retired[2]	0.40	0.20	**0.33**
Wealth (Mean) [1992 $]			
Non-pension Net Worth, not including IRA	215 543	216 382	**215 813**
IRA	16 860	25 525	**19 655**
Pension Wealth, not including 401(k)	77 633	108 358	**87 543**
401(k)	0	30 267	**9 762**
Social Security Wealth	143 182	182 013	**155 707**
(Expected) Lifetime Earnings	1 405 403	2 102 737	**1 630 318**
Wealth (Median) [1992 $]			
Non-pension Net Worth, not including IRA	78 000	117 400	**91 000**
IRA	0	4 000	**0**
Pension Wealth, not including 401(k)	4 213	51 381	**19 000**
401(k)	0	1 923	**0**
Social Security Wealth	137 074	190 738	**159 377**
(Expected) Lifetime Earnings	1 200 098	1 902 350	**1 457 998**
Number of Observations	4 969	2 249	**7 218**

Notes:
[1] The table is based on the Wave I household-level sample, excluding households with severely missing values for wealth and income. The figures are weighted by the Wave I household analysis weights from the HRS tracker file version 2.
[2] Retirement statuses are derived from the self-reported information and working statuses at Wave I–V. Households are categorized as 'retired' if the heads of the households are categorized as either partially or completely retired.

covered by 401(k)s, $1.4 million. These expected lifetime earnings measures are calculated using data on current and retrospective earnings, which, for years not observed in the data, are then used to estimate separate fixed-effects log earnings regressions for men and women by marital statuses (single and married/partnered) and three education groups (less than high school, high school graduate, and college and postgraduate graduate). The imputed earnings streams are summed to calculate the lifetime earnings measures, starting at the age people report taking their first full-time job and ending at the self-reported expected retirement date.

Our measure of defined benefit pension wealth uses the 'Pension Present Value Database' that Bob Peticolis and Tom Steinmeier have kindly made available on the HRS website, and in so doing, incorporates information on the specific details of the pension plans covering selected HRS respondents.[17] The program makes present value calculations of HRS pensions for Wave I respondents for nine different scenarios, corresponding to the Social Security Administration's low, intermediate and high long-term projections for interest rates, wage growth rates and inflation rates. For our study, we use the intermediate values for underlying assumptions with the Peticolis-Steinmeier DB pension wealth calculations.[18]

Following others in the literature (for example, Engen *et al.*, 1999, page 159), we do not use the Peticolis-Steinmeier calculations for valuing DC pensions. Gustman and Steinmeier (1999b) document discrepancies between reported and calculated pension values, showing the mean accumulations reported by respondents are only 69 per cent of the amounts calculated by using pension documents. It might seem that there is no *a priori* reason to choose between self-reports of DC pension wealth or calculations made on the basis of detailed plan documents. In this case, however, we view the self-reports to be more useful than the calculated values for two reasons. First, one could argue that it is people's perception of their DC wealth that will influence life-cycle consumption behavior. Second and more importantly, the pension calculation program assumes a constant contribution rate over time for participants of plans with voluntary contributions. If workers alter their contribution patterns (in particular, begin to increase contributions as they approach retirement and/or have children that leave the household), the calculated amounts will be overstated. Indeed, Gustman and Steinmeier (1999b) present evidence consistent with DC pension contributions increasing with age. Because of this, we use self-reported information to calculate DC pension wealth.[19]

We developed a simple social security simulation to calculate social security benefits for the respondent and spouse or, if higher, the couple, based on the actual and imputed earnings histories. Comparing wealth measures, we see that 401(k)-eligible households have greater IRA wealth, pension wealth, 401(k) wealth and social security wealth than households not eligible for 401(k)s. While median financial wealth in the forms of non-pension, non-IRA net worth is also larger for 401(k)-eligible households, it is equal at the mean.[20] Given that households not eligible for 401(k)s have lower lifetime income, this raises the possibility that 401(k)s displace non-401(k) wealth.

6.5.2 401(k)s and Subjective Views About Retirement in the HRS Cross-section

If 401(k)s increase wealth and eligibility for 401(k)s is randomly determined in the population, households eligible for 401(k)s should have greater satisfaction (or greater anticipated satisfaction) in retirement than households not eligible for 401(k)s. Of course, 401(k) eligibility is not determined randomly in a population. Workers with strong saving preferences are likely to gravitate toward employers offering 401(k)s. Employers may try to manipulate the characteristics of their workforce with 401(k)s if the taste for saving is positively correlated with other attributes (Ippolito, 1997). It is also clear from Table 6.1 that 401(k)-eligible households have higher income and greater educational attainment than households not eligible for 401(k)s, and income and education are typically positively correlated with wealth.

To address these concerns, we examine the correlation of 401(k) eligibility and subjective views about retirement, comparing respondents in households eligible and not eligible for 401(k)s within a lifetime income quintile conditioning on other observable characteristics.[21] Our identification assumption underlying the analysis is that after conditioning on observable characteristics, 401(k) eligibility is random for households within a given lifetime income quintile.

Our analysis focuses on two subjective questions. The first, which we refer to as 'retirement satisfaction' reads (for those who are retired): 'All in all, would you say that your retirement has turned out to be very satisfying, moderately satisfying, or not at all satisfying?' For those respondents not completely retired the question reads, 'When you think about the time when you [and your (husband/wife/partner)] will (completely) retire, are you looking forward to it, are you uneasy about it, or what?' In the regressions below, we group those 'uneasy' about retirement or 'not at all satisfied' in retirement together, and examine the characteristics correlated with these responses. One might be tempted to focus solely on those who have retired, since the interpretation of their responses seem more clear cut. But retirement dates are a choice variable that presumably is significantly influenced by one's financial well-being. Hence, restricting the sample based on retirement status could bias results.

The second question reads for those who are retired, 'Now for things that some people say are bad about retirement. Please tell me if, during your retirement, they have bothered you a lot, somewhat, a little, or not at all. Not having enough income to get by'. For those not completely retired: 'Now for things that worry some people about retirement. Please tell me if they worry you a lot, somewhat, a little, or not at all. Not having enough income to get by'. In the regressions below, we examine factors correlated with the responses 'not having enough income bothers me a lot'.

Table 6.2 shows the distribution of responses to these questions by lifetime income quintile. Overall, about 22 per cent of the population is not at all satisfied in retirement (or is uneasy about retirement) and 30 per cent are bothered a lot or worry a lot about not having enough income to get by in retirement. These concerns fall sharply with income and worries appear to be somewhat less prevalent for households eligible for 401(k)s relative to those who are not.

Table 6.2 Individual retirement outcomes by household lifetime income groups[1]

	Not at All Satisfied with Retirement[2]			Worried a Lot about Retirement Income[3]		
	401(k) Ineligible	401(k) Eligible	**Total**	401(k) Ineligible	401(k) Eligible	**Total**
1st Income Quintile [%]	33.8	31.2	**33.6**	55.3	59.4	**55.6**
2nd Income Quintile	25.8	26.1	**25.9**	38.4	33.9	**37.2**
3rd Income Quintile	20.7	19.6	**20.3**	29.5	24.9	**27.9**
4th Income Quintile	19.0	15.2	**17.2**	23.6	18.9	**21.4**
5th Income Quintile	18.1	18.0	**18.1**	14.9	16.0	**15.5**
All Income Quintiles	*23.9*	*19.1*	***22.2***	*33.9*	*22.7*	***29.9***
Number of Observations	5066	2671	**7737**	5224	2713	**7937**

Notes:

[1] Expected retirement outcomes are used for non-retirees. The figures are weighted by Wave I HRS individual analysis weights. The samples exclude respondents who were proxy (and thus were not asked these questions by construction), answered 'don't know', or refused to answer the questions.

[2] For completely-retired respondents, the question reads 'All in all, would you say that your retirement has turned out to be very satisfying, moderately satisfying, or not at all satisfying?' For not-completely-retired respondents, the question reads 'When you think about the time when you [and your (husband/wife/partner)] will (completely) retire, are you looking forward to it, are you uneasy about it, or what?' The answer 'uneasy' about retirement of the latter question is grouped together with the answer 'not at all satisfied' in retirement of the former.

[3] For completely-retired respondents, the question reads 'Now for things that some people say are bad about retirement. Please tell me if, during your retirement, they have bothered you a lot, somewhat, a little, or not at all. Not having enough income to get by.' For not-completely-retired respondents, the question reads 'Now for things that worry some people about retirement. Please tell me if they worry you a lot, somewhat, a little, or not at all. Not having enough income to get by.'

Table 6.3 presents probit regression coefficients (transformed into marginal effects) showing the factors correlated with, in column 1, not being at all satisfied in retirement (or being uneasy about retirement) and with, in column 2, being bothered a lot or worrying a lot about not having enough income to get by in retirement. Retirement concerns seem to be greater for women and they decline with age, though they are higher for those already retired. They are strongly correlated with being in poor health. They also, not surprisingly, fall with income and with net worth. One quite surprising result is that while worries about retirement income fall with education, dissatisfaction (and unease) about retirement increases with education.

Table 6.3 Correlations of subjective retirement views and 401(k) eligibility[1]

	Dependent Variables	
	Not at All Satisfied with Retirement	Worried a Lot about Retirement Income
Respondent's Characteristics		
Gender (male = 1)	−0.03**	−0.02*
	(0.01)	(0.01)
Age	0.02**	0.01
	(0.01)	(0.01)
Age^2	−0.00017**	−0.00014*
	(0.00007)	(0.00008)
Race (non-white = 1)	−0.02	−0.03**
	(0.01)	(0.01)
High School Graduate	0.02**	−0.04**
	(0.01)	(0.01)
College Graduate	0.04**	−0.05**
	(0.02)	(0.02)
Post-Graduate School Graduate	0.06**	−0.09**
	(0.02)	(0.02)
Marital Status (married = 1)	−0.07**	−0.06**
	(0.02)	(0.02)
Retiree (retire = 1)	0.06**	0.02*
	(0.01)	(0.01)
Forced to Retire	−0.16**	−0.21**
	(0.01)	(0.01)
Poor Health	0.17**	0.21**
	(0.02)	(0.02)
Household Characteristics		
Gender of Household's Head (male = 1)	0.02	−0.06**
	(0.01)	(0.01)
Two Income Earners	0.03**	0.05**

Table 6.3 (continued)

	Dependent Variables	
	Not at All Satisfied with Retirement	Worried a Lot about Retirement Income
	(0.01)	(0.01)
Family Size	0.01*	0.03**
	(0.01)	(0.01)
Have a Non-401(k) Pension	−0.03**	−0.06**
	(0.01)	(0.01)
2nd Income Quintile	−0.01	−0.04**
	(0.02)	(0.02)
3rd Income Quintile	−0.03*	−0.08**
	(0.02)	(0.02)
4th Income Quintile	−0.04**	−0.13**
	(0.02)	(0.02)
5th Income Quintile	−0.03	−0.15**
	(0.02)	(0.02)
1st Income Quintile x 401(k) Eligible	0.015	0.046
	(0.035)	(0.041)
2nd Income Quintile x 401(k) Eligible	0.012	−0.054**
	(0.021)	(0.021)
3rd Income Quintile x 401(k) Eligible	0.005	−0.061**
	(0.019)	(0.019)
4th Income Quintile x 401(k) Eligible	−0.033*	−0.045**
	(0.017)	(0.020)
5th Income Quintile x 401(k) Eligible	0.015	−0.010
	(0.019)	(0.023)
Net Worth	−0.17**	−0.42**
	(0.03)	(0.04)
Net Worth^2	0.06**	0.13**
	(0.02)	(0.02)
Net Worth^3	−0.006**	−0.011**
	(0.002)	(0.003)
R^2	0.063	0.146
Number of Observations	9 888	10 117

Notes:
[1] The results are marginal effects on probability of reporting a particular answer (Probit regressions). The sample sizes are larger than the one in Table 6.2 because a significant fraction of respondents who are not age-eligible as defined by the HRS are included. Standard errors are in parentheses.
*indicates significance at the 90% confidence level.
** indicates significance at the 95% confidence level.

The central coefficients of interest are the 401(k) eligibility indicator variables, interacted with the lifetime quintile indicators. These show only one marginally significant correlation between 401(k) eligibility and retirement satisfaction – that occurs in the fourth lifetime income quintile. But 401(k) eligibility is negatively, significantly correlated with being bothered a lot or worrying a lot about not having enough income to get by in retirement for respondents in households in the middle 60 per cent of the lifetime income quintiles. Moreover, the effects are fairly sizeable – around 5 percentage points, off a base that ranges from 21 to 37 percentage points.

Two questions arise from the analysis of subjective expectations. First, does the reduction in 'worry' correspond to observable differences in wealth between 401(k) eligible and ineligible households? We examine this issue in the next subsection. Second, how robust are the results on subjective expectations? On the latter question, the results depend somewhat on the treatment of respondents in the sample who say they will never retire (this is 845 of 6695 non-retired respondents in Wave I of the HRS). In the regression in Table 6.3, these respondents are dropped because expectations about retirement are not well defined for people who never plan to retire. The results are similar if the 'never retire' respondents are included in the sample and those who say that 'work is important because of the money' are included in the undesirable outcome. The results are somewhat different if the 'never retired' are included in the sample and all are treated as not having worries (or unease). In this specification, 401(k) eligibility is again negatively correlated with bad expectations in the third and fourth lifetime income quintiles, but it is positively correlated with bad outcomes in the first quintile.

6.5.3 401(k)s and Wealth Accumulation in the HRS

Table 6.4 reports coefficients from a cross-sectional regression examining correlations between 401(k) eligibility and net worth. The first column gives coefficients from an OLS regression. Because of our concern about outliers in the net worth data, the second column reports coefficients from a median regression. The regression uses only Wave I data and restricts the sample to households who are not retired because we do not want to consider asset accumulation (or decumulation) of retired households.[22] The dependent variable in these regressions is net worth, defined to include the value of defined benefit pension and defined contribution pension wealth. Like Table 6.3, the coefficients of primary interest in this specification are the interaction terms of 401(k) eligibility and lifetime income quintile. If 401(k)s increase overall net worth, we expect the interaction terms to be positive and significant.

Table 6.4 Regressions of Wave I net worth and 401(k) eligibility[1]

Dependent Variable = Wave I Net Worth Including Pension Wealth	OLS	Median Regression
Household Characteristics		
Gender (male = 1)	3.62	−9.41*
	(21.76)	(5.29)
Age	9.58	5.46
	(19.53)	(4.57)
Age^2	−0.03	−0.02
	(0.18)	(0.04)
Race (non-white = 1)	−61.45**	−25.98**
	(19.96)	(4.85)
High School Graduate	97.76**	40.21**
	(20.30)	(4.94)
College Graduate	213.08**	137.43**
	(29.19)	(7.11)
Post-Graduate School Graduate	387.09**	238.07**
	(31.41)	(7.65)
Marital Status (married = 1)	141.78**	51.05**
	(35.67)	(8.67)
Two Income Earners	−71.26**	−15.43**
	(25.23)	(6.13)
Family Size	−10.99	−8.47**
	(14.15)	(3.43)
Have a Non-401(k) Pension	−42.39**	27.54**
	(16.83)	(4.10)
2nd Income Quintile	49.26	24.76**
	(30.46)	(7.41)
3rd Income Quintile	122.37**	58.47**
	(34.01)	(8.27)
4th Income Quintile	179.08**	107.24**
	(37.59)	(9.14)
5th Income Quintile	471.33**	286.36**
	(39.77)	(9.68)
Poor Health	−97.72**	−22.28**
	(33.40)	(8.12)
1st Income Quintile x 401(k) Eligible	36.20	0.70
	(55.03)	(13.37)
2nd Income Quintile x 401(k) Eligible	−54.72	−1.94
	(37.54)	(9.13)
3rd Income Quintile x 401(k) Eligible	−47.57	6.16
	(33.99)	(8.28)

Table 6.4

Dependent Variable = Wave I Net Worth Including Pension Wealth	OLS	Median Regression
4th Income Quintile x 401(k) Eligible	−91.68**	−1.87
	(33.30)	(8.11)
5th Income Quintile x 401(k) Eligible	−110.97**	−28.81**
	(34.68)	(8.45)
Constant	−315.60	−210.29*
	(532.52)	(124.50)
R^2	0.15	0.17
Number of Observations	4736	4736

Notes:
[1] The sample excludes households whose heads were already retired at the Wave I interview. For married couples, we define the head as the partner with the higher lifetime income.
* indicates significance at the 90% confidence level.
** indicates significance at the 95% confidence level.

The key interaction terms provide little evidence that 401(k)s increase net worth. In the median regressions, which we believe are the most informative, the coefficients are small and insignificant, except in the top lifetime income quintile. There the coefficient of −28.8 suggesting those eligible for 401(k)s in the highest wealth quintile have $28 800 less private wealth than those who are not, after conditioning on observable characteristics. These results, coupled with the evidence from Table 6.3, suggest that 401(k)s help relieve anxiety about retirement living standards, perhaps because the value of 401(k)s are easy to keep track of, but they do little to increase wealth accumulation. The same transparency that relieves anxiety about retirement may also facilitate adjustments in other parts of the household's portfolio to mitigate positive effects of 401(k)s on wealth.

The other coefficients suggest that wealth is lower for non-white families, two-earner couples, and larger families; it increases sharply with educational attainment and with lifetime income; and it is higher for married couples and for families covered by a pension other than a 401(k) (in the median but not the mean regression). These coefficients are typical of regressions examining net worth, though the specification presented in this paper is unusual in that it conditions on lifetime income, and incorporates the value of defined benefit pensions in its wealth measure.

We conclude, like several recent papers on the topic, that there is little evidence in the HRS that 401(k)s increase private wealth accumulation. A conclusion like this must still be cautious, however. Wealth data are noisy, and this is particularly so when trying to use the HRS pension data. We have made painstaking efforts to mitigate potential problems, but problems may still remain. Other implicit assumptions enter into empirical analyses of 401(k)s. Analysts must make some attempt to condition on lifetime resources (see, for example, Gale, 1998). We do this explicitly by including dummy variables for the household's lifetime income quintile. But if 401(k)s and other fringe benefits are capitalized in wages, for example, households may be inappropriately classified. Moreover, 401(k)s may affect other margins of behavior, such as retirement. The literature has not grappled in a serious way with these issues.

6.6   CONCLUSIONS

We do three things in this chapter. First, we describe the institutional factors affecting retirement preparation in the United States – social security (public pensions), employer-provided pensions, and tax incentives for private saving. Second, we provide a brief survey of the literature on the adequacy of retirement preparation in the US. Third, we present new evidence on the efficacy of tax incentives for saving using data from the Health and Retirement Study.

A large number of tax provisions attempt to enhance the private saving leg of the three-legged stool. But there is little compelling evidence that they promote private, to say nothing of national, saving.[23] The provisions are also piecemeal, each with different eligibility rules, contribution limits and other rules. Moreover, the incentives would seem to be designed in a way to reduce their efficacy. In particular, the benefits of the up-front deduction and tax-free accumulation increase with marginal tax rates. Hence, high income households have the largest incentive to participate in the programs. They also are most likely to receive employer-provided pension benefits (and hence benefit disproportionately from that tax expenditure) and the greatest opportunity to displace saving that would otherwise occur.

The largest tax incentive for saving, 401(k) plans, appears to be significantly related to respondents worrying less about not having enough income in retirement. It is possible that the information provided about 401(k)s – quarterly reporting, newsletters and internet access – helps respondents to better understand the resources they have available for retirement. There is little evidence in the HRS, however, that 401(k) wealth significantly increases overall wealth accumulation. In the cross-sectional data (either 1992 or all years of the HRS pooled), 401(k) eligible households did not appear to have more aggregate wealth than households not eligible for 401(k)s. We conclude, therefore, that while there are many features of the US economy and tax system that are perhaps worth emulating, the patchwork of private saving incentives is not one of them.

NOTES

1. At the close of the first March trading day in 1992, March 2, the Vanguard Index 500 Fund (VFINX) was $33.0186. Eight years later on March 1, the Vanguard index closed at $127.2847, an increase of 285.5 per cent. The percentage increases over the intervening two-year intervals were 17.6, 46.0, 71.9 and 30.6.
2. See OECD Statistics: National Accounts, Main Aggregates, 1960–97.
3. In 2000, the OASDI program is financed by a 6.2 percentage point tax levied on employers and employees (for a combined 12.4 per cent tax) on earnings up to $76 200. These tax receipts are credited to the social security trust fund. To receive benefits a worker must have at least 40 quarters of employment in jobs covered by the social security system (most jobs are now covered), unless they are disabled. Benefits are based on average indexed monthly earnings (AIME) for the highest 35 years of earnings (inserting 0s for monthly earnings if workers have fewer than 35 years of positive earnings) using a formula that gives low-income workers a greater share of their AIME than high-income workers. Workers (who are not disabled) can begin drawing benefits as early as 62. Benefits payments increase (nonlinearly) as retirement is delayed until age 70, at which point benefits no longer increase with age of retirement.
4. From the 2001 Annual Report of the Board of Trustees of the Federal Old Age and Survivors Insurance and Disability Insurance Trust Fund, Office of the Chief Actuary, Social Security Administration.
5. From 'Private Pension Plan Bulletin', Abstract of 1995, Form 5500, Annual Reports, Spring 1999, Pension and Welfare Benefits Administration, Office of Policy and Research, Department of Labor, http://www.dol.gov/ebsa/programs/opr/bullet1995/e_8.htm.
6. Figures are from the FY2002 Federal Budget.
7. Specific institutional details on IRAs and other provisions discussed in this section can be found in http://www.fool.com/money/allaboutiras/allaboutiras.htm and http://www.fool.com/csc/csc.htm.
8. In 2001, annual contributions to a Roth IRA are limited to $2000 minus the taxpayer's deductible IRA contributions. The $2000 limit is phased out as adjusted gross income increases from $150 000 to $160 000 (married filing jointly) or $95 000 to $110 000 (single filer). There are several other types of less commonly used tax incentives for retirements. A Simplified Employee Pension (SEP-IRA) is set up by an employer for a firm's employees. In 2001, an employer may contribute up to $30 000 or 15 per cent of an employee's compensation annually to each employee's SEP-IRA. A Savings Incentive Match Plan for Employees IRA (SIMPLE-IRA) is set up by a small employer for a firm's employees. In 2001, employees could contribute up to $6000 per year to these IRAs and will receive some level of a matching percentage of pay from their employers. Between the employer and the employee, up to $12 000 may be contributed annually to the participant's account.
   In addition to SEPs and SIMPLEs, the self-employed (and partnerships and unincorporated businesses) can also set up Keogh plans as either a defined benefit or defined contribution plan. As defined contribution plans, they may be structured as a profit-sharing, a money-purchase, or a combined profit-sharing/money-purchase plan.
9. Congressional Budget Office (2001), for example, reports that after-tax income grew an average of 157 per cent between 1979 and 1997 for the top one per cent of the population, rose a modest 10 per cent – about one-half of one per cent per year – for the 20 per cent of Americans in the middle of the income spectrum and was effectively unchanged for those in the bottom fifth.
10. 'Binge Buyers: Many Baby Boomer Save Little, May Run Into Trouble Later On: They Don't Build Nest Eggs Nearly Rapidly Enough for an Easy Retirement', Bernard Wysocki Jr., 6/5/95, A1 Wall Street Journal.
11. Hamermesh (1984) used limited consumption data from the Retirement History Survey in 1973 and 1975 to measure the ability of households to sustain pre-retirement consumption levels. He finds households do not have sufficient wealth to maintain pre-retirement consumption and that they respond by reducing real consumption as they age. Hausman and Paquette (1987) also find evidence of inadequate wealth accumulation.

12. Also see Bernheim (1997) for a similar conclusion.
13. Gustman and Steinmeier (1999a) examine patterns of wealth accumulation in the Health and Retirement Study and also conclude '... it is hard to find evidence of a massive crisis in retirement undersaving of the type that has been promoted in the media' (p. 294). Kotlikoff *et al.* (1982) use data from the 1969, 1971 and 1973 waves of the Retirement History Survey to compare the ratio of consumption annuity a household would be able to purchase with their lifetime resources (including human capital and social security wealth) with the annuity a household could purchase with the resources they have for old age. They conclude 'The results in this paper suggest that there is currently no systematic problem of undersaving among the elderly population' (p. 1068).
14. Engen *et al.* (1999) make both of these points.
15. An appendix with details on data construction and definitions is available from either author on request.
16. An overview of the HRS is given in a Supplementary issue of the Journal of Human Resources, 1995 (volume 30). There, 22 authors discuss and assess the data quality of many dimensions of the initial wave of the HRS. Subsequent careful work with the HRS related to this paper includes Gustman *et al.* (1998), Moore and Mitchell (1998), Gustman and Steinmeier (1999a) and Gustman and Steinmeier (1999b).
17. See http://www.umich.edu/~hrswww/center/rescont2.html.
18. The intermediate Social Security Administration assumptions are 6.3 per cent for interest rates, 5 per cent for wage growth, and 4 per cent for inflation.
19. After documenting the problem, Gustman and Steinmeier (1999b) raise concerns about respondent misreporting, so they use the plan documents for DC wealth, adjusted downwards based on a regression analysis of self-reported and calculated pension wealth. This leads them to reduce the calculated DC pension amounts by roughly half for a calculated pension of $25 000 and almost two-thirds for a calculated pension of $100 000.
20. Non-IRA, non-pension net worth is a broad measure that includes stocks, bonds, mutual funds, checking and saving accounts, CDs, other financial assets, housing, real estate less all liabilities.
21. Engen and Gale (forthcoming) first used this approach.
22. The qualitative and quantitative results are similar when we pool all five existing waves of the HRS so the results shown in Table 6.4 are not simply an artifact of using the 1992 HRS cross-section.
23. The effect of tax incentives on national saving will depend on their effect on private saving plus the (negative) effect on public saving, due to the tax break associated with the incentives.

REFERENCES

Aaron, H.J. and J.B. Shoven (1999), *Should the United States Privatize Social Security?*, Cambridge, Massachusetts: The MIT Press.
Banks, J., R. Blundell and S. Tanner (1998), 'Is There a Retirement-Savings Puzzle?', *American Economic Review*, September, 769–88.
Bernheim, B.D. (1997), 'The Adequacy of Personal Retirement Saving: Issues and Options', in Wise, D. (ed.) *Facing the Age Wave*, Stanford, California: Hoover Institution Press.
Bernheim, B.D., J. Skinner and S.Weinberg (2001), 'What Accounts for the Variation in Retirement Wealth Among U.S. Households?', *American Economic Review*, **91**, 832–57.
Congressional Budget Office (2001), 'Historical Effective Tax Rates, 1979–97, Preliminary Edition', May, http://www.cbo.gov/ftpdoc.cfm?index=2838&type=1.
Engelhardt, G.V. (2000), 'Have 401(k)'s Increased Saving: Evidence from the Health

and Retirement Survey', Syracuse University Working Paper .

Engen, E.M. and W.G. Gale, forthcoming, 'The Effects of 401(k) Plans on Household Wealth: Differences Across Earnings Groups', *Journal of Public Economics* (and NBER Working Paper #8032).

Engen, E.M., W.G. Gale and J.K. Scholz (1996), 'The Illusory Effects of Saving Incentives', *Journal of Economic Perspectives*, Fall, 113–38.

Engen, E.M., W.G. Gale and C.R. Uccello (1999), 'The Adequacy of Retirement Saving', *Brookings Papers on Economic Activity*, **2**, 65–165.

Gale, W.G. (1998), 'The Effects of Pensions on Household Wealth: A Reevaluation of Theory and Evidence', *Journal of Political Economy*, **106** (4), 706–23.

Gale, W.G. and J. Sabelhaus (1999), 'Perspectives on the Household Saving Rate', *Brookings Papers on Economic Activity*, **1**, 181–224.

Gustman, A.L., O.S. Mitchell, A.A. Samwick and T.L. Steinmeier (1998), *Pensions and Social Security Wealth in the Health and Retirement Study*, Dartmouth College, University of Pennsylvania and Texas Tech University, April, mimeo.

Gustman, A.L. and T.L. Steinmeier (1999a), 'Effects of Pensions on Savings: Analysis with Data from the Health and Retirement Survey', *Carnegie-Rochester Conference Series on Public Policy*, **50**, 271–324.

Gustman, A.L. and T.L. Steinmeier, (1999b), *What People Don't Know About Their Pensions and Social Security: An Analysis Using Linked Data from the Health and Retirement Study*, Dartmouth College and Texas Tech University, mimeo.

Hamermesh, D.S. (1984), 'Consumption During Retirement: The Missing Link in the Life Cycle', *Review of Economics and Statistics*, **66** (1), 1–7.

Hausman, J.A. and L. Paquette (1987), 'Involuntary Early Retirement and Consumption', in Burtless, G. (eds), *Work, Health, and Income among the Elderly*, Studies in Social Economics series, Brookings Institution, Washington D.C., 151–75.

Heckman, J.J. (1996), 'Comment', in Feldstein and Poterba (eds), *Empirical Foundations of Household Taxation*, University of Chicago Press, 32–8 .

Ippolito, R.A. (1997), *Pension Plans and Employee Performance*, University of Chicago Press.

Kotlikoff, L.J., A. Spivak and L.H. Summers (1982), 'The Adequacy of Savings', *American Economic Review*, **72** (5), 1056–69.

Mitchell, O.S. (2000), 'New Trends in Pension Benefit and Retirement Provisions', Pension Research Council Working Paper 2000–1, Wharton School, University of Pennsylvania, (http://prc.wharton.upenn.edu/prc/prc.html).

Moore, J.F. and O.S. Mitchell (1998), 'Projected Retirement Wealth and Savings Adequacy in the Health and Retirement Survey', Pension Research Council Working Paper 98–1, Wharton School, University of Pennsylvania, (http://prc.wharton.upenn.edu/prc/prc.html).

Poterba, J.M., S.F. Venti, and D.A. Wise (1996), 'How Retirement Saving Programs Increase Saving', *Journal of Economic Perspectives*, Fall, 91–112.

7. Retirement benefit and pension taxation principles

Axel Börsch-Supan and Melanie Lührmann

7.1 INTRODUCTION

With the aging of the population the public pay-as-you-go (GRV – Gesetzliche Rentenversicherung) retirement insurance scheme is coming under increasing pressure. If current levels of retirement income are to be sustained in the future and direct and indirect contributions to the PAYG system kept reasonably stable, it is inevitable (and, for numerous reasons not discussed here, desirable) that a significant element of old-age pension provision is shifted to private and funded schemes.[1] As a result, the taxation treatment of payments to various old-age pension institutions and the taxation of retirement benefit and pension income itself are becoming increasingly important.[2]

The taxation approach adopted generates important signals. The preferential tax treatment or subsidization of old-age pension provision over and above that accorded to other savings measures could obviate the need for mandatory, supplementary old-age provision with all the ensuing negative psychological consequences (compulsory pensions) and economic side effects this would entail. Moreover, capital is so highly mobile that even a slight shift away from a 'level playing field' – relative taxation disadvantages for one type of investment compared with another – is enough to trigger major substitution movements into other forms of saving.

The current taxation of retirement benefits and pensions in the Federal Republic of Germany is, however, inconsistent and inherently contradictory. The situation is anything other than a 'level playing field'. This state of affairs has already been censured several times by the Federal Constitutional Court. The impending judgement of the Federal Constitutional Court on the taxation of retirement benefits and pensions will hopefully clarify matters. However, the onus is already on legislators to bring current inconsistent laws into line with clear principles. This chapter outlines rational principles for the taxation of retirement benefits and pensions and compares these with current practice in Germany and abroad.

National measures and corresponding reform are not only demanded by the Federal Constitutional Court in Karlsruhe. European integration and globalization are two further factors exercising additional pressure for more transparent tax treatment. Firstly, increasing mobility within the European Union dictates that clear rules be defined about when and which forms of old-age provision are tax-deductible, and when and which forms of pension benefits are subject to taxation in order to prevent distortions in mobility or dual and erroneous taxation. Secondly, the globalization of capital markets will compel harmonization of the taxes levied on capital, as capital flows to those locations where the after-tax returns on capital are greatest. Countries levying higher rates of tax on capital will therefore be forced to offer a higher gross yield which, in turn, will make them less attractive and will be unsustainable in the long term.

This chapter is structured into five sections which start with theoretical considerations and go on to deal with actual practice. In Section 7.2, we define the meaning of 'neutrality' in the context of taxes levied on retirement benefits and pensions and the taxation principles implied by this concept. We then discuss the reasons why, and to what extent, it would be appropriate to subject old-age provision to preferential tax treatment. Section 7.3 analyses four basic tax approaches employed in the European Union. We examine the extent to which these approaches are congruent with the principles of neutrality referred to above as well as their impact on revenues and rates of return. Section 7.4 discusses detailed problems relating to the taxation of retirement benefits and pensions during the contribution and benefit payment phases, such as the influence of inflation, the valuation of capital gains and the distortions which occur when, despite the varying tax rates to which a company's employees may be subject, a flat-rate tax is levied. Section 7.5 considers the extent to which the propensity to save in general and for old-age in particular can be encouraged and with which instruments. This section is empirical in character and based on our observation of relevant experiences in Germany and abroad in recent years. Section 7.6 compares the principles and insights developed in the first part of the chapter with actual taxation practice in Germany. Our conclusions have already been outlined at the beginning of this chapter: the taxation of retirement benefits and pensions in Germany is inconsistent and only reflects rational principles of taxation to a very limited extent. Consequently, this chapter concludes (7.7) with briefly formulated recommendations for the reform of retirement benefits and pensions in Germany.

7.2   NEUTRALITY IN THE TAXATION OF RETIREMENT BENEFITS AND PENSIONS

Governments must finance their budgets from taxes imposed on the productive factors of labour and capital as well as taxes on consumption expenditures. This must, in principle, also apply to the income and expenditure of pensioners. Initially economic and legal principles (maximizing the economic well-being of society and the principle of equal treatment anchored in the German constitution) require that taxes must be as neutral as possible, i.e. they should not prejudice or benefit one form of economic activity more than any other (Section 7.2.1 and 7.2.2) unless there are very good reasons for doing so of the type discussed in Section 7.2.3.

Strict neutrality, however, is a lofty and elusive aim, as the imposition of taxes on particular activities will always result in a reduction in such activities. This is just as true of taxes on incomes, which reduce the supply of labour or drain away the incentive to invest, as it is of taxes on consumption expenditures, which diminish demand for consumer goods. The quantitative calculation of incentive effects is far from straightforward. Deciding which rate of tax should be applied to which activity to ensure that the burden of taxation remains the same across all forms of taxation is highly problematic in practice. However, to begin with it is important to explain the meaning of the principality of neutrality in the context of the tax treatment of retirement benefits and pensions.

7.2.1   The Relevant Principle of Neutrality

There are two schools of thought which contend that taxes levied on retirement benefits and pensions should be neutral. The first school of thought argues that consumption and savings should be taxed equally. This would appear to make immediate sense given that the state is not supposed to influence the use to which income is put (i.e. what the balance between consumption and savings should be). If we accept this principle, taxes should be levied on all incomes with perfect evenness. This is known as comprehensive income taxation, a state of affairs brought about by taxing income from capital in the same way as earnings.

Although this principle appears to make perfect sense at first sight, a closer look reveals that it is in fact incorrect. The second school of thought points out, quite rightly, that saving is not an end in itself, but that it is merely a form of deferred consumption. If the principle of neutrality is applied correctly, this would require that the state make no distinction between current and future consumption. The state should therefore levy taxes on spending rather than on incomes. The actual act of consumption itself should be the focus of taxation. This is consequently referred to as the principle of consumption tax, even if this means in practice that expenditure for capital formation is deductible for income tax purposes.

A comparison of both principles clearly demonstrates that comprehensive income tax has a relatively greater discriminatory impact on the formation of savings than a consumption tax. A comprehensive tax on income discriminates in favour of current consumption and, as such, is not neutral with regard to present and future consumption. It acts as a disincentive to savings, particularly on individual private provision for old-age. The core principle of a rational method of taxing retirement benefits and pensions must therefore be based on the consumption tax principle.

7.2.2 Other Aspects of Neutrality

Neutrality also proves to be a multifaceted concept when looked at in greater detail. To begin with there is the principle of the equivalence of contributions to pay-as-you-go financed pensions. If the requirements of this principle are met, social insurance contributions to public retirement insurance and contributions to private (personal and occupational) pensions should both be regarded as an investment in the future. If the principle of equivalence is infringed, contributions to public retirement insurance schemes assume the character of a tax. Part of the contributions are thus deemed to be 'lost' and neutrality between statutory and private old-age provision no longer holds. This is the case, for example, whenever future generations pay more into the pay-as-you-go (PAYG) system than they are ever likely to receive back in the form of pension benefits. The principle of equivalence of pension insurance contributions has so far managed to limit these negative effects for the most part. Mixed financing (revenues from the energy tax and value-added tax which are earmarked for the public retirement insurance scheme) and the falling implicit rate of return offered by public retirement insurance will, however, systematically undermine the principle of equivalent contributions such that contributions to the public retirement insurance scheme will increasingly assume the character of a tax. If those paying social insurance contributions increasingly perceive their contributions as lost, this will generate disincentive effects as people try to opt out or dodge the system (evading contributions, e.g., in the form of bogus self-employment); at any rate, it is no longer regarded as worth working for (reduction in labour supply). A 'level playing field' in the tax treatment of old-age provision therefore depends on the highest possible level of contribution equivalence.

Neutrality also needs to be achieved on the international level. Employees who change their residence and place of work within the European Union should experience neither tax advantages nor disadvantages with regard to existing private pension schemes; this applies analogously to state social insurance. To date, the portability of retirement benefits and pensions is still limited. Occupational pensions and personal savings for old-age in particular are subject to different taxation regimes when transferred from one country to another.

A third important aspect of neutrality relates to the distribution over time of retirement income from capital. The principle of neutrality requires that benefit payments be given the same tax treatment, regardless of whether the capital saved is paid out in a lump sum or as an annuity guaranteeing a fixed income for the remainder of the beneficiary's life. The next section discusses why this aspect of neutrality is contentious.

7.2.3   Reasons for Diverging from the Principle of Neutrality

The principle of comprehensive income taxation is inequitable with regard to old-age pension provision; the principle of consumption tax, on the other hand, implies neutrality. There are, however, a number of reasons why we should go a step further and actually give preferential tax treatment to old-age pension provision.

The first argument applies to savings formation in general. The savings rate is very low in many countries.[3] An inadequately low savings rate leads to a high level of individual consumption in the short run, but also leads to a reduction in investments which are required for the high levels of long-term economic growth which pave the way for consumption at a later date. It is difficult to define in practice how high the ideal savings rate should be. As long as the rate of return on capital continues to be higher than the growth in total wage income we can be sure, however, that this ideal savings rate has not yet been reached. This is the case in almost all the OECD countries, including in the Federal Republic of Germany. In order to achieve neutrality *vis-à-vis* the consumption of present and future generations, savings should be preferred to consumption as long as the rate of return on capital continues to be higher than the growth in total wage income.

There are also a number of reasons why funded personal pensions should be given preferential tax treatment. The principal argument is that many people are simply short-sighted and only begin to make provision and to accumulate capital for their old-age once it is too late. Even if the paternalism implicit in this view – the state knows better how to plan for the future than its citizens – is unappealing in many respects, there is nonetheless plenty of empirical evidence corroborating the observation that young people find it difficult to plan for their old-age if this means deferring consumption. An additional factor is that most people have little intuitive grasp of interest and compound interest mechanisms and believe it is possible to compensate for the low contributions made during the first half of their working life by saving twice as much during the second half. Simple financial mathematics shows that this is not the case – in fact individuals would need to save four times as much. As it is not possible for the individual citizen to rectify this mistake once it has been made, paternalistic logic suggests that the state must encourage saving.

It also makes sense from a purely fiscal standpoint to deploy tax instruments to ensure adequate old-age provision. If retirement income drops below a defined threshold, the law currently requires that inadequate incomes be topped up by social assistance payments. This should only be an emergency measure, however, as otherwise the far-sighted will simply end up subsidizing the short-sighted. In the Federal Republic of Germany this would also result in federal side effects as social assistance is financed from Länder and local authority resources.

Finally, there are several more subtle reasons why efforts should be made to ensure that all citizens put aside savings to provide for their old-age. One important argument in this context is what is known as adverse selection. This is based on the observation that people who believe they have an above-average life expectancy are more likely to convert funded old-age pension provision into life annuities. Others prefer lump-sum payments. This means that, in Germany too, private life annuities are too expensive for most people.[4] This adverse selection of 'poor risks' can only be rectified by giving preferential tax treatment to life annuities relative to lump-sum payments, assuming we wish to avoid the instrument of the compulsory pension and the negative incentive effects associated with it. It is worth, however, considering some of the side effects which would ensue if lump-sum payments were to be given inferior treatment, e.g. in terms of paying off debts or moving to a smaller house. Clearly the devil is in the details.

In those countries in which pay-as-you-go systems are gradually being supplemented by funded systems, tax allowances for old-age pension provision have also been used to accelerate the transition from one system to the other and to spread the transition burden equally across several generations.[5] The requisite tax concessions are self-financing to the extent that the PAYG contribution burden regarded as 'lost' by employees drops, and results in a boost of labour productivity, a reduction in moonlighting, and a rise in capital productivity as institutional investors increase their participation in capital markets.[6]

7.3   TAXATION VARIANTS

Retirement benefits and pensions may be taxed in three phases:

- To begin with contributions may be taxed. In practice this means that contributions must be financed from taxed income and cannot be deducted from tax.
- Secondly, the capital income realized during the contribution phase can be subject to taxation. This would include tax on compound interest, dividends and capital gains.
- Finally, tax can be levied on retirement benefits and pensions themselves and thus be treated as any other form of income.

These tax options generate numerous taxation variants. We will analyze four combinations of these tax options that are common in the European Union:

- FFT – tax-free contributions, tax-free capital income during the accumulation phase, and taxable retirement benefits
- TFF – taxable contributions, tax-free capital income during the accumulation phase, and tax-free retirement benefits
- FTT – tax-free contributions, taxable capital income during the accumulation phase, and taxable retirement benefits
- TTF – taxable contributions, taxable capital income during the accumulation phase, and tax-free retirement benefits.

    In the classic case of deferred taxation, contributions are made from untaxed income (i.e. they are deductible from income tax), capital income is tax-free during the accumulation phase; on the other hand, benefit payments bear the full weight of taxation. We abbreviate this to 'FFT' where the three letters refer to the form of taxation during each of the three taxation phases: 'tax-*free*, tax-*free*, and *t*axable'. Deferred taxation clearly corresponds with the principle of consumption tax referred to in the preceding section.

    The classic form of comprehensive income taxation, on the other hand, is effective during the first and second phases. Contributions must be made from taxed income, and capital gains – not however pension benefits – are subject to taxation. This taxation variant is abbreviated to 'TTF', i.e. '*t*axable, *t*axable, tax-*free*'.

    These terms are somewhat confusing as both consumption tax and comprehensive income tax may be levied immediately or deferred. There are thus four potential combinations. Table 7.1 shows the simplest scenario for the two classic taxation variants (in bold) and the two alternative variants.

This comparison is based on the assumption that the same rate of tax applies in all taxation phases, that there is no inflation, and that a contribution of DM 1000 is paid throughout an average working life of 37 years. The interest rate is 3 per cent, the tax rate 22 per cent.[7]

Table 7.1 Comparison of taxation variants based on the simplest scenario

Variants	FFT	TFF	FTT	TTF
Taxation principle	**Consumption**		**Comprehensive income**	
Timing of taxation	**Deferred**	Immediate	Deferred	**Immediate**
Pre-tax contributions	**37 000**	37 000	37 000	**37 000**
Tax rate	0%	22%	0%	22%
After-tax contributions	**37 000**	28 860	37 000	**28 860**
Pre-tax capital income	**31 159**	24 304	28 445	**22 187**
Tax rate	0%	0%	22%	22%
After-tax capital income	31,159	24 304	22 187	**17 306**
Ultimate amount saved before tax	**68 159**	53 164	59 187	**46 166**
Tax rate	22%	0%	22%	0%
Net after-tax benefit	**53 164**	53 164	46 166	**46 166**

This simple scenario clarifies an important issue: initially it makes no difference at all whether tax is levied during the contributions or benefit phase. After-tax pension rights are not dependent on deferred taxation in any narrow sense, but on the neutrality between present and future consumption (the two variants, FFT and TFF in the left-hand column) or between consumption and savings (the variants FTT and TTF, in the right-hand column). As capital gains are not taxed in the first two cases, the after-tax and pre-tax rates of return are identical, while in the third and fourth cases they diverge owing to capital-gains taxation and consequently trigger the corresponding distortion effects. In the case of proportional taxes and no inflation, the only important principle is that of consumption tax.

If different tax rates apply during the earning and pension phases or if the rate of inflation alters the basis of taxes on capital income, the whole picture changes, however. This is demonstrated by Table 7.2. Different rates of tax emerge, for example, owing to the fact that income tax is progressive as pension benefits typically tend to be lower than earned income. Tax progression generates an incentive effect with regard to the deferred taxation of pensions which is stronger for consumption taxation than for income taxation.

Table 7.2 The influence of inflation and the progressive tax system*

Variants	FFT	TFF	FTT	TTF
Taxation principle	**Consumption**		**Comprehensive income**	
Timing of taxation	**Deferred**	Immediate	Deferred	**Immediate**
Pre-tax contributions	**37 000**	37 000	37 000	**37 000**
(Real) net after-tax benefit:				
Proportional tax system, no inflation	**53 164**	53 164	46 166	**46 166**
Progressive tax system, no inflation	**59 980**	53 164	52 085	**46 166**
Proportional tax system, 2.5% inflation	**53 164**	53 164	41 272	**41 272**
Progressive tax system, 2.5% inflation	**59 980**	53 164	46 564	**41 272**

Notes:
* Cf. Table 7.1. In this example, too, DM 1000 (in real terms) are invested over a period of 37 years at a 3 per cent rate of effective interest, or nominal 5.5 per cent with inflation. The final amount saved is paid out as a lump sum once retirement age is reached. In the case of proportional tax, employees and pensions are taxed at 22 per cent, in the case of progressive tax pensioners are only taxed at 12 per cent.

The bottom two rows of Table 7.2 show the impact of inflation on the four types of taxation. As the contributions paid in each year have been modified in the table such that they equal a real contribution DM 1000, a fall in the value of money results in no change in the deferred consumption tax on a real net payment of DM 53 164 (DM 59 980) in a proportional (progressive) tax system. Consumption tax does not exercise any additional distortion effects in this case either.

In the case of comprehensive income taxation where the capital income is also subject to taxation, inflation results in falling net benefit payments as fictitious capital gains are now subject to tax.[8] These lower net benefit payments are the outcome of interest on nominal amounts which lead to higher attributed capital gains than actually generated in real terms. Net, untaxed capital gains amount to DM 3116 so that, in the less advantageous case represented by immediate income tax, fictitious gains account for around a third of the real capital gains! Taxation of these fictitious gains results in a significant drop in net benefit payments and deferred and immediate income tax in particular become less attractive than the two consumption tax variants.

Inflation has the opposite effect if the rising nominal incomes which accompany inflation put the tax-paying retired and pensioners in a higher tax bracket and reduce the advantage which tax progression offers them.

Basically, in the case of a progressive tax system and under inflationary conditions, deferred taxation appears to result in higher net benefit payments than is the case with immediate taxation, and consumption tax has less distorting impact than comprehensive income tax. The most rational economic taxation principle would therefore be a deferred consumption tax, or the first variant, 'FFT', shown in Tables 7.1 and 7.2.

7.4 PRACTICAL ASPECTS OF DIFFERENT TAXATION PRINCIPLES

In addition to the theoretical considerations discussed in Section 7.2, there are a number of practical reasons in favour of the deferred 'FFT' type of taxation of retirement payments and pensions during the three taxation phases.

7.4.1 Taxation Treatment of Contributions

If taxes are to be levied during the contribution phase, the same tax rate must apply to contributions paid by employees and those paid by employers on behalf of their employees. If this is not the case, substitution will take place in the direction of the form of contribution subject to the lowest rate of tax and, as we will elucidate, this is usually to the disadvantage of employees subject to lower tax rates. This consideration is important for occupational pensions and proves to be a major obstacle for this taxation variant.

The principle of equal treatment can be upheld as long as the contributions paid by employers on behalf of their employees can be clearly assigned to individual employees such that they are included in the tax levied on employees in a similar way as other benefits in money's worth (value?). Problems arise, however, if employer contributions are either not clearly attributable to individual employees or if the amount of such contributions cannot be determined precisely. The first instance occurs if flat-rate contributions are paid into a fund for a group of employees which, for example, is managed by an industry organization. Flat-rate transfers of this type are made, *inter alia*, when the employer's contributions are based solely on the number of employees working for the company, but not on their actual level of income. Flat-rate taxation would then have to be based on the average actual income tax paid by the employees, in other words, subsequent to annual wage tax assessment or income tax return – an entirely impractical proposition. This approach would also be to the disadvantage of employees on a below-average marginal rate of taxation and would favour employees with higher incomes.

Similar problems arise where accruals are set up for pension promises. In this case the employer's contributions are derived implicitly from the value of the pension promise. This is usually calculated on the basis of an employee's expected salary on retirement, however. This final salary is not known at the time tax is levied and it is therefore impossible to arrive at an indisputable quantification of the appropriate taxation.

7.4.2   Tax Treatment of Capital Income

To begin with it is important to clarify that the taxation of capital income does not constitute a form of double taxation; this only occurs if capital assets are taxed. Capital income results from current factor income which increases gross national product and which, like every other form of factor income, is fundamentally subject to income tax treatment. This applies to interest, dividends and realized capital gains.

The problems begin with unrealized capital gains, the amount and distribution of which are indeterminate. The issue becomes even more problematic if pension funds are managed for whole groups of employees rather than for individuals. The same complex of problems which applies to the taxation of contributions then raises its head again: a blanket tax rate will disadvantage employees on lower incomes and favour employees with an above-average marginal rate of taxation.

Levying tax on the basis of nominal income is also problematic. It is especially important to make adjustments for inflation-based losses of value when taxing capital income as only real capital gains and interest have the character of factor income. The continued use of the nominal value principle in Germany is the source of considerable distortions as the example in Table 7.2 shows.

7.4.3   Tax Treatment of Benefit Payments

The taxation of benefit payments is much simpler in technical respects. This is also another reason why the deferred taxation of retirement benefits and pensions is by far the most common approach adopted in OECD countries.[9] When benefits are paid out, the distribution of capital assets among the owners (the pensioners) is clearly defined and the allocation problems referred to earlier are thus eradicated.

Practical problems arise with regard to the treatment of lump-sum payments in comparison with life annuities. The correct systematic treatment of life annuities is clear enough; they are taxed as recurring, regular benefit payments in the same way as any other income. If the accumulated capital is paid out as a lump sum, however, this may be subject to a very high marginal tax burden which becomes all the more critical the steeper the tax rate schedule is. In this case it would be feasible to spread the tax burden over several years, although any specific form of distribution is bound to be arbitrary.[10]

Leaving aside the problem of how to tax lump-sum payments, deferred taxation based on the consumption tax principle proves to be the most practical method of taxing retirement income and pensions from a technical point of view. This is true for both pay-as-you-go and funded approaches.

7.5   THE IMPACT OF TAX INCENTIVES ON SAVINGS IN GENERAL AND ON OLD-AGE PROVISION IN PARTICULAR

As discussed above in Section 7.2.3, there are numerous reasons why savings formation in general and old-age provision in particular should not be dealt with neutrally for tax purposes, but should in fact be given preferential treatment. This section examines empirical evidence regarding the potential efficacy of tax breaks. This issue has sparked off a prolonged controversy in the USA.[11]

7.5.1   The Incentive Effects of Taxation on Savings

Our starting point is the microeconomic insight that after-tax rates of return trigger contrary income and substitution effects. The substitution effect stimulates demand for investment instruments with a markedly high after-tax rate of return. If all forms of saving are encouraged, the substitution effect will reduce consumption and spur saving. The income effect works in the opposite direction. Tax concessions which increase the rate of return also mean that less money needs to be saved to attain a defined financial objective. There is therefore no *a priori* evidence as to whether encouraging saving through the tax system will generate any incentive effects at all.

The following example in which the substitution effect is eliminated and only the income effect is felt clarifies the problem:[12] if all employees save in order to build up a defined retirement income, state encouragement which boosts the after-tax rate of return of such savings will reduce both the private and state savings rate as employees will now need to pay less towards their retirement and the state will have taken on additional obligations. These will either increase the deficit or will need to be deducted from disposable incomes which in turn will push down the private savings rate further.

Empirically it is therefore important to estimate the magnitude of the income and substitution effect. Returning to the above example, this means that it is important to assess whether employees will respond to measures designed to encourage saving by aiming to achieve a higher level of ultimate savings. This is an extremely difficult empirical challenge, and despite the large number of such studies in this field the results remain controversial. Tax concessions do, in fact, appear to exercise a positive influence on the propensity to save; it is however considerably less dramatic than many partisan analysts tend to claim.[13] The reason why this is so should become clear in the following discussion of displacement effects.

7.5.2 Specific Incentive Effects on Old-Age Pension Provision

The outcomes which were cautiously formulated in the preceding section may not, initially, be interpreted to mean that specific methods of promoting old-age pension provision would have only a minor effect. On the contrary, in this respect the empirical evidence is incontrovertible.

Our experiences regarding the effect of government support for savings towards old-age pension provision largely originate from 'experiments' performed in the USA and Canada during the 1980s. Following the introduction of tax relief on 'individual retirement accounts' (IRAs) in the USA, the savings accumulated on these accounts rose dramatically. Subsequently contributions to these accounts fell in line with the trimming of the relevant tax relief.[14] As the level of tax breaks rose, so did the popularity of the '401(k) plans', a mixed form of company retirement and personal pension plan which experienced a huge boom during the 1990s.[15] Canada experimented with 'Registered Retirement Saving Plans' (RRSPs), the volume of which also rose in unison with the level of government support.[16]

There are also interesting parallels in Europe such as the 'opting out' rules in the United Kingdom and Hungary. These rules empower employees to opt between remaining in the pay-as-you-go state system or switching to private pension plans which are managed either by the employee or the employer and aided by government tax reliefs. Relatively simple calculations of rates of return show that the after-tax rate of return of privately funded pension plans is higher than that of the pay-as-you-go system for younger cohorts, but lower for older cohorts. Opting-out behaviour reflected this state of affairs precisely: employees clearly preferred the pension system which provided the respective higher, after-tax rate of return.[17]

Finally, econometric studies have been performed on the impact of tax relief on savings in the Federal Republic of Germany. These have been performed in particular on capital sum life insurance policies and savings and loan agreements.[18] These too show that state support of specific investment vehicles strengthens the attractiveness of the relevant form of saving.[19]

7.5.3 Substitution between Different Investment Vehicles

This outcome does not however mean that the effective encouragement of specific forms of saving inevitably leads to an increase in the general propensity to save. Subsequent to the preferential tax treatment of a particular investment vehicle there is, in general, a distinct substitution to other investment vehicles, i.e. there is a slackening in demand for forms of saving which are now at a disadvantage. If full substitution takes place, displacement occurs between different forms of saving without an increase in the rate of saving in the economy as a whole. If substitution is less than one to one, demand not only rises for the supported form of saving but there is also an increase in the rate of saving in the economy as a whole.[20]

Whether the support given to company retirement and personal pension plans in the USA resulted in a marked increase in the overall propensity to save or merely in an insignificant increase is a matter of dispute – as we indicated above. A comparison of the currently extremely low savings rate in the USA with the significantly higher rate in Germany is an inappropriate tool for assessing this issue, however. It is tempting but economically incorrect to draw conclusions about the impact of tax-related measures by comparing the savings rates in two economies. The reason is that the remaining macroeconomic and foreign trade pictures have just as much influence on the savings rate of both countries as support for a particular form of saving. Chile, the country with the longest and widest experience with funded and, during the transition phase, heavily subsidized old-age pension provision, offers the best data for the assessment of this issue, as the transition itself and the support provided during the transition process perhaps best qualify for 'experimental' status. In fact, it is possible to demonstrate convincingly that an increase in the overall savings rate in the Chilean economy is the result of the support given to old-age pension provision.[21]

7.6. TAXATION PRACTICE IN GERMANY

In Germany tax is levied during all three of the taxation phases described in Section 7.3. While the tax on civil servants' pensions and occupational pensions in the form of a pension promise or a provident fund is deferred, in other words levied on benefit payments, the contributions to occupational pension schemes in the form of direct insurance or pension funds are taxed. The last two forms of occupational pension scheme share some of the features of the public pay-as-you-go system: tax is due not on all the benefit payments accruing from these plans, but on the interest portion of payments. Finally, tax is levied on capital income from equity funds which can be used for old-age pension provision purposes, as well as on pension investment funds (AS funds) which also cover biometric risks.

German law also provides for numerous tax-free allowances and deduction options geared to special forms of saving which make this inconsistent array of tax variants even more complex and which exacerbate the inequities of the taxation system even further. Table 7.3 provides an overview.

The institutional breadth of public retirement insurance and private old-age pension provision and their taxation have significant monetary effects. These are calculated in Table 7.4, based again on the example in Tables 7.1 and 7.2, i.e. an annual contribution of DM 1000 invested over a working life of 37 years in various alternative forms of old-age pension provision: the public retirement insurance scheme, a civil servant pension, occupational pension, a capital sum life insurance policy and in an investment, equity or AS fund. For ease of comparison, the calculation assumes an identical rate of return of 3 per cent (including the pay-as-you-go scheme) and is based on a tax rate of 22 per cent. The net benefit amount corresponds, as in Table 7.2, with the capital value of the paid-out retirement benefit or pension (retirement benefit or pension rights). The calculation has been simplified to the extent that no account has been taken of maximum tax allowance amounts.

Table 7.4 shows that the current situation has not the remotest resemblance to a level playing field. Public retirement insurance easily receives the most preferential tax treatment; pension funds come off worst. The difference in the net benefit payments from the public retirement insurance scheme and an AS fund is almost 50 per cent of the amount paid out of the AS pension investment fund. The net benefit payments of pension forms which are subject to deferred taxation – public retirement insurance, civil servants pensions, and occupational pensions – tend to be higher than net benefit payments subject to the other tax principles. This corresponds with the results shown in Table 7.2. Public retirement and occupational pensions generate the highest net benefit payments as only a very minor share of the pension benefits (the interest portion) is taxed and, thanks to the very generous tax-free limit, usually no tax is levied at all. The most consistent application of the tax system would therefore require tax to be levied on pay-as-you-go pensions and removed on the capital income from AS funds.

Table 7.3 Various forms of tax levied on old-age pension provision in Germany

Form of old-age pension provision	Contribution side	Capital income	Benefit side
Public retirement insurance (GRV)	No tax levied Employee contributions partly deductible.	No tax levied	The interest portion is taxed at the usual rate of income tax.
Civil servants' pensions	No tax levied	No tax levied	Subject to income tax. A personal exemption amount of 40% of benefits, maximum of DM 6000, is tax-deductible
Occupational pension I (pension fund or direct insurance)	Subject to income tax 20% – maximum DM 3408 – of expenses of a provident nature are deductible	No tax levied	Interest portion subject to taxation
Occupational pension II (pension promise or provident fund)	No tax levied	No tax levied	Subject to income tax. A personal exemption amount of 40% of benefits, maximum DM 6000, is tax-deductible.
Capital sum life insurance	Subject to income tax. Fixed amounts are deductible as special expenses	No tax levied	No tax levied
AS pension investment funds and equity fund	Included in taxable income and taxed accordingly	Subject to income tax. DM 6000 or DM 12 000 savers' tax-free amount and income-related expenses are deductible.	No tax levied

Source: Federal Ministry of Finance.

Table 7.4 Comparison of the effects of different taxation rules

	GRV	Civil servant pension	Occupational pension[1]	Occupational pension[2]	Capital sum life insurance	AS or investment fund
Type	FFT/FFF*	FFT	FFT	TFT/TFF*	TFF	TTF/TFF[#]
Pre-tax contribution	37 000	37 000	37 000	37 000	37 000	37 000
Tax	0	0	0	6 510	8 140	8 140
After-tax contribution	37 000	37 000	37 000	30 490	28 860	28 860
Pre-tax capital income	31 160	31 160	31 160	25 670	24 300	24 300
Tax	0	0	0	0	0	7 000/0[#]
After-tax capital income	31 160	31 150	31 160	25 670	24 300	17 310/ 24 300[#]
Ultimate amount saved	68 160	68 150	68 160	56 160	53 160	46 170/ 53 160[#]
Tax	4 050/0*	14 990	9 000	33 400/0*	0	0
Net benefit payment	**64 110/ 68 160***	**53 160**	**59 160**	**52 830/ 56 160***	**53 160**	**46 170/ 53 160[#]**

Notes:
[a] GRV: Public retirement insurance; AS: Pension investment funds. The figures reflect a savings period of 37 years and an annual contribution of DM 1000, a real rate of interest of 3 per cent, a retirement age of 65 and an average tax rate of 22 per cent. Deductions are calculated on the basis of statutory percentage rates; no account is taken of maximum tax allowance amounts.
[b] The alternatives marked * account for the frequent cases in which the interest portion is so low that taxable income remains below the tax-free allowance so that no tax is levied.
[c] The alternatives marked # account for those cases where capital income is below the savers' tax-free amount plus income-related expenses totalling DM 6100 for single people and DM 12 000 for married people so that no tax is levied.
[1] Pension promise/provident fund.
[2] Direct insurance/pension fund.

From a microeconomic perspective, subjecting pay-as-you-go financed pensions to full taxation would imply a process of redistribution between young and old. Following indexing to net wages, the taxation of pensions within the normal income tax framework would imply that, assuming pension levels remain stable, absolute pension benefits would fall while contributions to the pension insurance scheme would rise. Additional redistribution effects would occur indirectly between the rich and poor, as well as between the various budgets and para-fiscal authorities of the German state. From a macroeconomic perspective, taxing pensions would result in a further reduction in the implicit rate of return of the pay-as-you-go scheme. This would trigger substitution towards more private savings. Taxing pensions might also serve as a political vehicle for – more or less elegantly – bringing the accustomed, but ultimately unsustainable, level of pension benefits down to a level at which they can be financed in the long term.

The unequal tax treatment of different forms of old-age pension provision cast occupational pensions and investments in AS pension investment funds in a highly unattractive light. While the unequal tax treatment of a pure capital investment in equities can be justified on paternalistic grounds, as this form of saving does not cover biometric risks, cf. Section 7.2.3, the other two investment vehicles do in fact cover these risks and, bearing in mind the problems associated with the pay-as-you-go scheme, represent a rational form of supplementary private old-age pension provision. As a result, it is difficult to field any cogent economic arguments for subjecting these forms to less advantageous tax treatment, especially as AS pension investment funds are, in this respect, at least equivalent to investments in capital sum life insurance policies. Nonetheless, account must be taken of the fact that the rate of return from both investment vehicles is not, as assumed here, identical but that the tax advantage enjoyed by life insurance policies is accompanied by disadvantages with regard to the rate of return.[22]

The asymmetric taxation of state and private old-age pension provision is not only reflected in different levels of net benefit payments but also exercises incentive effects and triggers substitution effects. These are apparent from the spread of different forms of private old-age pension provision in Germany. Of those investing in private forms of pension provision, 71.2 per cent have a life insurance policy but only 15.1 per cent an equity fund. Occupational pensions are the weakest pillar of pension provision in Germany. The volume of such schemes is less than half of that of life insurance policies and less than 10 per cent of public retirement insurance expenditure.[23]

7.7 CONCLUSIONS AND OUTLOOK

The tax discrimination between different forms of pension instruments in Germany outlined in the preceding section is scarcely justifiable; a consistent form of taxation would appear to be the appropriate remedy. The theoretical considerations regarding the postulate of neutrality show that the only appropriate consistent tax approach would be the deferred taxation of all retirement income. This is the most rational taxation form from an economic perspective as it is the only form which preserves neutrality between present and future consumption. Deferred taxation also poses the fewest practical tax imposition problems.

Deferred taxation based on the consumption tax principle can also be elegantly combined with tax support generated automatically by the progression effect. In other words, due to the fact that the tax rate tends to be lower during the benefit payment phase as retirement income is generally lower than income during the contribution phase. In addition, taxes are postponed to the future which, however, only has a transitory effect as shown in Section 7.3.

Whether the savings rate in Germany should or can be increased by means of tax incentives or not is an open question.[24] Regardless of this issue, the discussion presented in Section 7.2.3 shows that it would make sense to concentrate current state support for asset formation on old-age pension provision wherever possible in order to compensate to some extent for the natural temptation to postpone pension saving for as long as possible and for the intuitive difficulty of grasping interest and compound interest mechanisms. Bearing in mind experiences in the USA and Canada, we take the view that deferred taxation and the indirect support provided by the progression effect is preferable to a 'compulsory pension' and is also sufficient as an incentive for those on average and high incomes to save for their own old-age pensions. Additional subsidization may be necessary for those on low incomes in order to avoid mandatory measures and their associated negative incentive effects.

We do not underestimate the detailed problems involved in a transition to a consistent system of deferred taxation of all retirement benefits and pension income. The political problems posed by raising the level of taxation on state pensions (in line with civil servants' pensions) may well prove weightier than the financial burdens incurred during the transition period when tax is cut on contributions but has not yet begun to be levied on benefits. These difficulties should not, however, deter the German government from finally heeding the exhortations of the Constitutional Court and the economic imperatives of increasing European integration and introducing the deferred taxation of all retirement benefits and pension income as part of its impending pension and tax reform package.

NOTES

1.   The literature on pay-as-you-go versus funded systems runs into volumes. Börsch-Supan (1999) draws together the threads of current discussion on this theme in Germany.

2. By 'retirement benefits and pensions' we mean all income arising from provisions made for old-age. Retirement benefits includes PAYG-funded public retirement insurance schemes as well as the life annuities from funded private provision. Pensions include funded occupational pensions as well as PAYG-funded civil servant pensions.
3. The US provides the best-known example.
4. Cf., for example, Walliser und Winter (1999).
5. Examples may be found in the United Kingdom and Hungary (Palacios and Rocha, 1998).
6. Cf. *e.g.* Börsch-Supan *et al.* (2000).
7. The original version of this example is from Dilnot (1992).
8. In the case of immediate income tax, fictitious gains amount, for example, to DM 1304.
9. The World Bank (1999).
10. As suggested in Section 7.2.3, the state may also wish to encourage benefit payments in the form of life annuities more than lump-sum payments on paternalistic and other grounds.
11. Venti and Wise (1990) maintain that the introduction of IRAs increased the savings rate of American households; this is contested by Gale and Scholz (1994).
12. Dilnot (1992).
13. Cf. the summary of this debate in Skinner and Hubbard (1996).
14. Venti and Wise (1990).
15. Poterba, Venti and Wise (1994).
16. Burbidge and Davies (1994).
17. World Bank (1999).
18. Börsch-Supan and Stahl (1991), Brunsbach and Lang (1998), Lang (1998), Walliser and Winter (1999).
19. The econometric evidence is much less clear, however, than that offered by these quasi-experiments as the rate-of-return constructs used are often based on generalized assumptions. It is particularly difficult to quantify allowances for special expenses if the tax situation of the employee is not totally clear.
20. A consideration of all support measures must also take account of the general equilibrium effect attendant on the financing of support measures and – as described in section 7.5.1 – which reduces disposable income and, in turn and dependent on its spread, reduces consumption or savings.
21. Diamond (1994), Schmidt-Hebbel (1998). How far the experiences gained in a newly industrialized country may be regarded as representative for a highly-industrialized country such as Germany remains an open question.
22. This implies redistribution in favour of those with life insurance policies.
23. DIA (1999).
24. We believe it should and can, but this difficult issue is not the main focus of this chapter. Cf. Börsch-Supan *et al.* (2000).

REFERENCES

Börsch-Supan, A. (1999), 'Zur deutschen Diskussion eines Übergangs vom Umlage-zum Kapitaldeckungsverfahren in der deutschen Rentenversicherung', *Finanzarchiv*, May.

Börsch-Supan, A., F. Heir and J.K. Winter (2000), 'Pension Reform, Capital Markets, and the Rate of Return', Papier für den Workshop 'Reforming Old-Age Pension Systems', Herbert-Giersch-Stiftung, Magdeburg, 25–26 May.

Börsch-Supan, A. and K. Stahl (1991), 'Do Savings Programs Dedicated to Homeownership Increase Personal Savings? An Analysis of the West German Bausparkassensystem', *Journal of Public Economics*, **44**, 265–97.

Brunsbach, S. and O. Lang (1998), 'Steuervorteile und die Rendite des Lebensversicherungs-sparens', *Jahrbücher für Nationalökonomie und Statistik*, **217**, 185–213.

Burbidge, J.B. and J.B. Davies (1994), *Household Data on Saving Behavior in Canada*, in Poterba, J.M. (ed.), *International Comparisons of Household Saving*, Chicago: University of Chicago Press.

DIA (1999), *Die Deutschen und ihr Geld*, Cologne: Deutsches Institut für Altersvorsorge.

Diamond, P. (1994), 'Privatization of Social Security: Lessons from Chile', in *Revista Analisis Economico,* **9.1**.

Dilnot, A.W. (1992), 'Taxation of Private Pensions: Costs and Consequences', in OECD, *Private Pensions and Public Policy*, Paris: OECD.

Gale, W.G., and J.K. Scholz (1994), 'IRAs and Household Savings', *American Economic Review,* **84**, 1233–60.

Lang, O. (1998), *Steueranreize und Geldanlage im Lebenszyklus*, Baden-Baden: Nomos.

Palacios, R. and R. Rocha (1998), 'The Hungarian Pension System in Transition', *Social Protection Discussion Paper Series* # 9805, The World Bank, Washington, DC.

Poterba, J.M., S.F. Venti and D.A. Wise (1994), 401(k)-Plans and Tax-Deferred Saving, in D.A.Wise (ed.), *Studies in the Economics of Aging*, Chicago: University of Chicago Press.

Schmidt-Hebbel, K. (1998), 'Does Pension Reform Really Spur Productivity, Saving, and Growth?', The World Bank, Working Paper, August.

Skinner, J. and R.G. Hubbard (1996), 'Assessing the Effectiveness of Saving Incentives', *Journal of Economic Perspectives*, Fall.

Venti, S.F. and D.A. Wise (1990), 'Have IRAs Increased US Saving? Evidence from Consumer Expenditure Surveys', *Quarterly Journal of Economics,* **105**, 661–98.

Walliser, J. and J. Winter (1999), 'Tax incentives, bequest motives and the demand for life insurance: Evidence from Germany' Discussion Paper No. 99–28, Sonderforschungsbereich 504, University of Mannheim.

World Bank (1999), 'The Tax Treatment of Funded Pensions', *World Bank Pension Reform Primer,* **2.3**, Washington, DC.

PART 3

Pension portability issues

8. Tenuous property rights: The unraveling of defined benefit contracts in the US

Richard A. Ippolito

8.1 INTRODUCTION

Historically, pension coverage was dominated by defined benefit plans that pay annuities to workers often based on final salary and years of service. These plans have been an important source of retirement income, and feature prominently in 'implicit pension contract' models that help explain lower quit rates and earlier retirement ages.[1] Since the mid-1980s, however, these plans have lost substantial market share to defined contribution pensions in the private sector.[2] In the early 1980s, defined benefit plans covered about 85 per cent of covered workers in the private sector. By 2000, this share had fallen to less than 40 per cent, and reasonable extrapolations suggest that defined benefit plans will attain clear minority status over the next decade (Figure 8.1).

They have been replaced by defined contribution plans that essentially give property rights to pension assets to workers: these assets plus investment returns usually are paid in the form of a lump sum upon leaving the firm.[3] I argue that, following a change in law that undercut the basis for enforcement of the implicit pension contract that characterized defined benefit plans, defined contribution plans, which we can call 'bonded' pensions, are the only sustainable options in the new environment.[4]

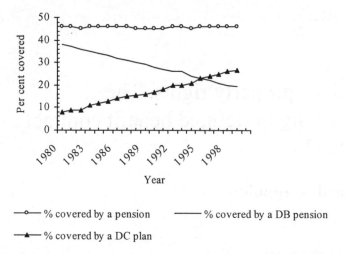

Source: US Department of Labor, Private Pension Plan Bulletin: Abstract of 1995 Form 5500 Annual Reports, Pension and Welfare Benefits Administration, Number 8, Spring 1999. Participants in 401(k) plans who do not contribute are not included as pension covered in these data.

Figure 8.1   Per cent of private labor force covered by type of pension, 1980–99

8.2   THE BASIC IDEA

Until the early 1980s, defined benefit plans terminated in conjunction with either firm failures or in the face of serious financial conditions arising with the plan sponsor (McGill 1970). I have argued that these events merely reflected the realizations of the downside of the implicit pension contract, that the imposition of pension losses on workers in failed firms is the *raison d'être* of unbonded pension plans.[5]

Beginning in the early 1980s a new kind of termination occurred, so-called terminations for reversions. In these transactions, which often were affiliated with corporate takeover events, firms unilaterally terminated the plans, took the excess assets into corporate profits, and often recreated essentially the same plan the next day. In effect, firms engaged in a pseudo-termination for the sole purpose of withdrawing pension monies. Since this two-step process accomplished what was clearly a violation of tax law in one step (plan sponsors are not permitted to take monies from the pension plan), a natural expectation is that the Internal Revenue Service (IRS) would have disallowed the transaction. They made the opposite ruling.

Supported by 'Guidelines' issued jointly by the US Departments of Labor, Treasury and Commerce, the IRS ruled that such transactions were permissible.[6]

In so ruling, the IRS essentially gave up its enforcement role to the implicit pension contract. As long as terminations were allowable only in the clearly demonstrable case where the plan sponsor encountered financial difficulty, then the firm's pension promise was bonded. Once the IRS abandoned its bonding role, the property rights to pensions became more tenuous.

The Pension Benefit Guaranty Corporation, which is the federal agency that guarantees the payment of legal liabilities in the event that a plan sponsor enters bankruptcy with underfunded plans, tracked only those terminations that conferred reversions in excess of $1 million. Starting in 1980, there were few such events. By 1985, there were 585. Through 1986, about 1500 plans were terminated with reversions of at least $1 million.[7] Only about $20 billion was taken in the form of reversions, amounting to only 2 per cent of excess assets as of 1986, but the trend was growing.

Congress reacted by instituting the first (non-deductible) reversion tax (10 per cent) in 1986. The tax was originally designed to recapture tax benefits embedded in reversions that flowed from the tax-exempt pension trust fund. But when the tax did not halt reversion events,[8] the Congress increased the tax to 15 per cent in 1988 and finally to a confiscatory 50 per cent. The last step had an unfortunate and presumably unintended effect. Not only did the tax make further unilateral terminations uneconomic, it also made uneconomic termination under conditions envisioned in the contract in the first place.

That is to say, the plan sponsor lost its opportunity to reduce its pension obligations by terminating the pension in the event of encountering financial difficulty, unless it carried zero excess assets. In effect, the new tax policy increased cost of imposing default risk on employees. Firms reacted strongly: they substantially reduced excess assets, and found a way to legally circumvent termination by converting their plans to 'cash balance', a variety of defined benefit plans.

The cumulative effect of reversions, defunding and cash balance conversions has worked to erode the trust that forms the basis for the implicit contract. Workers' estimate of the probability of termination depends in part on observations they make in the market. Each individual firm makes the termination decision because its workers no longer trust the firm, but this decision affects workers' estimate of termination in other firms, making it more likely that more terminations will ensue. Effectively a lemons market develops, which makes it uneconomic for honest firms to offer defined benefit plans. The adverse economics generated by this effect are exacerbated by the impact of reversion taxes on the expected cost of exposing workers to some default risk.

8.3 DEFAULT EXPOSURE: THE ESSENCE OF THE DEFINED BENEFIT PLANS

Contingent benefits are the core of defined benefit plans. If the plan does not terminate then workers at retirement are entitled to a benefit that is indexed to final wage.[9] This is called an 'ongoing' benefit. But if termination occurs earlier than retirement then workers are entitled to 'termination' or 'legal' benefit, which is a payable at retirement but is indexed to the wage on the date of termination. The difference between these calculations, which can be very large, is called the contingent benefit, or default exposure.

This exposure is easy to model, but more difficult to rationalize in an employee contract. It also is non-trivial to value, owing to its peculiar loss structure and imposition of undiversified exposure on workers. Whatever price workers pay for this asset, however, they are willing to pay less, the greater their estimate that the plan will terminate prior to their retirement date.

8.3.1 Pension Capital Losses

Consider a simple model of pensions. The worker starts at the firm at age zero, retires at age R, and dies at age D. I therefore can denote age and service by a. The quit rate is zero. I assume that there is no early retirement date. The pension annuity, A, is equal to service, a, times wage, w, times some generosity factor, b, there are no cost of living increases after retirement.[10]

$$A = baw \qquad (8.1)$$

The termination value of the pension benefit to some worker age a, earning wage w_a, if the firm terminates the pension is:

$$L_a^* = baw_a e^{-i(R-a)} \Omega, \qquad \text{where } \Omega = \int_0^{(D-R)} e^{-it} dt, \qquad (8.2)$$

where i is the market interest rate, and Ω is the present value of a \$1 annuity collected during retirement, evaluated at retirement age using interest rate i. The federal government guarantees the amount in (8.2), regardless of funding in the plan.[11]

If the firm does not terminate the pension, then the worker stays until age R, in which case he collects his pension indexed to his final wage. The ongoing value of the benefit based on current service evaluated at the same age a based on *current* service level a is:

$$L_a = baw_a e^{(g-i)(R-a)} \Omega, \qquad (8.3)$$

where g is the per annum wage growth (including overall increases plus within-firm merit or seniority increases). Contingent benefits at age a, C_a, equal the difference between these two pensions:

$$C_a = L_a - L_a^* . \tag{8.4}$$

Making the reasonable assumption that g is of the same order of magnitude as i then contingent benefits as a per cent of current wage are:

$$c_a = C_a / w_a = ba\Omega\left[1 - e^{-i(R-a)}\right]. \tag{8.5}$$

The capital loss structure in (8.5) is straightforward, and a fixture in pension economics. Setting R equal to 30, the interest rate to 6.4 per cent, and the generosity parameter to 1.1 per cent, the value of c_a is portrayed in Figure 8.2. The hill-like pattern of losses is familiar. Maximum losses are imposed on workers midstream in the contract, and gradually fall as workers approach retirement age.

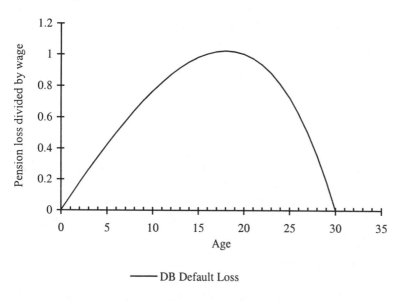

Figure 8.2 Pension capital losses from firm failure

8.3.2 The Economics of Default Risk in The Employee Contract

Default risk is not a 'natural' extension of a defined benefit plan. The firm can eliminate workers' exposure to pension default risk by funding the plan for ongoing liabilities, and writing the contract in a way that confers pension assets up to ongoing benefits to workers. Indeed, if firms had preferred this approach then the reversion tax legislation would have had no financial and economic consequences for the firm.

Virtually all firms elect to retain the ownership of pension assets; that is, workers hold the explicit property rights to termination benefits, not the assets that back them. Firms explicitly expose workers to default risk in the event that they encounter serious financial difficulty. This is a somewhat puzzling phenomenon, and one that has received little attention. The firm can borrow unsecured credit from the market at the appropriate default premium. Since all the idiosyncratic risk in defaults can be diversified away by market investors, the firm compensates investors for interest, expected default losses, plus any compensation to investors for accepting systematic risk.[12]

By forcing workers in effect to hold these securities, they are requiring workers to invest a substantial portion of their wealth in an undiversified portfolio; that is, one heavily laden with default risk in the firm. This means that the premium required by workers to accept this risk must be higher, and perhaps considerably higher, particularly in view of the fact that they may already be heavily invested in the firm in the form of firm-specific capital.[13] Why does the firm choose a more expensive form of financing?

One obvious candidate is that the firm calculates that workers at risk will be less likely to pose agency risk on the firm. It is more apparent how the bond makes sense when workers are unionized, because in this instance workers can act in concert and may find it optimal to hold up stockholders midway in the contract. I have made this argument elsewhere.[14]

Even if workers are not unionized, however, this does not mean that the impact on workers' long-term productivity is zero. If workers as a group have a common stake in the financial success of the firm then presumably they will create an environment where either shirking or an 'anti-management' attitude is frowned upon by fellow workers. If exposure to risks by workers can reduce default risks sufficiently, then the risk differential must be offset by improved financial performance.

8.3.3 Contingent Benefits

The essence of the implicit pension contract is that, if the firm is successful, the plan will not be terminated, and workers receive the full value of their ongoing pension benefits. If the firm encounters sufficient financial stress, however, it may terminate the plan, and pay workers termination benefits. If we sum all the ongoing and termination liabilities for workers in the firm then we have the total contingent benefits in the firm, C:

$$C = L - L^*. \tag{8.6}$$

These benefits are collectable by workers as long as the firm experiences favorable financial outcomes. Put differently, workers are secured bondholders in the firm up to the amount of legal pension liabilities, L^*. The amount, C, is the profit-sharing component of the pension.[15]

Historically, firms were allowed to fund for both termination and contingent benefits. Yet, because the firm legally owes workers only termination benefits, by convention, any assets in excess of termination benefits are referred to as 'excess assets'. Indeed, if the firm is fully funded for ongoing benefits, excess assets are exactly equal to contingent benefits.

The fact that the firm held the option to cancel contingent benefits did not convey ownership of the excess assets that backed these benefits in the eyes of the law. If the firm canceled contingent benefits, workers lost the contingent benefits, C. This loss represents workers' share of downside risk in the firm. Indeed, pension terminations have occurred most frequently in firms that evince financial stress.[16]

Upon termination, any excess assets (a normal condition in most plans) reverts to the firm, subject to normal corporate tax treatment.[17] That is, upon canceling contingent benefits, the firm automatically freed excess assets for corporate uses.

8.4 A NEW KIND OF TERMINATION

Plan termination traditionally signaled dire financial circumstances in the firm. Beginning in the early 1980s, sponsors discovered a new twist on termination, one seemingly designed to obtain access to excess assets for corporate profits. In other words, the plan sponsor is not permitted to take pension assets. But by terminating a plan and then recreating essentially the same plan, some sponsors argued that they could effectively do just that by the two-step termination process. These events became known as 'terminations for reversions'.

8.4.1 Terminations for Reversion

In a typical event, the firm would terminate the plan, purchasing annuities for their employees equal to the present value of termination benefits, L^*, then recreate an identical pension with past service credit, which recreated the full ongoing obligation, L. So as to not to overpay workers, they stipulated that the annuities paid in the new plan were offset dollar for dollar by the annuities purchased from the insurance company upon retirement. This stipulation reduced the liabilities in the new plan to the amount C. Thus, by adding the liabilities in the new plan to the old one, the firm recreated exactly the same liabilities it had prior to the termination: $L = L^* + C$. In effect, the firm effected a reversion without imposing capital losses on workers.

8.4.2 Breaking the Promise

Many 'terminations for reversions' occurred in conjunction with corporate events during the period. Excess assets sometimes were used to finance a leveraged buyout. The problem that arose for the market for defined benefit plans was that firms sometimes did not recreate the plan after termination, and instead created a defined contribution plan, effectively breaking the implicit pension contract. Indeed, Shleifer and Summers (1988) advanced the theory that the premiums affiliated with leveraged buyouts were attributable to the breaking of implicit contracts, effecting large transfers from workers and other stakeholders to stock holders.

In a study of 169 LBOs over the period 1980–87, William James and I found that these firms terminated 89 pensions within one year of the LBO. Only 22 were reestablishments; 27 had a new contribution benefit plan and 40 had no new plan. Consistent with other studies, we found that many firms in the latter group could be explained by plant closings and poor financial ratios.[18] But we could not explain the defined contribution replacement events in this way, and these accounted for one in every three terminations. Moreover, in a control (non-LBO) sample, we found that one-in-four terminations resulted in a defined contribution follow-on plan. It was not obvious from looking at financial data that these terminations were precipitated by financial problems (Ippolito and James, 1992).

8.4.3 The Internal Revenue Service Ruling

The tax rules dating to 1938 seemingly do not allow sponsors to access excess assets unless there is some evidence of errors by actuaries that cause the firm to contribute incorrect amounts to the fund.[19] Presumably, the intent of the language was to ensure that the pension trust fund, which was exempt from corporate taxation, not be used for purposes other than paying pension benefits.[20]

While many pension terminations occurred during the 1960s and 1970s, they were predominantly underfunded pensions affiliated with business failures (US Congress 1976). In 1971, the IRS issued a ruling in the context of a plan that terminated for 'business necessity'.[21] The IRS apparently allowed excess funds beyond those required to satisfy legal obligations to be considered as though they were attributable to actuarial error and eligible for reversion to the sponsor. This ruling had little practical importance for distress terminations, because typically firms in financial difficulty often defunded the plan of excess assets (through lower contributions) long before bankruptcy was encountered. Thus, prior to the 1980s, the law covering reversions was interpreted quite strictly, with an exception granted to firms in financial distress.

Following the initial 'terminations for reversion' in the early 1980s, the IRS issued a dramatically different ruling, and effectively established new tax policy for defined benefit pensions. It announced that upon any termination that fully satisfied the legal obligations of the plan, the firm could take excess assets into corporate profits. The ruling did not appear to be concerned that the tax-exempt pension trust seemingly was created by the Congress to support accumulations for the purpose of paying pension benefits.[22] Moreover, the ruling made it clear that the reversions were legal even if the only purpose of the termination was to capture a reversion.

This ruling substantially altered the economics of the implicit pension contract. An implicit contract requires a bonding mechanism for both parties. Workers are bonded by virtue of the fact that if the firm encounters severe financial difficulty, then they automatically absorb the downside default risk. For their part, firms were precluded from arbitrarily terminating the pension by a fairly strict tax code that prescribed the use of pension assets for the purpose of paying benefits. The new ruling, however, stripped the latter protection from the contract, and explicitly permitted a unilateral termination of the contract, regardless of the financial condition of the sponsor.

8.5 IMPLICATIONS OF REVERSION TAXES

8.5.1 Congressional Reaction

Congressional reaction to the new IRS tax policy was predictable, and it ultimately led to the enactment of a series of reversion taxes. In 1986, Congress enacted landmark legislation changing the corporate tax treatment of excess pension assets: it levied a 10 per cent (non-deductible) excise tax on reversions from defined benefit plans (known as 'the reversion tax'). While the tax rate was modest, it signaled a major alteration in Congressional interpretation on the ownership of excess pension assets, a signal that was reinforced in 1988 when the tax was increased to 15 per cent. In 1990, Congress affirmed the new ownership paradigm by increasing the reversion tax to 50 per cent.[23] These taxes ended the 'termination-for-reversion' phenomenon, but spawned an even more tumultuous period for defined benefit plans.

Ostensibly, the Congress was trying to recreate the 'old' environment in which reversions effectively were precluded. It did not perfectly replicate the old law. Indeed, it turns out that the taxes exacerbated the trend away from the implicit pension contract.

The reversion tax affects the value of defined benefit plans to the firm. Prior to 1986, firms could fund their plans so that pension assets covered both the termination liability and the contingent liability, but the firm held an option to cancel the contingent liability by terminating the plan and simultaneously removing the 'excess assets' backing the contingent liability. As a result of the reversion tax legislation, firms can continue to fund both components of the pension liability, but as long as the firm maintains excess assets in the plan, the payoff to canceling the contingent liability is severely diminished.

Effectively, the new rules mean that, to the extent that firms fund beyond termination benefits, they transform the contingent pension liability into additional secured debt, up to the amount of excess assets. Thus, if it terminates the pension, the firm now can reduce its pension debt burden by the full amount of contingent pension liabilities only if it maintains zero excess assets.

If the firm offers a defined benefit plan with no default risk, it can use the tax-free buildup to fund contingent benefits. If workers are exposed to default risk, the tax-free trust fund cannot be used to shelter assets that back the contingent benefits. Simply put, the cost of imposing default risk on workers is higher. The firm can reestablish the full value of its contingent pension debt by gradually reducing excess assets (through lower contributions).

8.5.2 Developments in Pension Funding

In effect, the reversion tax gave firms an opportunity to decide anew whether they wanted to continue to expose workers to default risk. If yes, then they would gradually reduce contributions until funding fell closer to termination liabilities. If no, they could forego the exposure by funding their plan closer to ongoing liabilities.[24] Judging by the reaction of sponsors, the vast majority decided to retain default risk. Beginning in 1986, and escalating since 1990, defunding in defined benefit plans was widespread and dramatic.

Figure 8.3 shows the average funding ratio for each year over the period 1980 to 1995 for a longitudinal sample of 1900 pension plans that I studied over this period (Ippolito, 2001). During the early 1980s, funding ratios generally increased, reflecting a rebounding from poor investment returns during the 1970s. But beginning in the mid-1980s, this growth noticeably flattened, and began falling significantly after 1990. In 1986, there was $125 in pension assets for every $100 in liabilities in the typical defined benefit plan. By 1995, there was only $107 in assets for every $100 liabilities.

The reduction is not explained by changing interest rates used to discount pension annuities. The funding ratios in the figure are calculated using the same 6.5 interest rate in all years. Nor is it explained by poor investment performance. The excess return for a balanced portfolio over the 1986–95 period was 5.4 per cent per annum (the dashed line in the figure reflects cumulative excess returns).[25] The pattern of funding ratios is not suggestive of gradual changes in the retirement market, say owing to increasing maturity of pensions, but of some stimulus that plausibly explains rapid and systematic change throughout the industry over a relatively short period. Tax policy is an obvious candidate.[26]

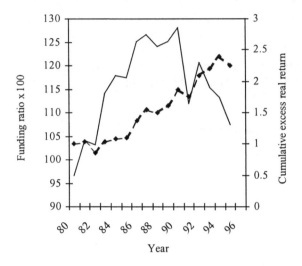

———— Funding ratio — –◆– – Cumulative excess real return

Source: Funding ratios: Longitudinal database, Form 5500 annual pension reports. All liabilities are adjusted to a 6.5 per cent interest rate and GAM 83 mortality table. Numbers reflect beginning-year values. Excess returns are equal to the return on a 50–50 portfolio of stocks and bonds minus the one-year Treasury bill rate from Ibbotson Associates, Stocks, Bonds, Bills and Inflation 1926–98.

Figure 8.3 Funding ratios, 1980–95

Cross-section distributions of funding ratios for 1986 and 1995 are shown in Figure 8.4, where both distributions reflect liabilities for the same 1900 longitudinal plans discounted at the same 6.5 per cent rate. The bar distribution shows funding ratios in 1995. The solid-line schedule shows the distribution in 1986. The change in funding policy over this period is apparent from inspection. In 1986, funding ratios are distributed widely, reflecting, among other things, a large difference in maturity levels across plans.[27] By 1995, the right tail of the distribution is mostly eliminated and the mass of the distribution is shifted markedly to the left.

The dashed-line schedules show the corresponding cumulative distributions. In 1986, 55 per cent of plans had funding ratios in excess of 120 per cent, and 30 per cent were in excess of 150 per cent. By 1995, these portions had fallen to about 30 and 10 per cent, respectively. Clearly, a dramatic change in pension funding occurred over the period, which predominantly affected the best-funded pensions.

New maximum full funding limits inaugurated in 1987 might explain some defunding.[28] In other words, since 1987, sponsors have been permitted to fund their plans only if assets are less than 150 per cent of terminated liabilities, whereas prior to 1986, sponsors were permitted to fund for ongoing benefits without regard to termination liabilities. I chose the interest and mortality tables in the calculations of pension liabilities to match these limits in 1995. If the rules were binding, then funding ratios would be bunched around 150 per cent. It is apparent from figure 8.4 that the mass of the distribution no longer is close to this limit.[29]

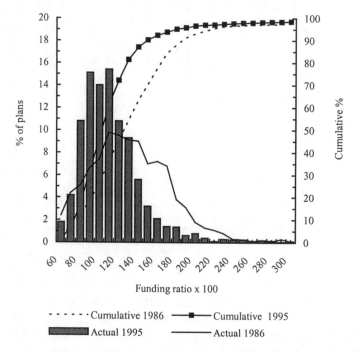

Source: Longitudinal database, Form 5500 annual pension reports. All liabilities are adjusted to a 6.5 % interest rate and GAM 83 mortality table. Numbers reflect beginning-year values Longitudinal database.

Figure 8.4 Funding ratios, 1986 versus 1995

I have reported more extensive results based on systematic study of pension funding elsewhere (Ippolito, 2001). I estimated the impact of reversion taxes on pension funding, holding constant pension funding limits, plan maturity and other confluences of time trends, and found strong evidence in favor of the reversion-tax theory of defunding. My estimates suggest that as of 1995, excess assets in the universe of defined benefit plans had fallen by 60 per cent, or about \$250 billion.[30]

8.5.3 Emerging Trend: Cash Balance Plans

One product created by reversion taxes is the so-called cash balance plan. The cash balance plans is created by a plan amendment to the existing defined benefit plan. It has the effect of awarding each participant an individual 'account'.[31] Typically, a worker's account is credited with the value of his or her accrued benefits (that is, the legally-mandated ERISA[32] benefit) as of the date of the amendment.[33] The plan guarantees a particular investment return on these monies that often is tied to a market instrument (for example, a Treasury bill rate).[34] This guarantee maintains the plan's legal status as 'defined benefit'. Future accruals are very much like traditional defined contribution plans; for example, the plan might award each account x per cent of pay for each year of service subsequent to the date of the amendment. Importantly, at the time of the switch to cash balance, pension assets in excess of the legal benefits in the old version of the plan are used to fund future contributions.

In effect, the cash balance conversion allows a plan sponsor to terminate its defined benefit plan, and reestablish a defined contribution plan in its place, without triggering the reversion tax on the excess assets that result from the termination. The available evidence suggests that the conversions are an important part of what we label the 'defined benefit universe'. The US Bureau of Labor Statistics estimates that six per cent of workers covered by defined benefit plans in the private sector were in cash balance plans in 1997 (US Department of Labor 1999). Moreover, this estimate is double the three per cent calculation in the same survey just two years earlier (Elliot and Moore, 2000). The trend continues sharply upwards. Based on preliminary data for the 1999 Form 5500 submissions, a better estimate for 1999 may be more like 20 per cent.[35]

8.6   A SIMPLE LEMONS MODEL

The cumulative effect of terminations for reversion, the reversion tax, defunding, and the drift towards defined contribution and cash balance plans, in combination, have increased the cost of the implicit pension contract. The essence of this idea can be demonstrated using a simple model in which two pension alternatives exist, defined contribution and defined benefit.

8.6.1   The Equivalence of Two Pensions

Consider a two-period model. Individuals are risk-neutral, pay no income tax, work in period one and retire in period two. The plan sponsor faces a corporate tax rate equal to τ. Workers can take a job in a firm that offers a defined contribution plan that pays cash wage $1 - \alpha$ at the start of period one. The amount α is deposited in a pension account that invests in riskless securities, and thus accumulates with interest rate, i. The property rights to the account convey fully and immediately to the worker. Pension plans assets accumulate at the tax-free rate (that is, earnings are not subject to corporate tax).

Alternatively, workers can take a job in a firm that offers a defined benefit pension plan. These firms pay wage w at the start of period one and award a pension P payable at the start of period two. The firm fully funds the pension and invests the assets in riskless securities. In this simple model, either the firm survives or not. The firm fails with probability v, in which case the pension is worthless. In the upside state, workers gain the property rights to the defined benefit pension. For simplicity, assume that the defined benefit pension equals the cash wage in a present value sense $(P = (1+i)w)$.

The expected present value of compensation in the defined benefit firm must equal the present value compensation in the defined contribution firm.

$$w + (1 - v)\, w\,(1 + i)\,/(1 + i) = 1 - \alpha + \alpha\,(1 + i)\,/(1 + i), \qquad (8.7)$$

which simplifies to:

$$w = 1 / (2 - v) . \qquad (8.8)$$

Workers require the wage rate, w, to just be willing to accept a job in a firm that offers a defined benefit plan. The numerator on the right-hand side of (8.8) is total compensation in the firm offering a defined contribution plan. If default risk is zero ($v = 0$) then the wage and the present value of the pension in the defined benefit firm each are ½. If default risk is positive, then in order to offset the chance that the pension will be zero owing to default risk, the wage plus present value pension in the DB firm must exceed unity in the good state.[36]

The cost for the firm to provide a defined benefit plan equals the cash wage, plus the product of the pension amount and the probability that the firm will not default:

$$C = w + (1 - v)\, w\,(1 + i)\,/(1 + i) . \qquad (8.9)$$

Substituting workers' required wage from (8.8), then it is obvious that the expected cost of offering the defined benefit plan is the same as offering a defined contribution plan:

$$C = 1. \tag{8.10}$$

If the firm does not fail, then defined benefit workers collect compensation in excess of their counterparts who work in defined contribution firms, and less if their firm encounters bankruptcy. This is the risk-sharing aspect of the defined benefit pension.

8.6.2 Impact of Reversion Taxes and Terminations

The accumulation for terminations and cash balance conversions causes workers to reevaluate the probability of termination. They do so not because they change their estimate of the firm's bankruptcy probability, but because they perceive some additional chance of termination or conversion to cash balance, independent of firm bankruptcy. They assess the probability of contract default as ε.

The new asking wage
I denote the new asking wage as $\hat{w}$. Recall my assumption that the pension equals the wage rate (that is, I assume 100 per cent replacement rate). The present value of the wage (and pension) in defined benefit firms must be the equivalent to the present value of compensation in firms offering defined contribution plans:

$$\hat{w} + (1 - v - \varepsilon)\,\hat{w}(1+i)/(1+i) = 1 - \alpha + \alpha(1+i)/(1+i). \tag{8.11}$$

Simplifying (8.11), the wage (and pension) in the defined benefit firm is:

$$\hat{w} = 1/(2 - v - \varepsilon). \tag{8.12}$$

The prospect of contract default increases the supply wage to defined benefit plan sponsors, and in particular, the change in supply wage is:

$$\hat{w} - w = \varepsilon / \left[(2 - v)(2 - v - \varepsilon) \right] > 0. \tag{8.13}$$

The higher is their perception of a unilateral contract default, the less workers are willing to pay (in the form of foregone wages) for the uncertain pension. This problem for the firm is apparent. If workers' estimation of contract default, ε, exceeds the firm's assessment , say ε^0 then a wedge develops between the value of the pension as perceived by workers, and the cost of providing the pension absorbed by the sponsor.

Add the reversion tax

We also need to take into account that, independent of the probability of termination, the effect of reversion tax policy is that firms can expose workers to default risk only by saving for the pension outside the tax-free trust fund. That means, earnings on deferred compensation that are subject to default and contractual risk are now subject to corporate income tax. The defined benefit pension therefore is discounted inside the firm at rate $1 + i(1 - \tau)$.

The cost of offering a defined benefit plan in the new environment is therefore equal to:

$$\hat{C} = \hat{w} + (1 - v - \varepsilon^0)\, \Gamma\, \hat{w}, \text{ where } \Gamma = (1 + i)/(1 + i(1 - \tau)) > 1. \quad (8.14)$$

Substituting workers' required wage from (8.12) gives us:

$$\hat{C} = \left[1 + (1 - v - \varepsilon^0)\, \Gamma \right] \div (1 - v - \varepsilon). \quad (8.15)$$

Thus, using (8.10), the increase in cost of offering a defined benefit plan expressed as a per cent of the new asking wage is:

$$\Delta c = (\hat{C} - C)/\hat{w} = (1 - v)(\Gamma - 1) - \varepsilon^0 \Gamma + \varepsilon. \quad (8.16)$$

Let the workers' perception of the unilateral termination probability, ε, equal the firm's own assessment of this probability, plus some amount, δ, which can be zero, positive or negative:

$$\varepsilon = \varepsilon^0 + \delta. \quad (8.17)$$

Substituting (8.17) into (8.16), we have:

$$\Delta c = (1 - v - \varepsilon^0)(\Gamma - 1) + \delta. \quad (8.18)$$

It is apparent that the cost of offering a defined benefit plan increases for two reasons. The first term is attributable to the *de facto* new tax on defined benefit pensions (which makes $\Gamma > 1$). The impact of the tax is larger, the smaller the probability that the firm will default on the pension promise, either owing to bankruptcy or contract default. Apart from the direct tax effect, the cost also increases in proportion to the amount by which workers overstate the probability of the firm reneging on the pension promise, as embodied in the term, δ.

8.6.3 The Makings of a Lemons Market

The bigger the wedge between workers' estimate and the firm's own assessment of unilateral termination, the larger is the cost of maintaining the defined benefit pension plan. Oddly, if workers underestimate their sponsor's likelihood of reneging then this error works in the direction of reducing the cost of offering the defined benefit plan.

We now have the makings of a lemons market. Suppose that workers assess their employer as having average trustworthiness; that is, they set ε equal to εbar, where εbar is the overall observed probability of reneging on the pension among all pension sponsors last period. I suppose that this average is an unbiased estimate of firms' collective perception; that is,

$$\varepsilon bar = (1/n) \sum_{j=1}^{n} \varepsilon_j^0 . \tag{8.19}$$

Thus, the error made by workers in the jth firm is δ_j:

$$\delta_j = \varepsilon bar - \varepsilon_j^0 . \tag{8.20}$$

For firms that are least trustworthy, that is, $\varepsilon_j^0 \gg \varepsilon bar$, the cost of offering defined benefit plans is more likely to fall because workers understate the true probability of unilateral default. These are the most likely sponsors to continue offering the defined benefit plan. For firms that are most trustworthy, that is, $\varepsilon_j^0 \ll \varepsilon bar$, the cost of offering their defined benefit plan increases significantly because workers overstate the true probability of unilateral termination, and therefore understate the true value of the plan. These firms are least likely to continue offering a defined benefit plan.

As the most trustworthy firms leave, the pool gradually becomes disproportionately populated with firms more likely to renege on the contract. As this process plays out, workers covered by defined benefit plans in the aggregate increase their collective estimate of εbar, a process that pushes the market closer to a corner solution.

To a trustworthy firm, the problem manifests itself in a growing perception that the generous pension plan it is offering, at considerable cost, seems to be heavily discounted by its covered workers. Workers, it will seem, attach more value to defined contribution pensions. As this wedge grows, the net benefits of offering the defined benefit variety become smaller. Put simply, if workers act as though the firm is less trustworthy than it really is, then the only profitable option for the firm is to fulfill its workers' expectations, by simply reneging on the promise. Once the firm defaults on its implicit contract, it has only one option, namely to offer a defined contribution or cash balance plan, which effectively are bonded. In other words, if workers believe that the firm is not trustworthy, then it will be.

8.6.4   Factors that Can Preserve Some Coverage

The only way in which this process can find equilibrium with a positive share of defined benefit coverage is for plan sponsors that are trustworthy to be able to convey their unusually high trustworthiness to employees, which is problematic if other firms with similar characteristics have either terminated their plans or converted to cash balance. Additionally, even if the firm is trustworthy, the question naturally arises whether the firm will be subject to a change in corporate ownership in which case it might not be trustworthy next period (Shleifer and Summers, 1988).

In the private sector, some bond is required to enforce the firm's part of the contract. This can occur if the firm is willing to forego exposing its workers to default risk, in which case it can contract to guaranty the payment of ongoing benefits by essentially awarding the workers ownership of pension assets. Unions can maintain their pensions because they are protected by explicit collective bargaining agreements, making it costly for the firm to renege.[37] In the public sector, defined benefit plans could be terminated, but presumably, if sufficient numbers of voters are public employees, and if they care intensely about the pension issue, a mechanism exists to effectively bond the pension. Otherwise, it is difficult to envision the mechanism by which the lemons market does not develop.

The most effective way to create a bond is simply to use a defined contribution plan. In these plans, vesting can be immediate (and usually occurs within two years). Workers effectively own their accounts, which means that they own all contributions plus earnings; and often, workers are given discretion on the portfolio composition of their accounts. When they depart the firm, they usually take the lump sum in their accounts with them. Put simply, the main attribute of defined contribution plans that distinguishes them from their defined benefit counterparts is that workers own all the pension assets. In effect, defined contribution plans are the ultimate solution to the unraveling of the implicit pension contract, because they offer perfect bonding of the pension promise.

8.7   CONCLUDING REMARKS

The recent history of pension plans in the United States shows the power of public policy, and the sensitivity of equilibrium to assigned property rights. Implicit contracts are by their nature tenuous. In the US, they were sustained largely by a tax policy that made it difficult to use pension assets for purposes other than paying pension benefits. In the event of (near) firm failure, firms typically reduced funding to limits below legal liabilities, and so, as a practical matter, the issue of reversions in the context of a 'distressed firm', was never an issue.

When the Internal Revenue Service changed its policy in 1983 to effectively allow all excess assets to revert to the plan sponsor, regardless of the nature of the termination, the pension institution began a process to find a new equilibrium. The Congress tried to rediscover the old equilibrium by instituting a series of reversion taxes. These taxes raised the cost of engaging in contract default. They also made it more costly to expose workers to financial default risk, which is a core feature of defined benefit plans. Firms reacted by engaging in widespread defunding, and converting to cash balance plans.

Without the bonding provided by the IRS, the only sustainable plans are those that have a bonding feature. Outside union plans, which are protected by explicit collective bargaining agreements, this bonding takes the form of defined contribution plans, the property rights to which reside with the participants themselves. The new equilibrium does not necessarily imply dramatic reductions in efficiency in the firm; nor does it necessarily imply a change in the distribution of pension wealth among participants. Defined contribution plans can reduce quitting and encourage retirement; accomplish desirable sorting (Ippolito, 1997); and expose workers to financial default risk (Ippolito, 2002). Firms must accomplish these outcomes, however, within the constraints of strictly bonded pensions.

NOTES

1. Basic data describing pensions trends is found in the US Department of Labor (1999). Studies that include summaries of the implicit contract literature include Quinn *et al.* 1990; Gustman *et al.* 1994; Hanushek and Maritato 1996; Ippolito 1997.
2. In this chapter, I deal exclusively with private pension plans. Public pensions still heavily favor the defined benefit variety and evince little of the trend towards defined contribution plans observed in the private sector. See EBRI (1997). I also deal exclusively with single employer plans, and thus, ignore the minority of plans that are multiemployer plans (plans that cover unionized workers that work for any number of employers, like the Teamsters or Ladies Garment Workers). Coverage in multiemployer plans has remained primarily defined benefit.
3. Workers can roll these amounts into Individual Retirement Accounts without triggering a tax penalty.
4. Part of the change reflects employment shifts from traditional defined benefit firms and industries (for example, large, unionized firms in the manufacturing sector), to firms and industries that traditionally favored defined contribution plans (for example, smaller, non-union firms in the service sector). But these studies also reveal a sharp decline in employer preferences for defined benefit plans across all portions of the private sector. Several studies have used standard statistical methods to disentangle the portion of the reduction in defined benefit market share over time (Clark and McDermed, 1990, Kruse, 1995, Ippolito, 1997, Gustman and Steinmeier, 1992). Generally, these studies conclude that about half of the reduction in defined benefit share is explained by employment shifts, and the remaining half by preference changes away from these types of plans. Most of the shift is affiliated with new plan formation and not plan termination with defined contribution replacement (Kruse, 1995; Papke *et al.*, 1996; and Ippolito and Thompson, 2000). Also see Hustead (1990).

5. See Ippolito (1985).
6. The Joint Implementation Guidelines essentially required all legal liabilities be satisfied upon termination; that the payouts be made in the form of annuities purchased from an insurance company; and that the discount rate used to value liabilities be no higher than the one used by the Pension Benefit Guaranty Corporation. Essentially, the guidelines called for a satisfaction of legal, and not ongoing, liabilities. See 23 Tax Notes 1088 (4 June 1984).
7. The Pension Benefit Guaranty Corporation tracked these totals. Summaries can be found in PBGC Annual Reports throughout the 1980s. My numbers are taken from the 1989 report.
8. About $2 billion in reversions was taken in 1987 and again in 1988.
9. In many plans, the final wage is the average of the 'high-3' or 'high-5', but in pension nomenclature, these are known as 'final salary' plans, and are usually modeled as though the benefit was indexed to the last wage.
10. Some plans pay flat benefits instead of indexing the pension to service and salary, but as long as the flat benefit is increased periodically, the same analysis pertains. Flat benefit plans almost always cover union workers. See US Department of Labor (1999) for the distribution of defined benefit characteristics.
11. Upon termination, vesting for all participants is automatic. With few reductions, the Pension Benefit Guaranty Corporation guarantees the termination benefit.
12. In the context of the Capital Asset Pricing Model then if it is more likely for bankruptcies to occur in poor economic conditions then the beta value on these securities is positive, and thus, there is some additional compensation paid to investors to accept the risk of losses when the market portfolio is 'down'.
13. This means that discounting the pension promise by the riskless interest rate is incorrect, but I not address this complication here.
14. Ippolito (1985).
15. Perhaps, we could think of workers as either 'super' unsecured bondholder, in the sense that the bond can be made valueless upon the firm encountering a condition short of bankruptcy, or alternatively as workers selling a call option to the firm that comes into the money upon the firm encountering a serious financial condition.
16. See note 18.
17. Even if firms do not exercise the option to cancel contingent benefits, the existence of excess assets serves as implicit collateral for general creditors of the firm. In the event of bankruptcy, overfunded pension plans can be terminated with the excess assets distributed to the creditors. Generally, their pension funding positively influences firms' credit ratings; see Carroll and Niehaus (1998).
18. Most studies have shown a relation between reversion events and the financial condition of the plan sponsor. See, for example, Mitchell and Mulherin (1989), Mittelstaedt (1989), Petersen (1992), Thomas (1989), Stone (1987), and VanDerhei (1987).
19. The common understanding about reversions stems from Section 401(a)(2) of the Internal Revenue Code, and Section 1.401–2(b) of the regulations that interpret the Code. These regulations permit 'the employer to recover at termination of the plan trust and only at the termination of the trust, any balance, *which is due to erroneous actuarial computation* [my emphasis]'.
20. For a full history of reversion law, see Stein (1989).
21. See ruling 71–152.
22. See ruling 83–52.
23. If the sponsor gives 25 per cent of the reversion to the participants (in the form of contributions to some other plan), the excise tax is reduced to 20 per cent. The reversion also is subject to the normal 34 per cent corporate tax, potentially leaving the firm only 16 cents for each dollar of reversion.
24. Plan sponsors face constraints in funding. It may be difficult to either reduce funding to the level of termination liabilities or to raise funding to equal ongoing liabilities, but sponsors have substantial flexibility in how well to fund their plans within pretty wide bounds.
25. I use a 50–50 mix of S&P returns and the Solomon bond index returns for the years 1986 through 1994. The excess return is $r = \frac{1}{2} r_s + \frac{1}{2} r_b - r_t$, where r_s is the nominal returns on S&P stocks, r_b is the nominal return on long-term corporate bonds, and r_t is the one-year treasury bill

rate. All data are from Ibbotson Associates, Stocks, Bonds, Bills and Inflation (1998). Since pension data reflect beginning-year values, the returns I use are lagged one year to correspond to the observations on pension funding.

26. One idea we can rule out is the notion that defunding might reflect attempts by firms trying to defend themselves against a threatened takeover: The *raison d'être* of reversion taxes is to prevent the excess from being used for corporate purposes.

27. Maturity refers to how many young workers are in the firm compared to older workers and retirees. Plans that have disproportionate numbers of young workers means that wage projections in ongoing benefits are important, which makes the difference between legal and ongoing benefits quite large. Since contribution rules are tied to ongoing benefits, assets in the plan normally are much higher relative to termination liabilities (the index used in Figure 8.3), as compared to plans that have mostly older workers and retirees.

28. Numerous restrictions have been made to limit the amount of overfunding in defined benefit plans. Most of these are redundant to the full funding limit of 1988. For a more complete description of all the limits, see ERISA Industry Committee (1996); also see Hustead (1989).

29. Effective in 1988, Congress enacted a new full funding limit on defined benefit plans, which imposed the 150 per cent limit. Prior to this time, they were permitted to fund for ongoing benefits. Numerous other restrictions have been made to limit the amount of overfunding in defined benefit plans. Most of these are redundant to the full funding limit of 1988. For a complete description of various interferences in pension funding and other regulations, see ERISA Industry Committee (1996).

30. My estimates suggest that new full funding limits were of minor importance, once account was taken of reversion taxes, a result consistent with Gale (1994). If the reversion tax were eliminated, and sponsors reverted to their pre-reversion tax contribution behavior then the impact of the limits would become binding for many more firms, thereby leading to larger marginal effects.

31. The account is a bookkeeping entry, which records the opening balance, plus new contributions made by the employer plus interest, but the assets backing the accounts are still held in a pool managed by the sponsor. The earnings credited to each account typically do not reflect actual earnings in the fund, but are guaranteed the interest rate as stated in the plan document. Thus, there is some chance that the overall fund could have less money than the sum of the 'accounts'.

32. ERISA, or The Employee Retirement Income Security Act of 1974, is the basis for much regulation of private pensions; it includes oversight of fiduciary, vesting, disclosure and funding issues, and authorizes the Pension Benefit Guaranty Corporation to provide mandatory pension insurance to all defined benefit plans. Termination benefits are regulated in non-forfeiture rules.

33. The ERISA benefit is that amount that is owed workers if the plan terminated immediately. Sometimes, the plan credits some participants' accounts with something less than this amount, but if the employee quits, he cannot receive a benefit with a value less than his accrued benefit at the time of his departure. Legally, the plan does not set up individual accounts for the participants, but instead maintains a pooled asset account that may hold investment instruments entirely different than the guaranteed return stated in the plan. But the plan reports 'account values' to participants as though they have individually owned accounts.

34. When the amendment is made, the sponsor calculates the present value of legal pension liabilities and creates individual account balances usually in these amounts. Assets beyond these amounts ('excess assets') are retained in the plan. The firm awards future contributions to each worker's account on the basis of some formula (often a per cent of pay). The key feature of the cash balance plan is that it requires only an amendment to the plan, not termination, and thus does not trigger the reversion tax on excess assets in the plan. The firm can make future contributions to employees' accounts from excess assets.

35. This estimate is based on about 50 per cent of records received for that year. The 1999 cycle is the first in which the questions asked whether defined benefit plans in fact are cash balance. Cash balance conversions are concentrated in larger plans.

36. The expected value of compensation in the DB firms is $(1 - v)[2/(2 - v)] + v/(2 - v) = 1$.

37. Absent binding language, if the firm and union allow an agreement to expire, without replacing it in the interim then technically the firm might be able to terminate the pension. Presumably, the

union could react in ways that could make this action costly for the firm. These events must be exceedingly rare.

REFERENCES

Carroll, T. and G. Niehaus (1998), 'Pension Plan Funding and Corporate Debt Ratings', *Journal of Risk and Insurance,* **65**, 427–44.

Clark, R. and A. McDermed (1990), *The Choice of Pension Plans in a Changing Environment*, Washington, DC, American Enterprise Institute.

EBRI Databook on Employee Benefits (1997), Washington, DC, Employee Benefits Research Institute.

Elliot, K. and J. Moore (2000), 'Cash Balance Pension Plans: The New Wave', *Compensation and Working Conditions*, **5**, 3–11.

ERISA Industry Committee (1996), 'Getting the Job Done: A White Paper on Emerging Pension Issues', Washington, DC.

Gale, W. (1994), 'Public Policies and Private Pension Contributions', *Journal of Money, Credit and Banking*, **26**, 710–34.

Gustman, A. and T. Steinmeier (1992), 'The Stampede Towards Defined Contribution Plans', *Industrial Relations*, **31**, 361-9.

Gustman, A., O. Mitchell and T. Steinmeier (1994), 'The Role of Pensions in the Labor Market: A Survey of the Literature', *Industrial Labor Relations Review*, **47**, 417–38.

Hanushek, E. and N. Maritato (1996), *Assessing Knowledge of Retirement Behavior*, Washington DC: National Academy Press.

Hustead, E. (1990), *Pension Plan Expense Study for the PBGC*, Washington, DC: Hay Huggins Co.

Hustead, E. (1989), *OBRA 1987: The Impact of Limiting Contributions to Defined Benefit Plans*, Washington, DC: Hay Huggins Co.

Ippolito, R.A. (2002), 'Replicating Default Risk in a Defined Benefit Pension Plan', *Financial Analysts Journal*, **58**, 31–41.

Ippolito, R.A. (2001), 'Reversion Taxes, Contingent Benefits and The Decline in Pension Funding', *Journal of Law and Economics*, **44**, 199–232.

Ippolito, R.A. (1997), *Pension Plans and Employee Performance*, Chicago: University of Chicago Press.

Ippolito, R.A. (1985), 'The Economic Function of Underfunded Pension Plans', *Journal of Law and Economics*, **28**, 611–51.

Ippolito, R.A. and J. Thompson (2000), 'The Survival Rate of Defined Benefit Plans', *Industrial Relations*, **39**, 228–45.

Ippolito, R.A. and W. James (1992), 'LBOs, Reversions and Implicit Contracts', *Journal of Finance*, **47**, 139–67.

Kruse, D. (1995), 'Pension Substitution in the 1980s: Why the Shift Towards Defined Contribution Plans?', *Industrial Relations*, **34**, 218–41.

McGill, D. (1970), *Guarantee Fund for Private Pension Obligations*, Homewood, IL: Richard D. Irwin.

Mitchell, M. and J.H. Mulherin (1989), 'The Stock Price Response to Pension Terminations and the Relation of Terminations with Corporate Takeovers', *Financial Management*, **18**, 41–56.

Mittelstaedt, H.F. (1989), 'An Empirical Analysis of the Factors Underlying the Decision to Remove Excess Assets from Overfunded Pension Plans', *Journal of Accounting and Economics*, **11**, 399–418.

Niehaus, G. and T. Yu (2000), *Cash Balance Plan Conversions: An Implicit Contract Perspective*, University of South Carolina.

Papke, L., M. Petersen and J. Poterba (1996), 'Did 401k Plans Replace Other Employer-Provided Pensions?' In D. Wise (ed.) *Further Studies in the Economics of Aging*, Chicago: University of Chicago Press, 219–236.

Petersen, M.A. (1992), 'Pension Terminations and Worker-Shareholder Wealth Transfers', *Quarterly Journal of Economics*, **107**, 1033–56.

Quinn, J., R. Burkhauser and D. Myers (1990), *Passing the Torch: The Influence of Economic Incentives on Work and Retirement*, Kalamazoo, MI: Upjohn Institute.

Shleifer, A. and L. Summers (1988), 'Breach of Trust in Hostile Takeovers', in A. Auerbach (ed.) (1988), *Corporate Takeovers: Causes and Consequences*, Chicago: University of Chicago Press.

Stein, N. (1989), 'Reversions from Pension Plans: History, Policies, and Prospects', *New York University Tax Law Review*, **44**, 259.

Stone, M. (1987), 'A Financing Explanation for Overfunded Pension Plan Terminations', *Journal of Accounting Research*, **25**, 317–26.

Thomas, J. (1989), 'Why Do Firms Terminate Overfunded Pension Plans?', *Journal of Accounting and Economics*, **11**, 361–98.

US Congress (1976), Senate. Committee on Labor and Public Welfare. Subcommittee on Labor. 'Legislative History of ERISA', 3 Vols. 94th Cong., 2d sess.

US Department of Labor (1999), 'Employee Benefits in Medium and Large Private Establishments 1997', Bureau of Labor Statistics Bulletin, **2517**.

VanDerhei, J. (1987), 'The Effect of Voluntary Terminations of Overfunded Pension Plans on Shareholder Wealth', *Journal of Risk and Insurance*, **54**, 131–56.

9. Occupational pensions and job mobility in the European Union[*]

Vincenzo Andrietti

9.1 INTRODUCTION

Pension portability reforms undertaken in recent years in European Union (EU) countries have often been inspired by the need for a more mobile labour force to adjust rapidly to shifts in demand (an efficiency argument). Motivating portability reforms on efficiency grounds is consistent with the 'spot contract view' of the labour market[1] where the lack of pension portability is seen as a causal determinant of the lower turnover rate of pension workers. However, such an interpretation does not receive unanimous support in the literature. First, within the implicit contract paradigm dominating labour economics literature in the last two decades, non-portable pensions can raise productivity by preserving productive job matches, stimulating investments in workers, or creating incentives for workers not to shirk. Second, there is a lack of consensus in the empirical literature regarding the role played by financial disincentives (pension losses), compensation premiums and self-selection in explaining the lower mobility rates of pension workers. Finally, most of the empirical literature analyses US data producing evidence which cannot be directly applied to countries characterized by rather different occupational pension systems.

---

[*] This chapter has been awarded the 'Premio de Investigación Cátedra Uni2 – Complutense de Economía Europea de 2001'. Financial support from a *Marie Curie Fellowship* of the European Community programme *Improving Human Potential* under contract number HPMF-CT-2000–00504 and from the Center for Research on Pensions and Welfare Policies (CeRP) is gratefully acknowledged. I am indebted to Vincent Hildebrand and Franco Peracchi for their helpful comments on previous drafts of this chapter. The usual disclaimer applies.

Although the issue of pension portability has been high on the EU policy agenda in the last two decades, no comparative studies have been produced to support the ongoing policy discussion with empirical evidence. At the EU level, the application of workers' freedom of movement principle would require full portability of pension rights between countries, on the assumption that portability losses would prevent an efficient rate of job mobility in the EU area. The empirical analysis we propose in this chapter aims to answer the following question: does a lack of pension portability represent an impediment to within-country mobility in EU countries? A positive answer would imply reframing the EU policy discussion in terms of within-borders portability as a necessary first step to achieve cross-borders portability. Alternatively, if portability constraints were found to have no effect at country-specific level, there would still be reason to suspect the lack of cross-borders portability arrangements to be an impediment for the mobility of labour between countries. While the latter hypothesis cannot be investigated with currently available data, very little empirical research has been produced to evaluate the effects of occupational pensions and their portability rules on job mobility choices within EU countries. The main aim of this chapter is to fill this gap using recent releases of data from the European Community Household Panel (ECHP) survey. The analysis is limited to four EU Member States – Denmark, Ireland, the Netherlands and the United Kingdom – where occupational pension plans play an important role in the provision of retirement income, covering a large portion of the private sector workforce. We find that, among the countries under study, pension-covered workers are significantly less likely to move only in the United Kingdom, while pension portability losses do not generally act as a significant impediment to labour mobility. Although these results are consistent with the pension portability options guaranteed by defined contribution (DC) plans in Denmark and by industry-wide and company defined benefit (DB) plans in the Netherlands, they provide some surprising evidence for the United Kingdom and for Ireland, where DB employer provided pensions typically have limited portability. The finding of positive wage premiums accruing to pension workers in the latter two countries is rather consistent with the view that individuals are simply less likely to leave 'good' jobs (jobs offering a pension plan as well as a better wage profile).

The chapter is organized as follows. The next section outlines the issue of pension portability and reviews the related empirical literature. Section 9.3 summarizes legislation regulating occupational pensions portability at EU as well as at national level. Section 9.4 introduces the empirical model of interfirm job mobility. Section 9.5 discusses the data. Section 9.6 presents the results. Section 9.7 concludes.

9.2   PENSION PORTABILITY

Pension portability can be defined as the capacity of workers covered by an occupational pension plan[2] to carry the actuarially fair value of their accrued rights from one job to the next. When a mover is not entitled to full preservation of his/her accrued rights, either in the old or in the new scheme, pension portability is not guaranteed and a portability loss is expected to arise. The latter can be defined as the shortfall of actual retirement benefits from those that would have been paid if there had been no change in scheme membership as a consequence of job separations during the career. Occupational pension plans, independently of their nature and subject to country-specific pension regulations, usually define a vesting period representing the minimum length of service to be completed in order to obtain pension rights' entitlement. Workers leaving the plan before completion of the vesting period forfeit their pension rights. Portability losses related to vesting are usually small in magnitude, given the short length of the vesting period, while portability losses arising to vested early leavers could be sizeable.   In this respect, the distinction between DB and DC plans becomes relevant. In DC plans employer contributions are accumulated into individual accounts and invested on behalf of the employee. The annual pension accrual rate[3] is constant over the worker career, and vested workers are entitled to an actuarially fair lump-sum distribution of their accrued rights upon leaving. Alternatively, DB plans are characterized by a 'backloaded' structure of pension rights' accrual.[4] In a traditional DB plan the sponsoring employer promises to the worker the payment of a pension annuity of the following form:

$$P(R) = b(R - t_{k-1})W(R), \qquad\qquad (9.1)$$

where $P(R)$ is the pension annuity accrued at retirement age R, $(R - t_{k-1})$ represents the years of pensionable service accumulated at retirement, b is the annual (percentage) accrual rate and $W(R)$ is the wage earned immediately before retirement. Pension contributions paid in the early years of membership will generally be set at a higher level than is required to fund pension benefits on the basis of the individual's current salary, because the actuary will anticipate salary increases which can be expected in the future. Where an individual leaves prior to pensionable age, he/she will accordingly have paid too much for the benefit to which he/she is entitled, given that upon leaving the pension rights accrued under the scheme freeze and do not grow in line with any other salary increases which he/she may receive from subsequent employment. This actuarial practice is consistent with the implicit pension contract view (Ippolito, 1985), which predicts a portability loss proportional to the difference between retirement and separation wages arising to early leavers. Alternatively, the spot pension contract view, proposed by Bulow (1982), argues that pension contributions are determined on the basis of current wage earnings, and therefore no portability loss arises to early leavers. Ippolito (1985) and Kotlikoff and Wise (1985) provide empirical evidence supporting the implicit contract view of pensions. Following this approach, the value of pension rights that the worker would be entitled to if he/she stays with the firm until retirement – the *Stay Pension Wealth* – calculated at time t_k is based on current service, $(t_k - t_{k-1})$, and retirement wage earnings, $W(R) = W(t_k)e^{g^e(R-t_k)}$:

$$P^{Stay} = b(t_k - t_{k-1})A(t_k)W(t_k)e^{g^e(R-t_k)}e^{-i^e(R-t_k)} \qquad (9.2)$$

where $A(t_k)$ is the annuity factor transforming the pension annuity into pension wealth, i^e is the long term expected discount rate at which the pension annuity is discounted from retirement to current age and g^e is the expected rate of nominal wage growth. The value of pension rights that the worker would be entitled to upon leaving a DB plan before retirement – the *Leave Pension Wealth* – calculated at time t_k is based on current service, $(t_k - t_{k-1})$, and current wage, $W(t_k)$:

$$P^{Leave} = b(t_k - t_{k-1})A(t_k)W(t_k)e^{-i^e(R-t_k)}. \qquad (9.3)$$

Assuming that pension-covered movers immediately find another job with the same pension plan and with the same wage profile, and that $g^e = i^e$, the portability loss arising to vested workers is defined as:

$$P^{Loss} = P^{Stay} - P^{Leave} = b(t_k - t_{k-1})A(t_k)W(t_k)(1 - e^{-i^e(R-t_k)}), \qquad (9.4)$$

while for unvested workers, the portability loss is defined as:

$$P^{Loss} = P^{Stay} = b(t_k - t_{k-1})A(t_k)W(t_k). \qquad (9.5)$$

The pension portability loss has a concave shape relative to age. Its basic pattern does not depend upon the worker joining the firm at any specific age or upon actuarial assumptions, although the latter two affect its magnitude. The 'new pension economics' literature of the early 1990s includes pension portability loss[5] as well as compensation premiums accruing to pension-covered workers[6] or self-selection of workers into pension-covered jobs[7] as potential explanations to the well-documented low mobility rate for pension-covered workers.[8] In Allen *et al.* (1993) pension portability losses are assumed to act both as a mobility deterrent for pension-covered workers and as a self-selection device, inducing 'stable' workers to join pension-covered jobs while screening out workers who are likely to quit or to be laid off. Estimating a switching bivariate probit model of pension coverage and turnover on 1975–82 PSID data, Allen, *et al.* (1993) conclude that the main reason why a lower turnover rate is observed among workers participating in DB plans seems to be the prospect of a pension wealth loss. In contrast, they find little evidence of sorting on unobservables. A different research approach, similar to the one adopted in this chapter, is followed by Gustman and Steinmeier (1993). They question the causal interpretation usually attributed to the strong negative correlation between portability losses and job mobility suggesting, as an alternative explanation, that implicit contracts may provide the payment of compensation premiums to pension-covered workers. Using the 1984 release of the SIPP data, Gustman and Steinmeier (1993) model the individual job mobility decision as depending on current as well as on alternative job lifetime wage earnings, on a constructed pension backloading variable and on a set of other regressors proxying mobility costs. Imposing joint normality on the wage and the mobility equation error terms, they estimate the model through a maximum likelihood procedure. However, their self-selection mechanism differs from standard switching regression models with endogenous switching, including the one presented in this chapter. In particular, Gustman and Steinmeier (1993) assume a different definition of actual and counterfactual wages: stayers' wages are observed for all individuals in period one job, while the alternative (mover) wages are observed only for those who have changed job between period one and period two. These assumptions allow them to compute an actual wage differential for movers (as opposed to the usual one derived from counterfactuals imputation) while providing enough information to estimate an additional parameter – the correlation among unobservables in the current and alternative wage equations – which is not identifiable in the standard setting of a switching regression model with endogenous switching. Their empirical findings suggest that efficiency wage premiums rather than backloaded pension accrual patterns are the primary cause for the lower turnover rates of workers covered by DB pension plans. Similar results are provided by Andrietti and Hildebrand (2001) estimating the model presented here on SIPP pooled panel data covering the period 1984–94.

Empirical models have mainly been tested on US data, while there is almost no evidence on pension-mobility patterns for EU countries.[9] The main aim of the chapter is to fill this gap, using recent available releases of data from the European Community Household Panel (ECHP) survey.

9.3 PENSION PORTABILITY IN EU COUNTRIES

For EU countries an institutional argument adds to the traditional economic portability arguments. The principle of workers' freedom of movement, stated by the Treaty of Rome, calls for the elimination of any obstacle to labour mobility. Accordingly, a directive was recently issued[10] aiming to preserve the supplementary pension rights of workers moving within the EU area. Although the directive reaffirms the principle that each worker should be able to move to a job in another Member State without suffering portability losses from occupational pension arrangements, it is still unclear how to reach this objective. Indeed, a necessary preliminary step for cross-borders portability – often overlooked in policy discussions – is to achieve full portability within countries. Under this perspective, it becomes important to analyse the effect of pension plans and their portability rules on labour mobility in a sample of EU countries characterized by different occupational pension arrangements. In this section we describe the legislation regulating pension portability in the countries under study and applied to within-country mobility.[11] This is also summarized in Table 9.3.

Denmark
In Denmark, the typical plan is DC. Vesting usually depends upon the contractual scheme's nature. Private pension funds, regulated by the *Pensions and Savings Fund Act*, provide immediate vesting rights for employees' contributions, while employer contributions are vested only after five years. Group insurance arrangements, regulated by the *Tax on Pension Schemes Act*, require a minimum age of 30 for early leavers as a further condition for full vesting. Employees are entitled to a tax-free transfer value once they move job.

Ireland
In Ireland the 1990 *Pension Act* requires full vesting after five years of scheme membership of which two are after 1 January 1991. Moreover, vested workers leaving a DB scheme from 1 January 1996, are entitled to deferred retirement benefits indexed to the Consumer Price Index up to a 4 per cent maximum. As an alternative to deferred benefits, early leavers have the right to request the transfer of their accrued pension rights to a new employer's pension scheme or to a Life Assurance Company Retirement Bond.

The Netherlands
In the Netherlands the vesting period is set to one year. In the case of a worker leaving before the required vesting period, he/she is entitled to a refund of his/her own contributions. Employers are not required to index

deferred pension benefits or pensions in payment. Early leavers' deferred benefits are usually voluntarily indexed by sponsoring employers. However, indexation of preserved benefits is required whenever the scheme provides indexation for pensions in payment. Substantial changes in employer-provided pension regulation aiming to improve pension portability were introduced in 1987 and in 1994. The 1987 *Pensions and Savings Fund Act* introduced the obligation for pension schemes to entitle early leavers with a deferred benefit proportional to the length of plan membership. Moreover, occupational pension members changing job after July 1994 have been given the statutory right of transferring their accrued rights to another pension scheme. In the Netherlands, portability of pension rights differs between industry-wide plans and company pension plans. Industry-wide plans guarantee portability of pensionable service within a particular industry, enabling workers to change jobs without losing service credit when they resume work with another employer in the plan. Alternatively, company pension plans satisfying particular requisites can transfer deferred benefits of their workers through five portability clearing-houses called 'transfer circuits'. A job leaver has the option of keeping the vested rights in the former employer's plan or to use a clearing-house for transferring them to the new employer's plan. Again, these transfer circuits operate for company plans within a particular industry, so that only people moving jobs within a particular industry are not penalized.

The United Kingdom
A number of legislative changes have contributed to improve the situation of early leavers over the last 25 years. Before 1975, early leavers in the United Kingdom had no legal right to transfer their accrued pension entitlements to a new scheme or even to have a deferred pension from their old scheme. Under the current rules, the vesting period is set at two years of pension plan membership. In particular, vested early leavers from DB plans can have their accrued rights preserved in the pension scheme as deferred benefits, to be revalued until retirement guaranteeing a minimum Limited Price Indexation in line with the Retail Price Index (RPI), up to a maximum of 5 per cent. Alternatively they can take a tax-free transfer value to a different occupational pension scheme (either DB or DC) or to an approved personal pension or purchase a retirement annuity.

9.4   THE MODEL

The model presented in this section[12] focuses on the role played by structural wage differentials and expected portability losses in the job mobility decision, while testing for the existence of compensation premiums accruing to pension workers. We assume exogeneity of pension participation choices but we account for potential selectivity bias arising when the individual mobility choice is endogenous due to potential correlation between the unobservables determining the choice and alternative prospective wages. The model is based on a binary representation of the job mobility decision. Individuals in the sample are assumed to observe the lifetime wage earnings profile in their current job as well as in their next best alternative. They also perceive a variety of pecuniary and non-pecuniary mobility costs either due to the loss of accumulated firm-specific human capital or to family and relocation costs. In addition, workers participating in DB plans expect to suffer a pension wealth loss while moving to a new job, due to the limited portability of their accrued pension rights. The mobility choice of individual i is represented by the binary random variable $I_i = 1\{I_i^* > 0\}$, where $1\{\}$ is the usual indicator function and I_i^* is the lifetime net gain from mobility. We specify the latter as follows:

$$I_i^* \equiv Y_{mi} - Y_{si} - C_i \underset{<}{\overset{>}{\quad}} 0, \quad i = 1,....n, \qquad (9.6)$$

where Y_{mi} is the expected present value of lifetime earnings on the assumption that the individual moves into his/her best alternative job, Y_{si} is the expected present value of lifetime earnings on the assumption that the individual remains in his/her current job, C_i is the expected present value of costs associated with mobility. The individual mobility choice in (9.6) is based on an *ex ante* comparison. The individual moves to a different job if his/her expected lifetime earnings gains exceed mobility costs. Otherwise he/she stays in his/her current job.

In representing the individual decision empirically we have two main problems. First, we do not observe lifetime wage earnings for actual movers and stayers. We assume current earnings to be the best predictor of lifetime earnings. The second problem is that we cannot observe the counterfactual wage for each individual, that is what the individual would have earned had he/she taken the alternative mobility choice. What we observe is the wage conditional on the choice actually taken. In order to obtain predictions of the counterfactual wage for each individual we use the estimated coefficients of the actual movers and stayers. Given that the event $\{I_i^* > 0\}$ is equivalent to the event $\{I_i^+ = I_i^* / Y_{si} > 0\}$ and that mobility costs are not directly observable, we can specify the selection index as follows:

$$I_i^* = \gamma(\ln Y_{mi} - \ln Y_{si}) - \boldsymbol{\beta}_c' \mathbf{X}_{ci} - v_{ci}, \quad i = 1,....n, \qquad (9.7)$$

where $\mathbf{X}_{ci}$ is a vector of personal and job specific mobility costs predictors, $\boldsymbol{\beta}_c$ is a vector of unknown parameters, and v_{ci} is a continuous random variable distributed independently of $\mathbf{X}_{ci}$ with zero mean and variance σ_c^2. Wage equations for movers and stayers are modelled using a semilog form:

$$\ln Y_{mi} = \boldsymbol{\beta}_m' \mathbf{X}_i + v_{mi} \quad i = 1,....m, \tag{9.8}$$

$$\ln Y_{si} = \boldsymbol{\beta}_s' \mathbf{X}_i + v_{si} \quad i = m+1,....n, \tag{9.9}$$

where $\ln Y_{mi}$ is the natural logarithm of hourly net wage for movers, $\ln Y_{si}$ is the natural logarithm of hourly net wage for stayers, $\mathbf{X}_i$ is a vector of personal and job specific variables including education level, gender, experience and its square, occupational pension participation, type of contract, industry, occupation and employer size dummies, $\boldsymbol{\beta}_m, \boldsymbol{\beta}_s$ are vectors of unknown parameters, and v_{mi}, v_{si} are continuous random errors containing unobservable variables, such as individual abilities and specific capital that are useful in the chosen job, distributed independently of $\mathbf{X}_i$ with zero mean and unknown variances σ_m^2, σ_s^2. Equations (9.7), (9.8), and (9.9) represent our structural model of interfirm job mobility. Substituting from (9.8) and (9.9) into (9.7) yields a reduced form selection index:

$$I_i^* \equiv \boldsymbol{\beta}' \mathbf{W}_i + v_i \quad i = 1,....n, \tag{9.10}$$

where $\mathbf{W}_i = [\mathbf{X}_i, \mathbf{X}_{ci}]$, $\boldsymbol{\beta} = [\gamma(\boldsymbol{\beta}_m - \boldsymbol{\beta}_s) - \boldsymbol{\beta}_c]$, and $v_i = (\gamma(v_{mi} - v_{si}) - v_{ci})$. The decision rule (9.10) selects individuals into movers and stayers according to their largest expected present value. Therefore, wages actually observed in each group are not random samples of the population but truncated samples. Selectivity bias in wage equations estimation arises from any correlation between the unobserved determinants of mobility choices and wages. Only if such a correlation were not present, the usual ordinary least square method could be used to consistently estimate the wage equation parameters on the selected subsample. In general, however, this does not occur. Consistent estimates of the above model are obtained using Heckman's (1979) two-step correction. It is assumed that the error terms (v_{mi}, v_{si}, v_i) are independent of $(\mathbf{X}_i, \mathbf{W}_i)$ and have a trivariate normal distribution, with a zero mean vector and unknown variance covariance matrix:

$$\Sigma = \begin{bmatrix} \sigma_m^2 & \sigma_{sm} & \sigma_{vm} \\ \sigma_{ms} & \sigma_s^2 & \sigma_{vs} \\ \sigma_{mv} & \sigma_{sv} & 1 \end{bmatrix},$$

where v_i is assumed to have a unit variance, since the parameters of the reduced form probit equation (9.10) are estimable only up to a scale factor. Estimation of selection corrected wage equations allows us to predict wages for actual movers and stayers as well as to impute counterfactual wages for each individual's unobserved mobility status, conditional on his/her own observed characteristics:

$$\ln \tilde{Y}_{mi} = \hat{\beta}'_m X_i + \hat{\sigma}_{mv} \hat{\lambda}_{mi} , \quad i = 1,....n, \tag{9.11}$$

$$\ln \tilde{Y}_{si} = \hat{\beta}'_s X_i + \hat{\sigma}_{sv} \hat{\lambda}_{si} , \quad i = 1,....n, \tag{9.12}$$

where $\hat{\lambda}_{si}$ and $\hat{\lambda}_{mi}$ are the inverse Mills' ratios – estimated from the first-step reduced form probit – accounting for non randomness of job mobility choices. The following step is to compute the individual *ex ante* structural wage differential:

$$\ln \tilde{Y}_{mi} - \ln \tilde{Y}_{si} = \left(\hat{\beta}'_m - \hat{\beta}'_s \right) X_i + \left(\hat{\sigma}_{mv} \hat{\lambda}_{mi} - \hat{\sigma}_{sv} \hat{\lambda}_{si} \right), \quad i = 1,....n, \tag{9.13}$$

The first term on the right-hand side of (9.13) represents differences between systematic components of wages in the alternative and in the current job, while the second term accounts for random differences not captured by wage equations but important in determining the mobility choice. The imputed wage differential is then substituted in (9.7) to obtain a structural probit equation:

$$I_i^* = \gamma (\ln \tilde{Y}_{mi} - \ln \tilde{Y}_{si}) - \beta'_c X_{ci} + \varepsilon_i, \quad i = 1,....n, \tag{9.14}$$

where: $\varepsilon_i = \gamma (\hat{v}_{mi} - \hat{v}_{si}) - v_{ci}$.

Maximum likelihood estimation of equation (9.14) allows us to obtain estimates of the structural parameters related to the main determinants of the individual mobility choice. The model requires identifying exclusion restrictions. In particular, identification of wage equations parameters requires that at least one exogenous variable belonging to the vector X_{ci} be not contained in X_i.[13] In our model, some of the variables determining mobility costs can be assumed not to directly affect the wage determination process and are therefore excluded from wage equation.[14] An F-test of their joint significance supports their validity as joint instruments for the job mobility choice.

9.5   DATA: THE ECHP SURVEY

The European Community Household Panel (ECHP) survey is a standardized, multi-purpose, annual longitudinal survey[15] collected since 1994 in most of the EU Member States under Eurostat coordination. It is structured in the form of annual interviews to a selected representative sample of household members in each country. Our empirical analysis is limited to a sample of four countries – Denmark, Ireland, the Netherlands and the United Kingdom – where occupational pensions play a major role in the provision of retirement income. For each country a longitudinal dataset linking wave 2 (1995) to wave 3 (1996) has been used. We have selected a sample of individuals aged between 20 and 59 employed for at least 30 hours per week (full-time) in the private, non agricultural sector at the beginning of the observation period. Job mobility is defined as a change of employer between interview dates without an intervening spell of unemployment. Only transitions to full-time jobs are considered. Under this definition job mobility can be interpreted as the outcome of individuals' maximizing behaviour.[16] After dropping from the sample individuals with missing information in the relevant variables as well as those experiencing a job move with an intervening spell of unemployment (interpreted here as an involuntary move) we were left with: 1040 observations for Denmark, 943 observations for Ireland, 1542 observations for the Netherlands and 1017 observations for the United Kingdom.

For the purposes of our analysis we need to know if the worker was covered by an occupational pension plan at the time when the job mobility decision was taken, and, if that is the case, to obtain a description of the plan design and characteristics. From the second wave (1995) ECHP respondents were asked: 'Are you a member of a job-related or occupational pension scheme?' and: 'Do you contribute at present to a private pension scheme?', where private pension scheme refers here to individual voluntary retirement plans offered by private sector financial institutions. Occupational and private pensions participation rates – defined on a base of full-time private sector employees – are reported in Table 9.1. Relying on occupational pension participation figures we can divide the countries under consideration in two groups. In Denmark and in the Netherlands occupational pension plans have been established mainly at industry-wide level through employers' federations and trade unions. The high degree of union coverage and the mandatory nature of participation in industry-wide funds have guaranteed pension coverage of large sections (around 80 per cent) of the private sector workforce. Ireland and the United Kingdom belong to a second group of countries that seem to have followed a different pattern of development, with participation rates ranging between 40 and 50 per cent. These lower participation rates can be explained by the fact that occupational pension plan provision/participation has been preserved as an employer/employee choice. The figures are consistent with those provided by national and EU sources reported in Table 9.2.

Table 9.1 Occupational and private pension participation

	Denmark	Ireland	Netherlands	UK
Occupational Pension Plan	77.4	40.2	80.4	50.1
Private Pension Plan	46.7	8.5	12.8	25.7
Sample Size	1040	943	1542	1017

Base: Full Time Private Sector Employees.
Source: Our Elaboration on ECHP 1995 data.

Table 9.2 Participation by pension plan type in EU countries

	Denmark*	Ireland**	Netherlands*	UK***
Defined Benefit Plan	1	32	84	40
Defined Contribution Plan	79	10	1	10
Occupational Pension Plan	80	42	85	50

Sources:
* Commission of the European Communities (1997).
** Hughes and Nolan (1996).
*** Government Actuary's Department (2000).

Table 9.2 also reports pension participation rates by plan type for the countries under consideration. DB plans are dominant in all countries except Denmark, where almost only DC plans are found. Given that our data do not provide any information on the nature of the plan, for the purposes of our empirical analysis we assume that all pension-covered workers participate in DC plans in Denmark and in DB plans in the remaining countries. The calculation of pension portability losses is based on the typical DB plan found in each country, whose characteristics are reported in Table 9.3.[17] These assumptions seem to be a reasonable approximation, given the low proportion of workers covered by DC plans in Ireland, in the Netherlands and in the United Kingdom, and given the fact that the tight legal and administrative regulation of occupational pension plans as well as competition between pension funds has led to a considerable degree of similarity between the features of most DB schemes in these countries.

Tables 9.4 to 9.7 provide some preliminary empirical evidence on the relationship among job mobility rates, occupational pension participation and wages in the countries under consideration. First, in all the countries under consideration but Denmark there is evidence of a negative relationship

Table 9.3 Portability rules and assumptions for calculation of pension losses

	Ireland	Netherlands	UK
Annual Accrual Rate	1/60	1.75%	1/60
Pensionable Wage	Final Wage	Final Wage	Final Wage
Retirement Age	60	60	60
Inflation Rate*	2.5%	1.9%	3.4%
Post-Retirement Benefits Indexation	0.5 (CPI)	0.5 (CPI)	RPI up to 3.5
Vesting Period	5 years	1 year	2 years
Early Leavers' Indexation	No	Yes – Optional	Inflation up to 5%
Transfer to Another Employer Provided Plan	Legal Right	Legal Right	Legal Right
		Transfer Circuits	
		Industry-wide Plans	
Long Term Nominal Interest Rate*	8.2%	6.9%	8.2%

Source:
* OECD (1999).

between pension participation and job mobility. A second piece of evidence is that in all the countries under consideration but Denmark pension workers, either stayers or movers, are better-paid than no-pension workers. This could reflect either worker- or job-specific attributes. If the entire wage differential between workers with and without an occupational pension was due to individual characteristics, such as unmeasured ability, the wage on any alternative job would be identical to the current one, and no wage losses would result from a move. If wage on the current job was instead just a reflection of job-specific rather than personal characteristics, identical workers would be paid more on pension jobs than on no-pension jobs, either as a result of rent-sharing or because of some productivity-enhancing scheme requiring efficiency wage payments. In the empirical model we test for the existence of compensating wage premiums accruing to pension workers by means of occupational pension participation dummy variables in the wage equations.

Table 9.4 Denmark. Job mobility, wages and pension participation

	No Pension		Pension	
	Stayer	Mover	Stayer	Mover
Observations	209	26	730	75
Mobility (%)	11.06		9.32	
Mobility (%) to Pension Job		81		89
Pearson Chi Squared Test	0.633, pr: 0.426			
Hourly wage 1995 (Euro)	7.24	6.87	7.27	7.14

Source: Our elaboration on ECHP data.

Table 9.5 Ireland. Job mobility, wages and pension participation

	No Pension		Pension	
	Stayer	Mover	Stayer	Mover
Observations	498	66	357	22
Mobility (%)	11.70		5.80	
Mobility (%) to Pension Job		14		41
Pearson Chi Squared Test	9.317, pr: 0.002			
Hourly wage 1995 (Euro)	5.85	5.75	9.09	6.65

Source: Our elaboration on ECHP data.

Table 9.6 The Netherlands. Job mobility, wages and pension participation

	No Pension		Pension	
	Stayer	Mover	Stayer	Mover
Observations	269	34	1178	61
Mobility (%)		11.22		4.92
Mobility (%) to Pension Job		38		79
Pearson Chi Squared Test		16.7, pr: 0.000		
Hourly wage 1995 (Euro)	6.11	5.28	7.66	8.1

Source: Our elaboration on ECHP data.

Table 9.7 The United Kingdom. Job mobility, wages and pension participation

	No Pension		Pension	
	Stayer	Mover	Stayer	Mover
Observations	470	37	502	8
Mobility (%)		7.30		1.57
Mobility (%) to Pension Job		22		37.5
Pearson Chi Squared Test		19.3, pr: 0.000		
Hourly wage 1995 (Euro)	6.38	5.51	8.49	8.54

Source: Our elaboration on ECHP data.

9.6   EMPIRICAL RESULTS

The empirical model is estimated under two different specifications. The first includes among the mobility costs just a dummy variable indicating occupational pension participation. For Ireland, the Netherlands and the United Kingdom, we estimate a second specification of the model including also the individual expected pension portability loss among the mobility costs. The latter specification aims to capture the role of the opportunity cost of leaving a DB plan (in terms of lost pension rights' accruals) on job mobility decisions. Given that pension participation choices are not explicitly modelled, the validity of our results rests on the assumption that selection of workers into pension jobs is based on observable variables included in our specification.

9.6.1 Reduced Form Probit Estimates

Reduced form probit estimates provide very limited information about the validity of the theoretical framework captured by equations (9.7) – (9.9), giving only the total effect of each regressor on the probability of job mobility. Moreover, the sign of most variables included in the reduced form probit equation is *a priori* uncertain, thus raising interpretation problems on estimated coefficients' values. The reduced form estimates, not reported here, are used to derive Heckman's two-steps consistent estimates of the wage equations.

9.6.2 Selectivity in Wage Equations

Tables 9.8 and 9.9 present sample-selection corrected wage equations for movers and stayers. Given that the estimated parameters are not sensitive to the different specifications adopted, we only report wages estimated under the first specification (model 1). The reported *t*-values are computed correcting the variance-covariance matrix of the estimated coefficients following the Heckman procedure.[18] Earnings equations, and consequently mobility choices, can be thought of as being affected by two kinds of variables: the observed ones and the unobserved ones. The latter two are captured by the inverse Mills' ratios. In particular, the coefficients obtained on $\hat{\lambda}_m$ and $\hat{\lambda}_s$ signal if there is positive or negative selection bias in the movers'/stayers' categories. The reported *t*-values for $\hat{\lambda}$ coefficients simply test for the null hypothesis that $\hat{\lambda}_{m,s} = 0$ (no sample selection). Unobservables play a significant role in Denmark and in Ireland, indicating negative selection of stayers. Turning to the role of pensions as wage determinants, if occupational pensions were merely a vehicle for tax-preferred retirement saving, with no implications for employee productivity, a trade-off between cash wages and pension participation should be observed. On the other hand, if workers participating in an occupational pension receive more training, are more stable, or are less likely to shirk, some of this firm-specific productivity gain will likely result in higher wages.[19] Our empirical findings are consistent with the above predictions. We find evidence that where DB pensions are dominant – Ireland, the Netherlands, the United Kingdom – stayers in occupational pensions earn a significant wage premium, while we find some insignificant evidence of a wage-pension trade-off in Denmark, where DC plans are widespread. The effect of occupational pension participation on movers' wages is not significant at standard levels in all the countries under consideration. In the context of our modelling approach it is interesting to note that occupational pension participation is associated with an individual compensation premium. The latter, determined for each individual as the difference between the coefficients on the pension participation dummies in the stayers' and movers' wage equations, turns out to range from 22 per cent in Ireland to 3.5 per cent in the United Kingdom. These findings are consistent with the Gustman and Steinmeier (1993) view that individuals are less likely to leave jobs offering occupational pensions as well as higher wages.

Table 9.8 Stayers' wage equation. Model 1

	Denmark	Ireland	Netherlands	UK
Female	−0.144	−0.166	−0.145	−0.159
	(7.44)**	(6.63)**	(9.69)**	(7.04)**
Third-Level Education	0.092	0.115	0.177	0.265
	(4.24)**	(3.44)**	(10.20)**	(9.89)**
Experience	0.016	0.022	0.021	0.024
	(4.91)**	(4.80)**	(10.07)**	(5.84)**
Experience Squared/100	−0.036	−0.037	−0.037	−0.051
	(5.17)**	(3.81)**	(7.28)**	(5.68)**
Managers and Professionals$_t$	0.252	0.283	0.233	0.307
	(9.60)**	(7.85)**	(12.35)**	(9.67)**
White Collar Workers$_t$	0.097	0.054	0.057	0.142
	(4.13)**	(1.94)*	(3.13)**	(4.89)**
Construction$_t$	0.094	0.000	−0.085	0.011
	(2.90)**	(0.00)	(3.90)**	(0.22)
Services$_t$	0.012	−0.049	−0.038	−0.019
	(0.56)	(1.91)**	(2.70)**	(0.86)
Employer Size$_t$: 100–499	0.025	0.145	0.009	0.038
	(1.26)	(5.54)**	(0.63)	(1.29)
Employer Size$_t$: 500+	0.081	0.180	0.068	0.156
	(3.40)**	(5.12)**	(4.35)**	(5.18)**
Temporary Employment Contract$_t$	−0.042	−0.006	0.002	−0.093
	(1.31)	(0.13)	(0.35)	(1.69)*
Occupational Pension Plan$_t$	−0.027	0.154	0.052	0.135
	(1.16)	(5.26)**	(3.10)**	(5.77)**
Lambda$_s$	0.321	0.282	0.06	−0.056
	(3.15)**	(1.69)*	(0.70)	(0.37)
F-Test	43.15	64.14	81.31	55.56
Adjusted *R*-squared	0.37	0.49	0.42	0.42
Number of Observations	939	855	1447	972

Table 9.9 Movers' wage equation. Model 1

	Denmark	Ireland	Netherlands	UK
Female	−0.109	−0.174	−0.175	0.012
	(1.99)**	(2.60)**	(2.94)**	(0.10)
Third-Level Education	0.012	0.220	0.231	0.289
	(0.20)	(2.70)**	(3.62)**	(2.01)**
Experience	0.003	0.011	0.009	0.013
	(0.33)	(0.88)	(1.01)	(0.53)
Experience Squared/100	−0.023	−0.022	0.01	−0.046
	(0.87)	(0.60)	(0.41)	(0.86)
Managers and Professionals$_t$	0.367	0.255	0.32	0.372
	(5.04)**	(2.69)**	(3.77)**	(2.24)**
White Collar Workers$_t$	0.085	−0.026	0.148	0.164
	(1.30)	(0.33)	(1.84)*	(1.18)
Construction$_t$	−0.038	0.270	−0.178	0.026
	(0.45)	(2.41)**	(2.09)**	(0.11)
Services$_t$	−0.039	0.079	−0.078	−0.081
	(0.53)	(1.16)	(1.22)	(0.66)
Employer Size$_t$: 100–499	−0.026	0.188	0.030	0.024
	(0.45)	(2.51)**	(0.51)	(0.20)
Employer Size$_t$: 500+	−0.009	−0.055	0.092	0.120
	(0.11)	(0.39)	(1.46)	(0.35)
Temp. Employment Contract$_t$	0.054	−0.145	−0.07	−0.20
	(0.77)	(1.55)	(0.51)	(1.39)
Occupational Pension Plan$_t$	−0.034	−0.066	0.067	0.098
	(0.52)	(0.76)	(1.26)	(0.79)
Lambda$_m$	0.095	0.174	−0.02	0.020
	(1.07)	(1.27)	(0.22)	(0.22)
F-test	3.69	5.44	8.09	1.65
Adjusted R-squared	0.26	0.40	0.50	0.16
Number of Observations	101	88	95	45

9.6.3 Structural Probit Estimates

Maximum likelihood estimation of the individual probability of interfirm job mobility, as expressed by the structural probit equation (9.14) allows us to disentangle the structural coefficients of the mobility costs equation.[20] For each country a likelihood ratio test of the overall fit of model specification leads to rejection of the null hypothesis that all slope coefficients are equal to zero. The results relative to model 1 are reported in Table 9.10.

Table 9.10 Structural form probit equation. Model 1

	Denmark	Ireland	Netherlands	UK
Wage Differential	0.083	0.223	0.57	−0.381
	(0.66)	(2.45)**	(0.50)	(4.35)**
Not Married	0.002	−0.017	−0.016	−0.011
	(0.10)	(0.63)	(1.22)	(1.16)
Female	−0.032	−0.015	−0.007	0.101
	(1.87)*	(0.87)	(0.53)	(3.55)**
Children	0.010	−0.018	0.034	−0.001
	(0.48)	(0.82)	(1.78)*	(0.05)
Household Size	0.001	0.007	−0.013	−0.005
	(0.15)	(1.33)	(1.78)*	(1.21)
House Tenant	0.042	0.002	−0.021	−0.004
	(1.77)*	(0.08)	(1.88)*	(0.41)
Age	−0.003	−0.014	−0.001	−0.005
	(0.69)	(2.75)**	(0.78)	(1.72)*
Third-Level Education	0.006	0.014	0.006	0.039
	(0.33)	(0.47)	(0.33)	(2.35)**
Experience	0.004	0.008	−0.000	−0.001
	(0.87)	(1.38)	(0.18)	(0.22)
Experience Squared/100	−0.014	0.004	−0.005	0.003
	(1.83)*	(0.43)	(0.53)	(0.89)
Employer Size$_{t-1}$: 100–499	−0.022	0.008	−0.004	−0.019
	(1.18)	(0.44)	(0.38)	(1.97)**
Employer Size$_{t-1}$: 500+	−0.008	0.070	−0.001	−0.032
	(0.33)	(1.49)	(0.06)	(3.12)**
Temp. Employment Contract$_{t-1}$	0.120	0.068	0.123	−0.010
	(3.31)**	(2.05)**	(4.51)**	(0.72)
Occupational Pension Plan$_{t-1}$	−0.002	0.010	−0.011	−0.032
	(0.13)	(0.42)	(0.87)	(2.71)**
Private Pension Plan	0.009	0.002	0.027	0.010
	(0.51)	(0.07)	(1.67)*	(0.88)
Employer Provided Training	−0.034	−0.008	−0.023	−0.007
	(1.73)*	(0.44)	(2.17)**	(0.76)
Log-likelihood	−299.4	−264.8	−315.5	−151.8
Wald Chi2	69.79	67.37	68.19	56.38
Pseudo $R2$	0.0968	0.0947	0.1156	0.1764
Number of Observations	1040	943	1542	1017
Observed P	0.0971	0.0933	0.0616	0.0442
Predicted P(X)	0.0757	0.0729	0.0427	0.0229

We find that female workers are significantly less likely to change employer than their male colleagues only in Denmark. A prediction of the migration literature is that renting a house generally makes individuals more likely to move, as job change often implies a change of residence. However, this may not be true where the housing rental market is characterized by queues, such as in the Netherlands and in the United Kingdom. Our results generally support these predictions, although the estimates are statistically significant at standard levels only in Denmark and in the Netherlands. Education endows a worker with skills, increasing his/her ability to adjust to change and to gather information on alternative job opportunities, contributing to reduce mobility costs and thus increasing job mobility. However, we find that higher education significantly increases mobility only in the United Kingdom. In general, it is also expected that younger and less experienced workers are more willing to bear the fixed costs of moving in order to accept a better job, while it is likely that an older worker, having accumulated more firm specific capital, is endowed with a greater firm attachment. However, experience, being linearly dependent on age, also reflects different stages in the life cycle and the probability of changing jobs could decline non-linearly with experience because of changing preferences. We find that age has a negative and significant effect on the probability of job mobility in Ireland and in the United Kingdom. Experience variables present mixed signs, while being generally insignificant. Larger firms are expected to be related to lower job mobility rates, but we find significant evidence of such an effect only for the United Kingdom. Alternatively, temporary workers are found to be significantly more likely to move in all the countries under consideration but in the United Kingdom. Employer provided training has a negative effect on the probability of job mobility in all the countries under consideration, being significant at standard levels in Denmark and in the Netherlands.

Our model assumes that an individual's decision to change jobs responds positively to a wage differential defined as the lifetime earnings gain from moving. The finding of positive and significant effects of the wage differential on the probability of job mobility in Ireland and in the Netherlands constitutes evidence supporting the model.[21]

Consistently with their full portability, private pension plans offered by financial institutions are generally found to have a positive impact on the probability of job mobility, although this is true at standard significance levels only in the Netherlands under the first model specification. Turning to the role of occupational pensions on job mobility decisions, we find that participation in an occupational pension plan significantly reduces the probability of job mobility by 3.2 per cent in the United Kingdom. This result explains more than half of the mobility differential between pension and non-pension workers reported in Table 9.7. In the other countries under consideration occupational pension participation does not significantly affect the probability of job mobility. Table 9.11 reports the results for model 2, whose specification includes the pension portability loss computed as in Section 9.2. The results for the Netherlands and the United Kingdom are not sensitive to the inclusion in the structural probit equation of a pension portability loss variable, aimed at capturing the effect of the individual's perceived opportunity cost of leaving a DB plan. In the United Kingdom pension-covered workers preserve a significantly lower probability of job mobility, but among them workers suffering higher pension losses are not significantly less likely to move. In the Netherlands occupational pensions continue not to affect significantly job mobility, neither directly nor through pension portability losses. A peculiar result is found for Ireland, where pension portability loss turns out to have a negative and significant effect on the probability of job mobility of pension workers. However, while predicting job mobility at the individual level such an effect is compensated, even for the workers suffering the highest portability loss, by the magnitude of the positive coefficients on the pension participation dummy, which is also statistically significant.[22]

On the basis of the above findings, it seems that pension portability losses do not have an important effect on the mobility decisions of pension workers. However, while interpreting the role of occupational pensions on job mobility choices using the results presented in this section one should keep in mind the assumptions underlying them. First, incorrectly including people who actually belong to DC schemes with people who belong to DB schemes – as we did for lack of information in the data – could lead to underestimate the effect of the latter type of coverage on job mobility choices.[23] A further caveat is due to the truncated nature of the available job tenure data needed to calculate the pension loss, which leads to underestimate the actual expected loss. Second, it can be the case that pension participants in the United Kingdom give more importance to the fact of participating in a pension plan *per se* or that they do not have or are not able to handle the information needed to calculate pension losses.[24] Finally, it could be that occupational pension participants are intrinsically less likely to move. This would be the case if pension participation choices were not randomly made and were based rather on unobservables simultaneously affecting future job mobility choices.

9.7   CONCLUSIONS

This chapter provides a comparative empirical analysis of pension portability in a sample of EU Member States. DB pension plans play an important labour market role in Ireland, in the Netherlands and in the United Kingdom,

Table 9.11 Structural form probit equation. Model 2

	Ireland	Netherlands	UK
Wage Differential	0.204	0.272	−0.390
	(2.72)**	(2.06)**	(4.62)**
Not Married	−0.014	−0.012	−0.011
	(0.58)	(0.90)	(1.15)
Female	−0.015	−0.019	0.106
	(0.97)	(0.14)	(3.73)**
Children	−0.012	0.035	0.000
	(0.61)	(1.73)	(0.02)
Household Size	0.006	−0.012	−0.005
	(1.09)	(1.86)*	(1.21)
House Tenant	0.003	−0.018	−0.004
	(0.10)	(1.65)	(0.41)
Age	−0.009	−0.001	−0.005
	(1.94)*	(0.76)	(1.71)*
Third-Level Education	0.004	−0.008	0.039
	(0.15)	(0.54)	(2.38)**
Experience	0.006	0.002	−0.001
	(1.12)	(0.81)	(0.34)
Experience Squared/100	0.000	−0.015	0.003
	(0.05)	(1.56)	(0.89)
Employer Size$_{t-1}$: 100–499	0.009	−0.007	−0.018
	(0.52)	(0.64)	(1.94)*
Employer Size$_{t-1}$: 500+	0.069	−0.005	−0.032
	(1.71)*	(0.38)	(3.14)**
Temp. Employment Contract$_{t-1}$	0.049	0.128	−0.010
	(1.74)*	(4.63)**	(0.78)
Pension Portability Loss/1000	−0.004	−0.0006	0.000
	(2.70)**	(0.49)	(0.08)
Occupational Pension Plan$_{t-1}$	0.055	−0.01	−0.031
	(2.04)**	(0.76)	(2.26)**
Private Pension Plan	−0.001	0.019	0.010
	(0.05)	(1.13)**	(0.87)
Employer Provided Training	−0.004	−0.020	−0.007
	(0.22)	(2.14)**	(0.76)
Log-likelihood	−258.6	−313.4	−150.05
Wald Chi2	71.2	71.91	60.34
Pseudo *R* 2	0.1158	0.1216	0.1858
Number of Observations	943	1542	1017
Observed *P*	0.0933	0.0616	0.0442
Predicted *P* (X)	0.0648	0.042	0.0223

covering large sections of private sector workforce. Alternatively, DC plans are dominant in Denmark. Pension portability reforms in the former countries over the last two decades have been propelled by the need for a more mobile labour force. Using recent releases of the ECHP data, we provide novel empirical evidence answering the question whether the lack of pension portability characterizing most DB plans represents an impediment to job mobility within EU countries. We find that, among the countries under consideration, workers participating in DB pension plans are significantly less likely to move only in the United Kingdom, while pension portability losses do not generally act as a significant impediment to labour mobility. We also find that occupational pension plans in Denmark do not significantly affect job mobility choices. Although these results are consistent with the pension portability options guaranteed by DC plans in Denmark and by industry-wide and company DB plans in the Netherlands, they provide somewhat surprising evidence for the United Kingdom and for Ireland, where DB pensions typically have limited portability. However, the finding of substantial compensation premiums accruing to stayers in pension jobs in the latter countries is more in line with the view that workers are less likely to leave good jobs. From a policy perspective, our results cast doubt on the effectiveness of reforms aimed at improving labour market efficiency through portability measures. In the context of national pension policies focused on the reduction of social security benefits and in the light of the upward trend of the participation of women in the workforce, a more convincing argument in favour of increased pension portability would be ensuring retirement income adequacy to multiple-job changers, and particularly to women, whose careers are usually characterized by frequent interruptions.

NOTES

1. See Dorsey (1995).
2. Occupational pension plans are employer-sponsored plans aiming to supplement retirement income provided by public statutory schemes.
3. Defined as the increment of accrued pension rights from continuing employment, net of returns on accumulated pension rights.
4. The term 'backloading' is sometimes used to refer to a weighting scheme whereby the pension formula explicitly gives greater weight to later than to earlier years of employment. In the context of this chapter, backloading refers to the positive slope of the pension accrual profile that results even when all years of work receive equal weight in the pension benefit formula.
5. Allen *et al*. (1988).
6. Gustman and Steinmeier (1993).
7. Allen *et al*. (1993).
8. Mitchell (1982, 1983).
9. Although some evidence is provided by McCormick and Hughes (1984), Henley *et al*. (1994) and Mealli and Pudney (1996) for the United Kingdom.

10. The *Council Directive 98/49/EC*.
11. For an institutional analysis of cross-borders pension portability in the EU see Andrietti (2001).
12. This model was pionereed by Roy (1951) and since then has been applied to the analysis of a wide variety of individual choices, ranging from education levels (Willis and Rosen 1979), migration (Robinson and Tomes 1982), sector of employment (Rees and Shah 1986) and job mobility (Borjas and Rosen 1980, Marshall and Zarkin 1987). These studies focus on the economic consequences – in terms of returns – of the choice taken, while we are investigating rather the factors affecting job mobility choices. A model similar to ours was proposed by Gustman and Steinmeier (1993), although their estimation methodology is on a different treatment of self-selection and on a different set of assumptions.
13. This avoids multicollinearity between regressors in the wage equation in case of linearity of the inverse Mills' ratio. However, in principle, identification could be attained even only relying on non-linearity of the latter.
14. The variables excluded from the wage equations are: Not Married, Children, Household Size, House Tenant, Age, Temporary Employment Contract$_{t-1}$, Employer Provided Training, Employer Size$_{t-1}$ dummies, Occupational Pension Plan$_{t-1}$, Private Pension Plan, Pension Portability Loss. All these variables refer to the beginning of the observation period.
15. For a critical analysis of the ECHP survey structure, see Peracchi (2000).
16. Although an individual-initiated separation (quit) could be followed by an unemployment spell while a firm-initiated separation (layoff) could produce a job-to-job transition, still there are good reasons to use the above definition. First, even if the ECHP data allow us to distinguish between quits and layoffs, a comparative empirical analysis focused on quits could not include the United Kingdom, due to missing data. Where the quit/layoff distinction is available, we have found a very high correlation between quits and job-to-job transitions without intervening unemployment. Moreover, self-reported causes of job mobility could suffer from measurement error, while the event of no unemployment experience between a job-to-job transition seems to offer a more objective measure of voluntary job mobility.
17. We assume, following Ippolito (1985), that $g^e = i^e$. Notice that the variable measuring job tenure is left truncated for those who started to work with the current – 1995 – employer before 1981. This leads to an underestimation of pension portability losses for workers with longer – truncated – tenures. We also account for the fact that in the Netherlands portability losses only arise for pension-covered inter-industry movers. Thus, in computing the potential pension losses arising for pension-covered stayers we include as a weight the predicted probability of inter-industry mobility. The latter is derived estimating a probit model of inter-industry mobility among actual movers.
18. See Heckman (1979). The routine for computation of the correct standard errors, programmed in Stata – version 7, is available upon request from the author. Reported *t*-values followed by one (two) asterisks are significant at 90 (95) per cent level.
19. Some of this rent would represent a compensating wage premium to offset the cost of reduced mobility.
20. The parameter estimates represent the effect of a one unit change in the independent variable on the probability of job mobility, evaluated at the sample means. Those marked with one (two) asterisk are significant at 10 (5) per cent level. Standard errors are bootstrapped to account for the fact that wage differentials are estimated rather than observed. The base case individual is male, married, without children, house owner, with education lower than third level, not participating in an occupational or private pension, not receiving employer-provided training, employed under a permanent contract in a small firm.
21. However, we also find a negative and significant impact of the wage differential on job mobility choices for the United Kingdom. The latter result is likely due to the poor fit of the movers' wage equation.
22. Note that the latter results could be affected by the high degree of collinearity among the pension participation dummy and the pension loss variable.

23. However, note that Gustman and Steinmeier (1993) and Andrietti and Hildebrand (2001) find no evidence that mobility is differently affected by whether the employer's plan is of the DB or DC form in the US.
24. Mitchell (1988) provides evidence consistent with this argument for the US.

REFERENCES

Allen, S., R. Clark and A. McDermed (1988), 'Why do pensions reduce mobility?', NBER Working Paper # 2509.

Allen, S., R. Clark and A. McDermed (1993), 'Pensions, bonding and lifetime jobs', *Journal of Human Resources*, **28** (3), 502–17.

Andrietti, V. (2001), 'Portability of supplementary pension rights in the European Union', *International Social Security Review*, **54** (1), 59–83.

Andrietti, V. and V. Hildebrand (2001), 'Pension portability and labour mobility in the United States. New evidence from SIPP data', CeRP Working Paper # 10.

Borjas, G. J. and S. Rosen (1980), 'Income prospects and job mobility of younger men' in R. Ehrenberg (ed.) *Research in Labor Economics 3*, Greenwich: Ct. JAI Press, 159–81.

Bulow, J. (1982), 'What are corporate pension liabilities?', *Quarterly Journal of Economics*, **97** (3), 435–52.

Dorsey, S. (1995), 'Pension portability and labor market efficiency: a survey of the literature', *Industrial and Labor Relations Review*, **48** (1), 276–292.

Government Actuary's Department (2000), *Occupational Pensions Schemes 1995: Tenth Survey by the Government Actuary*, London: HMSO.

Gustman, A. L. and T. L. Steinmeier (1993), 'Pension portability and labor mobility. Evidence from the Survey of Income and Program Participation', *Journal of Public Economics*, **50**, 299–323.

Heckman, J. (1979), 'Sample selection as a specification error', *Econometrica*, **41**, 153–61.

Henley, A., R. Disney and A. Carruth (1994), 'Job tenure and asset holdings', *Economic Journal*, **104**, 338–49.

Hughes, G. and B. J. Whelan (1996), *Occupational and Personal Pension Coverage 1995*, Dublin, Economic and Social Research Institute.

Ippolito, R. (1985), 'The labor contract and true economic pension liabilities', *American Economic Review*, **75** (5), 1031–43.

Kotlikoff, L. and D. Wise (1985), 'Labor compensation and the structure of private pension plans: evidence for contractual versus spot labor markets' in Wise, D. (ed.) *Pensions, Labor, and Individual Choice*, Chicago: University of Chicago Press.

Marshall, R. C. and G. A. Zarkin (1987), 'The effect of job tenure on wage offers', *Journal of Labor Economics*, **5** (3), 301–24.

McCormick, B. and G. Hughes (1984), 'The influence of pensions on job mobility', *Journal of Public Economics*, **23** (1–2), 183–206.

Mealli, F. and S. Pudney (1996), 'Occupational pensions and job mobility in Britain: estimation of a random-effects competing risks model', *Journal of Applied Econometrics*, **11**, 293–320.

Mitchell, O. S. (1982), 'Fringe benefits and labor mobility', *Journal of Human Resources*, **17** (2), 287–98.

Mitchell, O. S. (1983), 'Fringe benefits and the cost of changing jobs', *Industrial and Labor Relations Review*, **37**, 70–8.

Mitchell, O. S. (1988), 'Worker knowledge of pension provisions', *Journal of Labor Economics*, **26** (1), 21–39.

OECD (1999), *Economic Outlook*, Paris: OECD Press.

Peracchi, F. (2000), 'The European Community Household Panel Survey', in W. Voges (ed.), *Dynamic Approaches to Comparative Social Research*, Aldershot: Avery Publishers.

Rees, H. and A. Shah (1986), 'An empirical analysis of self-employment in the UK', *Journal of Applied Econometrics*, **1**, 95–108.

Robinson, C. and N. Tomes (1982), 'Self-selection and interprovincial migration in Canada', *Canadian Journal of Economics*, **14** (3), 517–35.

Roy, A. D. (1951), 'Some thoughts on the distribution of earnings', Oxford Economic Papers - New Series, 3, 135–46.

Willis, R. J. and S. Rosen (1979), 'Education and self-selection', *Journal of Political Economy*, **87**, s7–s35.

Index